A scientist, adventurer, writer, speaker, Africa nut, public transport buff, and accidental photographer Ian M Packham has written for a range of outlets including *Adventure Travel* magazine and Bradt's *Bus-Pass Britain Rides Again*. He was a runner-up in *National Geographic Traveller (UK)*'s travel writing competition in 2013.

A quest for challenge has taken Ian to the summit of Mount Kenya, and, by way of a PhD in Biomedical Sciences, the length of Hadrian's Wall. He completed his circumnavigation of Africa by public transport – the first solo and unassisted journey of its kind – at the end of September 2012.

Encircle Africa: Around Africa by Public Transport is his first book.

Visit www.encircleafrica.org for regular updates.

Encircle Africa

Around Africa by Public Transport

First published in 2013 by The Cloister House Press

A CIP record for this book is available from the British Library

ISBN 9781909465145

Author's Note

I travel because it challenges my preconceptions of the world, and about what I can and cannot do. Using public transport forces me into immersing with local cultures.

Since returning from encircling Africa I have gone on a different type of journey that has challenged me just as much. *Encircle Africa: Around Africa by Public Transport* is the result of both. It's the result of a private and personal endeavour, with no editor or proofreader who wasn't a family member. Like the journey, converting my notes and memories into a workable narrative was down to me alone, and not as easy as experiencing them first hand. The result is less an African adventure story than one of honest *reportage*: how I experienced Africa – that catch-all term for 54 nations, 2000 languages, and one billion people – daily, over 396 days.

I hope you enjoy the result as much as I have struggled with writing it, and also hope just some of the joy, vibrancy, fun and kindness of a hideously misrepresented continent comes through as a powerful contrast to the rare moments I was in over my head.

Ian M Packham
London, nine months on

To my mother, who hates me travelling

And sorry I could not travel both
And be one traveller, long I stood
And looked down one as far as I could
To where it bent in the undergrowth;

Then took the other, as just as fair,
And having perhaps the better claim,
Because it was grassy and wanted wear;
Though as for that the passing there
Had worn them really about the same,

And both that morning equally lay
In leaves no step trodden black.
Oh, I kept the first for another day!
Yet knowing how way leads on to way,
I doubted if I should ever come back.

I shall be telling this with a sigh
Somewhere ages and ages hence:
Two roads diverged in a wood, and I –
I took the one less travelled by,
And that has made all the difference.

Robert Frost, *The Road Not Taken*

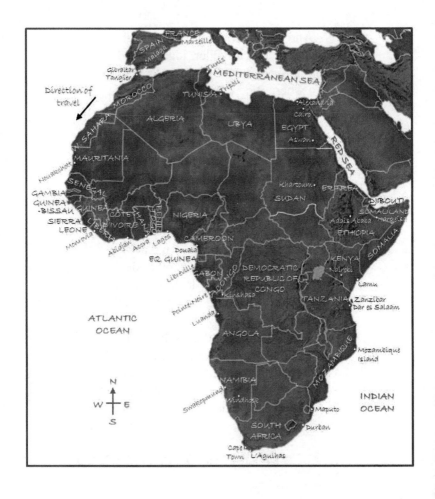

Gibraltar

The summer Mediterranean lies before me in all its
magnetic blueness. Somewhere out there, beyond the blue
throbbing line of the horizon lies Africa

Lawrence Durrell, *Justine*

'I normally tell people to have a good holiday,' he says,
passing me a bundle of clean banknotes. 'But in your case,
have the time of your life.'

As I stand alone at Europa Point facing the oldest continent
on earth I'm not sure how I should feel about the journey I'm
about to begin, though I know I'm the most nervous I've ever
been. Africa has a reputation for darkness; one I hope to
dispel. Describing my plan to circumnavigate Africa at the
currency counter of a post office in suburban Birmingham is
suddenly very different to actually standing at the very edge
of Europe with Africa such a short distance away.

The continent looms back at me through the candy floss
cloud that hides the upper reaches of Jebel Musa, thought to
be the southern ancient pillar of Hercules. It was from here
the hero tore Europe and Africa apart. At Europa Point, Gibraltar's southernmost, only 14 kilometres of strait separates
me from a journey of 13 months and 40,000 km following
Africa's coast.

Captured from Castile in 1704 and ceded to Britain in
perpetuity by treaty nine years later, Gibraltar is a British
territory immediately distinct from Britain. Its 300 years of
cultural fusion has produced a peculiar Anglo-Andalusian

atmosphere that pervades peninsula living, best represented by locals dropping sterling onto the collection plates of Roman Catholic churches.

I find its heart along Main Street, midway between the border with Spain to the north, and the Rock. As I make my way through Landport gate, a series of tunnels and fortifications as unlike a simple gateway as I could find anywhere, heading away from Spain and towards the towering limestone outcrop, the final dose of bright summer sun is beaten back by a heavy rainstorm raging in from Africa. Within the echoing tunnels West African immigrants crouch on their ankles wordlessly hoping for loose change, looking as out of their depth as I feel.

I reach the base of the Rock as the sky clears. A cable car journey means I'm all too quickly rising beside its steep flanks and meeting with its famed Barbary macaques – Europe's only free-living non-human primates. Invisible from the city below, the macaques cling to a small area of nature reserve on the upper Rock, leaping onto anyone who dares to stand still. I keep moving, unlike the macaques, who never wander far from the constantly replenished piles of neatly chopped fruits and vegetables on the roadside.

The paths eventually lead me back to the Rock's crowded lower reaches, via natural caves, hand-dug siege tunnels and an ancient Moorish castle. I am spurred on further only by the pungent scent of late summer blooms picked out by the earlier heavy African rain. Building after building relates Britain's military presence on the peninsula and Gibraltar's shifting cultural identity, marking the ease with which the perception of cultural and national frontiers as solid boundaries changes. The Rock remains ever present as I pass officers' cottages and the Trafalgar cemetery to one of the largest places of Islamic worship in Europe. The calm of the late afternoon is suddenly broken by the sound of British fighter jets tearing around Gibraltar Bay in tandem.

At the Ibrahim al-Ibrahim mosque the waters of the Mediterranean at the strait are still. Africa unravels ahead of me. Even with the cloud blotting out much of its coastline, masking Ceuta to the east, and the Punta Cires promontory with Tangier to the west, it seems to stretch on indefinitely. A journey of 40,000 km suddenly seems a long one.

My plan for the journey pretty much comes down to 'turn right at Tangier and keep going until you reach Tangier': heading west around the continent, I only have to keep salt water on my right hand side to get back to where I begin. I cannot get any closer to Africa without setting foot there.

The first thing I have to do to get closer to Africa is walk away from it. The road signs north of Main Street on Gibraltar's sole north-south artery show a series of roads spanning out from the territory. *SPAIN SPAIN SPAIN* stands out from them like a warning. It seems right to begin a 13 month overland circumnavigation by reaching Africa without recourse to air travel, and so my inevitable rendezvous with public transport begins at a bus station a short distance away in La Línea, beyond Gibraltar's border with Spain.

The ease with which I cross the border – the polished Spanish policeman giving my passport only the most cursory of glances before waving me on – belies the troubled relationship between the neighbours that ensured this frontier was not fully open until I was two years old. I board a bus travelling to Algeciras, across Gibraltar Bay, for one of the fast ferries to Tangier, and Africa.

Morocco – Western Sahara – Mauritania

If you ever get the chance, go there. It feels like…going
home

Bob Geldof, *Geldof in Africa*

Tangier's old port has acted as a gateway to Africa for
centuries. I also use Tangier as my gateway to the continent,
but I do not reach the city through its ancient port. Below the
whitewashed outer walls of the medina, it lies abandoned, its
functions transferred to a soulless state-of-the-art facility that
provides the berths needed for the ranks of ferries like my
own arriving from Europe. The new port of Tanger-Med is so
far out of town I spend half the afternoon battling with public
transport to reach Tangier's historic medina heart. I spend the
other half of the afternoon wishing I hadn't. Centuries of
travellers have given Tangier's entrepreneurs plenty of time
to get their patter right, and they hound me from my first
steps in the open at one of the medina's gates.

Its seediness is even more difficult to ignore than the self-
appointed guides hopping around me in the alleyways pre-
tending to escort me to the American Legation building or
Kasbah museum. There is all the latent charm of the glue
addicts that block my passage, yelling incoherently as they
inhale deeply from sweaty plastic bags. I exit the medina into
the wide avenues of the new town only for men to pop up
from among the afternoon shoppers to offer me hashish in
snatched whispers.

I wander away from them all: the old port, the medina, and
the hustlers, along the waterfront and allow myself to relax. I

indulge in a flavour-filled lamb tagine as a darkening sky marks the progress from afternoon to evening of my first day in Africa. But the quality of the food, the romanticism of the muezzin calling *Allahu akbar*, and the golden sun bathing the empty old port below the whitewashed jumble of medina buildings cannot convince me to stay in Tangier any longer. I'm eager to climb aboard the next available bus and start south; my schedule a delicate balance of hard travel and more leisurely cultural immersion. Leaving Tangier means I will not see the Mediterranean for another 10 months.

The interior of the coach to Morocco's capital is as uncomfortably hot as the quivering dark tarmac surface of the coastal highway to Rabat. The countryside behind the sealed and curtained windows is dead in the mid-afternoon heat.

With the late afternoon sun igniting the orange-yellow walls of the 400 year old medina, I end up on an old semaphore platform looking out across the point where the River Bou Regreg flows into the Atlantic. The wide traffic-laden avenues of the new town are filled with banks, trendy cafés, and modernity; the old walled city is quite different: a confusion of noisy lanes full of bustling pedestrians.

Le Tour Hassan, a minaret begun in 1195 by sultan Yacoub al-Mansour stands over the Bou Regreg a short distance upstream; a minaret without a mosque. Building of the square Moorish tower, the colour of the medina's walls, was abandoned at a height of 44 metres after the sultan's death. Beside it, a paved open space dotted with regimented lines of columns leads to the mausoleum of Mohammed V and his son Hassan II, the first of independent Morocco's kings. Ornately dressed mounted guards holding awkward flagstaffs stand at either side of its entrance, struggling to maintain the stability of Morocco's flag.

I encounter neatly marshalled protestors chanting Arabic slogans a short time later. Arriving at the medina walls they pause, eyeing the burgeoning police presence. From the quiet humdrum of city life there is a shout that provokes the police into action. Dozens of fast moving bodies rush past where I sit in the shade, crossing the square followed by slower moving police smiling behind riot shields; the first indication I get that Morocco isn't the modern democratic state it portrays itself to be.

I continue south, to Casablanca, by train. Casablanca is as laid back as Rabat, but also hectic with traffic and sinking under the weight of industrial drabness. Even the Atlantic looks bleak, a polluted haze hiding much of the town as it extends along the coastline from my position at the mosque of Hassan II, a modern mirror of Rabat's unfinished Tour Hassan.

Though the train network meets the definition of public transport as would be recognised in Europe, I soon realise that the term *public transport* in Africa translates roughly into 'any vehicle willing to take me and my backpack anywhere for a fee', and often refers to rickety bush and shared taxis. It's a shared taxi that takes me south along the coast road in the close embrace of a large Moroccan businessman, the sun kissing the horizon. From the *gare routiere*, a catch-all term for a jumble of shared taxis, buses, and coaches, I board a late night coach to Agadir.

Agadir turns out to be a European beach resort, the coast lined with the fast-food restaurants I avoid at home, and the sort of hustlers that pushed me into leaving Tangier so rapidly. Towards evening, in wandering around the old souq with walls the colour of sun-bleached sand I find the real Agadir. Round women in colourful shawls bring to mind Russian dolls, swaying from side to side as they walk with grim determination about the souq to complete their evening shopping. An entire department store of goods is laid out neatly on the ground, only to be packed away at nightfall and unpacked again the next morning. I am treated like any other shopper, no one bothering me as I examine the stacks of crockery.

The landscape becomes visibly dryer even before my coach to Tan Tan rises to cross the Anti-Atlas mountains. From the claustrophobic, crowded population centres of Morocco's north there is suddenly nothing but space and security posts, with *gendarmerie royale* checkpoints into and out of every town. The distance between towns in the south of Morocco is so great I find there is little else to do but move on. It takes most of the day to travel the 320 km between Agadir and Tan Tan, arriving just as the temperature drops with the onset of nightfall. In a week of travel I reach the same latitude as Fuerteventura in the Canary Islands, travelling over 1000 km from Tangier.

Though the coach departing for Tarfaya is already full, I am led to a shared taxi needing one final passenger. I share the Mercedes' back seat with three others, while another two share the passenger seat. Small avalanches of sand slip onto the perfect road surface from car-high dunes, pointing to my proximity to the Sahara Desert. Camels amble on the hot tarmac ahead of a small flock of flamingos simmering in the heat haze of a caustic lake where locals are harvesting salt.

The Hotel Bahia's name betrays Tarfaya's history as part of Spanish Sahara rather than French Morocco. The heat inside my room drives me out into the bleached and shadeless town, where donkey carts are still a preference over motor vehicles. In the 1920s, the town was an important landing site for France's international airmail service. Pilots including Antoine de Saint-Exupery became celebrities for flying biplanes from southern France along the northwest African coast to Tarfaya, described by the town's small museum as deep within 'the Mauritanian desert', before reaching Dakar and finally Brazil.

Clearly these flights were a risky business with many of the museum's photographs showing Saint-Exupery's biplane upside down on the landing strip. A slowly rusting cast metal monument of a biplane sits the right way up at the location of the landing strip, part of the town's coastline. The beach is too littered to enable any aircraft to land now, plastic scattered for miles along the wavefront among the sand and rocks. Opposite the monument, the island fort of Casa Del Mar tells of a time in the late nineteenth century when Tarfaya was the site of a British trading post.

However much I enjoy the quiet aimless life of Tarfaya and its look of gradual return to sand, it is time to move on. A town which I can leisurely walk around – a mini circumnavigation – in 30 minutes cannot hold me for long. Tarfaya is a frontier town, the last place of any population before the unmanned border between Morocco and Western Sahara.

I pass into Western Sahara by shared taxi without crossing any legally enforced frontier or needing my passport. The temperature at midday nudges 40°C; Western Sahara is well described by its name. Morocco would also like the international community to believe the county is part of historic 'greater Morocco'. The vast numbers of flags depicting Morocco's green pentagram star on its red background attempt to secure this point of view. Neither the United Nations, nor the Sahrawi people who used to call it home, are quite so sure. Most now live in refugee camps in Algeria. A UN brokered referendum on independence is long overdue. It was agreed in principle before Nelson Mandela was released from prison in 1990.

The scenery beside the road beyond the disputed border is the same drab semi-desert that recalls my journey into Tarfaya, from where 350,000 Moroccans headed south in 1975 to settle Western Sahara, even before Spain had relinquished its colonial authority. Meanwhile, Moroccan troops had already invaded from the northwest.

Moroccans now outnumber Sahrawi three to one in the Sahrawi's *de facto* capital, Laayoune, and I sense an air of distrust. Large police riot vans are parked perpendicularly across pavements, forcing me to walk along the road. The large UN presence is noticeable from the blue flags mounted on the front of perfectly polished white SUVs parked outside the First Great Western. I only meet one person willing to admit to being Sahrawi. I meet him in a teahouse in the evening. 'Europe had given its colonies independence, but Morocco will not give independence to Western Sahara' he tells me quietly in English, pain in his voice. I cannot think of any response, the short conversation dries up, and I leave the teahouse disappointed in myself.

With nothing to keep me longer in Laayoune other than some decent food and the quantity of vowels I book an overnight coach to Dakhla, Western Sahara's second city. In doing so, I miss my first real chance to cross paths with Portugal's early explorers of Africa. Diogo Cão's first port of call after Lisbon was Cape Bojador in Western Sahara, a name now more synonymous with a Sahrawi refugee camp in the Algerian Sahara.

With the destinations of arriving coaches written in Arabic, a language I can only get to grips with given several days of guessing, it takes luck and a two hour wait to find the coach bound for Dakhla and fight my way to an empty seat. In the darkness of the countryside there is little to see or do but rest until the coach pulls up smoothly to a non-descript corner of a non-descript Dakhla square come early morning.

Without a map I wander aimlessly along the streets stemming from the square until I bump into Colin. At eight in the morning he's finishing off a night's labour building a workshop for a friend.

'Of course, you're not the first person to do something like this' he says, hearing my plans, wiping the grease from his hands with a rag.

'Well, actually – '

'But that's not why you're doing it. You'll learn so much: about yourself, and the world. It's well worth doing. You can only understand the world if you get out and experience it for yourself.' He is right, I reason, accepting his offer of a lift into the centre of town – in the opposite direction to the one I had been heading in. In researching the journey, it was only a late discovery that I could be the first to complete an African circumnavigation this way.

As someone who has made a home in Western Sahara I ask Colin about the UN presence.

'They maintain the ceasefire, which is 20 years old, so they don't do a lot really' he says. 'It's seen as a chance to get some rest and recuperation. The weather's pleasant all year round, and the lack of income tax helps people like me. Plus, fuel and food stuffs are heavily subsidised to entice Moroccans into staying.'

As he buys me breakfast I realise he is either worldly-wise or a conspiracy theorist of the grandest order. 'You'll be fine in Mauritania,' he says between bites of sweet pastry. 'You're not a target. Britain doesn't pay the ransom, which means they have to kill you, which is a hell of a lot of bother for the terrorists. The French, yes, they have a bounty of $10,000 on their heads because their government pays. The Dutch, Swiss, and Germans even. And they're not going to bother with a traveller like you anyway. People think it's random, but terrorism is a business.'

Dakhla sits on a pencil-thin peninsula of land, separated from the rest of Western Sahara by a salt water lagoon. Leaving the peninsula a day later I get the passenger seat in a Mercedes 190 driven by a black Mauritanian in flowing blue boubou and wrap-around sunglasses. Both our skin colours mark us out as foreign. Much of the back is packed with badly hidden foodstuffs, the necks of cooking oil bottles sticking out beneath plastic bag covers, worth smuggling because of the huge hike in prices that comes with leaving Moroccan subsidies.

South of Dakhla the Mercedes crosses the Tropic of Cancer, passing a small sign beside the empty road at speed, the first definitive recognition of the distance I have already travelled from Tangier. A thin ribbon of flat aquamarine Atlantic water on my right divides the cloudless deep blue sky from the dusty flat land that allows me to see for miles. Save for the last checkpoints in Moroccan-controlled territory a herd of camels led by their cameleer is the only thing that forces a shift to a lower gear until the border.

The Mauritanian section of my guidebook – 15 thin pages – reads: 'hot (November to March), very hot (April to October)'. The three kilometre no man's land between borders is a slow drive over surface bedrock that runs between aging minefields without any sense of what might be a safe path. It's hot and dusty, and I am glad when my arrival at a small family-run *auberge* in Nouadhibou is followed quickly by the offer of sweet peppermint tea, the Sahara's drink of choice where Mercedes' are the Sahara's vehicle of choice.

I soon forget Colin's words and the worry brought about by the heavy fortifications around the Spanish consulate on the busy Boulevard Median. Following the road towards the port, as the stevedores head in the opposite direction having finished for the day, I feel comfortably out of place in this francophone black African country run by Arabs, and far more comfortable than my stomach, which takes on a concern rating closing in on seven out of 10: containing instances of mild peril. The cause is the great clouds of flies that blanket every surface, including my food. A large black man, with the brown stains on his teeth and eyes that mark him out as a hashish smoker, beckons me into his shed-like showroom covered in carvings shipped in from Senegal to the south.

'*Ça va?* Where are you from? What are you doing in Africa – you work here?' he asks.

'No, I'm a tourist I suppose. I'm heading for Senegal, then South Africa and then Tangier.'

'You'll fly from Dakar to South Africa?'

'No, no. I'm going by bush taxi.'

'And then from South Africa you'll fly back to Tangier?'

'No. After South Africa I go to Mozambique, and Tanzania …and finally back to Morocco.' He smiles, and tries, not very hard, to sell me something from his stock.

'Who *does* buy your stuff?' I ask.

'Tourists' he replies, 'but at the moment there aren't any, because of the trouble with al-Qaeda; they have been scared off.'

As I make to leave he pulls a cowry shell pendant from a nail and places it around my neck. 'To give you good luck on your travels; the first money.'

'I don't know what to say. Thank you.'

'It's nothing. *Au revoir.*'

There isn't much to do on the road to Mauritania's capital Nouakchott other than sit bolt upright in the minibus belonging to the Bon Voyage travel agency to prevent myself getting knee-capped, and shield my eyes from the sheets of sand cast across the vehicle by a side wind. With the windows slid shut the minibus acts like a greenhouse. There is nothing to the view on either side of the road other than occasional temporary looking structures and a single abandoned shipping container.

When the minibus breaks down about two hours in, with nothing but the road of any substance, it feels more like the driver is pulling off the black surface onto the sand for a break. Some passengers grab onward transport almost immediately, arms outstretched to oncoming traffic while hiding in the folds of their clothing from the spiralling sand. I'm left to sit it out in the baking heat of the vehicle, not quite sure whether I should be doing the same.

A relief expedition in the form of the second Bon Voyage minibus of the day arrives an hour later. Our bags are shifted from the roof rack to the rack of the other vehicle, and the protective netting used as an impromptu tow-rope for the remaining 200 km to Nouakchott.

The city looks so unlike any idea I have of a capital that I first mistake our stopping for another breakdown. It's rather like an overnight camp was hastily erected sometime in 1960 and forgotten about, five kilometres from the ocean, if not the sand. Clambering from the minibus it falls from my clothes in small drifts. The heat is intense, and without the relieving breeze of the Atlantic it feels like I've been sat on by a very large man without particularly good personal hygiene.

I wander the city streets at random; causing the hotel owner to call me over thinking I'm lost. I take respite in a small street café where I meet Ali, a professional footballer from Zimbabwe with even less French than I have.

'Africa has everything, *everything*' he says, 'Gold, iron, everything! If only we could unite like Europe. But our leaders are incapable. They don't try. They only want to make themselves rich.'

'Africa is still young isn't it? It needs time. It took Europe 1000 years' I reply.

'That is a good point; that is a good point. One day I pray Africa will be like Europe. Not like here, look around, there is sand in the streets, and bad smells. One day.' He adds then, 'Somehow'. It's a word he uses a lot.

While the sun is still rising I am in a shared taxi on my way to Rosso, the north bank of the River Senegal, and the Mauritanian side of the border with the country of the same name. Though the border sweeps down to within three kilometres of Saint-Louis, following the route of the river for much of its course, the absence of transport and paved roads limit me to crossing here.

The land south of Nouakchott is noticeably greener than that north, despite drifting orange-red sand dunes. I'm helped part of the way though the confusion of border formalities by a Gambian called Manko, who's concerned I'll be ripped off and shuffles me towards a vast crowd of Africans fighting to get near the tiny window of the immigration office. I end up behind French businessman François. He kindly organises for both our passports to receive the speed service, whereby they are taken directly to the office and jump the huddled queuing masses.

I end up on the same pirogue as François too; a quicker way to cross the latté-coloured waters than the ferry that has just come in to dock and is already overcrowded. It's a demonstration of how the idea of public transport differs in Africa to the west. There is both a public ferry that makes the crossing so slowly passengers are unsure who will be in power when they get to the other side, and a faster service of privately owned pirogues that make the crossing ten times faster at twenty times the price. The short river crossing gives us time to talk more properly, during which François offers me a lift to Saint-Louis on his way to Dakar.

'I live in Abidjan, in Côte d'Ivoire, but travel to Nouakchott and Dakar for business. I'm involved in the export of raw materials. I used to be able to fly between Nouakchott and Dakar, and then on to Abidjan' he explains. 'But Mauritania and Senegal fought a sort of war and now there are no flights between the two so I *have* to travel by road.'

Senegal & The Gambia

No other part of the earth has fewer bays or inlets in its
coast…the name of its people and towns are absolutely
unpronounceable except by the natives

Pliny the Elder, *Natural History*

François gets me through the immigration requirements in the
small near open-air structure on the Senegalese side of the
river, and into his shining yellow taxi, the air conditioning
battling the build-up in sticky heat along the highway to
Saint-Louis without much success.

He drops me off at a campsite on the Langue de Barbarie, a
narrowing spit of land that separates the final stretches of the
River Senegal from the Atlantic. It's the home of fishermen,
boat builders, and market stalls stacked high with fresh and
smoked fish. Colourfully painted fishing boats are beached all
along the stretch of riverbank from the campsite to the bridge
joining the Langue to the Île de N'Dar, Saint-Louis' historic
colonial heart. Abstract images dominate the decoration:
circles, swastikas, and more rarely the logo of Barcelona football club. Men saw vast orange hardwood trunks into planks
and shape them into boats, pinning the planks together with
iron reinforcing rods.

The UNESCO-listed heart of Saint-Louis was France's
first permanent settlement in the region and became capital of
French West Africa. I'm delayed in seeing any of its colonial
relics beyond Place Faidherbe by Muktar, a fisherman who
starts talking to me in the shady gardens there.

'Where are you from?' he asks. 'You're English! I have *never* seen an Englishman speaking French! Normally the tourists, they come and they walk around the market all high and mighty taking photos, not saying a word, but you are different; you are calm.'

'Thank you, but I think you're just saying that because it will look good if I end up writing a book and include this conversation.'

'You have been to the fish market?' he goes on. I nod. 'You think there are a lot of fish?' I nod again, remembering the neat stacks of smoked fish.

'Yes? No. No fish. The fish are in permanent decline. I go out in my boat for five days at a time but bigger boats go out for 80 days – '

'Wait – 80 days?' I say incredulously. 'You can go around the world in that time.'

'Yes, 80 days; three months. The boats are contracted to North Korea for two or three or five years. All the fish they catch are dried and sent to there. They use pirogues with a net slung between them and drag in everything: shark, ray, marlin, tuna. There is nothing left for me. My grandfather used to say "liberty has no price", but my children cannot afford to be fishermen.'

Leaving Muktar beside his simple-hulled pirogue, I move about the island via as many air conditioned patisseries and bars as I can locate until dusk settles over the river and brings a certain peace to the island, struggling like the air conditioning of François' taxi with the increased humidity since the Mauritanian border. My incidental movements take me past Saint-Louis' charming colonial buildings; gardeners clearing the grounds of the off-white Governor's Palace that dominates the area around Place Faidherbe.

I manage to cool off in the Atlantic, the water tinted purple by the dying sun. A few spots of rain clear to leave a night sky with incredibly bright stars, free from the effects of light pollution, while the waves run noisily onto the beach with the reassuring constancy of the breath of a loved one. Throughout the night, crabs come out of their burrows in the sandy soil and investigate the guy ropes of my tent with sharp snaps of their claws that keep me awake.

I rejoin the Senegalese mainland via the Hôtel de la Poste, celebrating the life of another early airmail pilot, Jean Mermoz. The hotel sits at one end of the only means of leaving the island without getting my feet wet. The eight iron sections of the nineteenth century French-built Pont Faidherbe arch 500 metres across the river to the old *gare routiere*.

The new *gare routiere* is another three kilometres south of the bridge. From there I claim a seat in a shared taxi that takes me in comparative comfort through to the abysmal traffic that starts on the outskirts of Dakar, the Senegalese capital.

The fences of a luxury hotel prevent me reaching the Atlantic from the city centre, so I track the coast northwest towards the Pointe des Almadies as best I can from a distance. For several kilometres, until the Monument to African Renaissance becomes the major feature on the land-scape, access to the ocean remains blocked by plush housing developments and the construction of a new shopping centre.

The monument sits on a flattened hilltop, and standing at 49 metres, it's taller than the Statue of Liberty. A muscular, bare chested African supports a woman at his side as he hoists a small child onto his shoulder. The child points roughly west, over the top of the nearby Mamelles lighthouse to the open ocean, within sight of a man sleeping rough on the monument's manicured grass banks.

I follow the direction of the child's pointing arm past a starving grey mare towards the Pointe des Almadies, the most westerly point of Africa, the continent ending with a second lighthouse on an outcrop of rock among the waves.

While the Pointe de Almadies is the westernmost point in Africa, the southernmost point in Dakar is Cape Manuel. There are no luxury developments barring access here, a quiet area of stunning ocean scenery in a sometimes chaotic city, from where I can see Gorée Island, and exchange pleasantries with French expatriates enjoying the chance to exercise without the onslaught of hawkers that reside around the streets outside the international hotels of the centre.

I take the 20 minute boat journey on one of the regular ferry services from Dakar's international port to Gorée Island two kilometres offshore, an island with a history intrinsically linked with European colonialism and slavery. A sticky climb up the basalt rock takes me away from the weekend crowds and screams of enjoyment from the narrow beach. I find myself alone with colourful lizards basking on the bare rocks and beneath eagles trying to grab fish from each other's talons while waves crash below me. There is a holiday atmosphere, a dilapidated Marseille without the yachts. There is a serenity that has little to do with its history as a port used in the Atlantic slave trade and more to do with the absence of road traffic. While famous for the trade, few slaves left Africa from Gorée, the majority leaving this part of West Africa from Saint-Louis and The Gambia's ports.

Gorée was first colonised by Portugal; then swapped between rule by the Dutch, Portuguese, the Dutch again, the British, and eventually the French until Senegalese independence. As one of the earliest sites to witness a European presence it received visits from notables including Vasco da Gama on his way beyond the Cape of Good Hope to Africa's Indian Ocean coast. The *maison des esclaves*, a sort of warehouse built to store first slaves and later peanuts, lies quietly on a side street as one of the island's oldest buildings. A back door drops steeply to the Atlantic waves, a figurative door of no return for up to 12 million people.

*

From the dusty lanes of Gorée I'm back on Dakar's broken pavements by early evening trying to avoid a pair of eagerly approaching hawkers, shirts for sale hanging over their arms. One of the pair points to my shoes before grabbing me at the knee. It stops me dead in my tracks. I'm suddenly aware how open I am to attack, my compact camera in an unbuttoned side pocket, day bag and other valuables like my passport on me. His grip is firm. I can't knock his hand away, shouting at him all the while in English. He lets go, and I walk quickly away thinking it's over. I notice the street isn't empty. There are locals minding their own business; a takeaway coffee cart on bicycle wheels being pushed up the street behind me.

My attacker grabs my knee for a second time, stopping me again. His partner dives into my back pocket, pulling out my stash of folded tissues, dropping them to the pavement when he realises their worthlessness. It gives me time to sprint away, to disappear into the crowds as quickly as I can.

My trust in people is shaken. In a month of travel I haven't worried about my belongings or my personal safety. I have felt safer in Africa than I have back home in England. Everyone suddenly seems hostile in my eyes. With the adrenaline surge everyone is a potential assailant and I don't start to relax again until I leave Dakar far behind and reach the end of the paved road at Joal-Fadiout on foot carrying my backpack, the shared taxi from Dakar ending its journey five kilometres earlier. Drizzle turns to a heavy onslaught of fat raindrops, taking the shine from the coastline of Senegal's Petite Côte beaches.

Mainland Joal is connected to Fadiout by a modern wooden bridge that carries foot passengers over a kilometre of lagoon sand to a manmade island whose ground level lies just above that of the high tide mark. Shells crunch under my feet among the narrow pathways leading around the low housing to its church. The island appears to be a historic Christian enclave, with free-roaming pigs, and religious shrines as well as its church. A carved wooden shrine to Mary the mother of Christ has the dates 1710 – 1966 inscribed on its plinth, while a painted concrete sculpture of her son has *11.11.1999* scratched beneath it.

In contrast, Joal is little more than an endless strip of uninteresting buildings where I settle down to a ghastly meal of cold, dry, grey and unrefined couscous smeared onto a plate together with flavourless sauce containing the vestiges of meat; the only hot meal I can find. I look to feign a full stomach and leave hungry when I am approached by a drunk, his unsteady eyes on my meal. His speech is so slurred I'm unsure whether he speaks to me in English or French. I stay, eating every last couscous grain as the man babbles on incoherently. With a clean plate I can make my excuses and find the patron, a woman equally eager to be rid of my table guest.

With a pillow like a volume of the *Encyclopaedia Britannica* I am up early to continue my journey on to Ndangane by shared taxi. Held together by a combination of hope and goodwill from driver and passengers, the cracks of the windscreen fixed with sticky tape, I am distracted from the rust spots on the roof by the sun reflecting off the silver sequins of the shawl of the Muslim teenager on the row of seats in front of me. A raised muddy road leads us out of Joal towards the confluence of the Siné and Saloum rivers, a region of bays, lagoons, and islands. The road soon narrows to a single-lane track flanked by tall walls of vegetation sheltering a plethora of birds.

'There are lots of French, Italians and English here, but no Spanish' says a piroguer in Ndangane, mistaking me for an Iberian. A heavily tanned and very skinny lady doesn't make the same mistake, looking for English speakers to talk with. An Alaskan living permanently in the village she admits to speaking no French before going on to give me a variety of dubious tips for saving money on my journey, such as visiting Senegalese families at meal times.

'They will feed you, for free; they will!' she says, taking a plastic cup out of her bag and helping herself to a jug of water. I sense isolation between her and the locals of what is a traditional close-knit village unused to western ideas of personal space and single travel. She informs me she gives massages for 500 West African Francs; I'm unsure whether she means anything more.

Another piroguer offers me passage to Toubakouta for 100,000 West African Francs, about £150; a week's budget. Though I'm tempted by the idea I make my excuses and seek out something a little more public and a lot less expensive.

It rapidly turns into one of those days when I have absolutely no idea what is going on for the majority of the time, with people simply pushing me between different modes of transport. Just a short distance from Ndangane I am able to catch a *ndiaga ndiaya* minivan to a quiet road junction with the N2 national highway. The tar is patchy, the suspension less than perfect. It looks like I will be stuck at the junction for some time. Barely any vehicles pass by, and when they do they are already full, but somehow I only have to wait a few minutes until I'm able to clamber onto a roughly welded coach.

A little while later I'm ushered off the coach and onto another more comfortable one without any real explanation, ending up on the trans-Gambia highway at Kaolack. I'm rushed to a motorbike taxi that takes me from the transport depot at the north of town to the *garage sud*. From here, it's simple to reach Toubakouta, I'm assured by two young friendly Gambians describing themselves as businessmen – which could mean anything from tea boy to multimillionaire – returning home after a holiday in Senegal. Like Ali in Nouakchott, Modou and Amodou think Africa will only be able to compete with Europe and the United States as a United States of Africa.

'But every country wants its own president, you know?' says Modou, with Amodou nodding furiously beside him. 'It costs money we don't have. Africa is poor. Life in Africa is hard, fucking hard.'

I have to leave Modou and Amodou at the junction outside Toubakouta where I am thrust onto another mototaxi for the final part of the day's journey. It takes me seven hours and the same number of modes of transport to reach Toubakouta; 75 km away through the mangroves by boat, 400 km by land. When Pliny the Elder wrote of the unbending simplicity of Africa's coastline he clearly wasn't talking about the Siné-Saloum delta.

I am out of Senegal and into The Gambia quickly, via Karang, the closest border crossing to the Atlantic. Having entered my first Anglophone country of the trip I transfer into a shared taxi for the journey to Barra, a town wedged between the Atlantic coast and the banks of the River Gambia. Entirely surrounded by Senegal, Africa's smallest country is little more than a valley for the river that has dominated its life for centuries.

To get across the river mouth I join the tightly packed crowd waiting for the gates of the port to be opened for the ferry. As the gate opens the crowd surges forward, catching several women unaware. A woman immediately in front of me is twisted around to face the crowd and narrowly avoids causing a crush as she digs among our feet for a lost sandal. Those ahead of me have already sprinted towards the ferry's short vehicle deck and I'm told to copy them and run if I want to get aboard.

I wait out the very stately progress across the river standing in a walkway of an upper deck, catching a breeze through a large window cut out of the ship's metalwork. Small speedboats zip past us, their passengers highlighted by the orange lifejackets they are made to wear. Those less lucky than me stand on the narrow metal steps, or squeeze between the vehicles on deck, resting their goods on the bonnets. There are several thousand people, along with their bags and market produce crammed aboard. I'm the only foreigner. It doesn't exactly chime with the Gambia Port Authority's motto of 'innovation and excellence', though it is a friendly journey. I don't feel at risk from the pickpockets I am warned about.

Wodu welcomes me in Wolof before thanking me for visiting the country as I suck on a bag of drinking water, grinding a hole in one corner with my incisors. Touted as the Smiling Coast, to me it feels like an English county town. It's small enough to remain friendly, unhurried, and ordered. The relative modernity, cleanliness, and state of repair of Banjul's taxis – the windscreens unbroken and chassis weld free – suggest at least one part of the country's motto: 'progress, prosperity, peace', is being met.

I walk an L-shaped path around two of Banjul's sides in about half an hour. Like the country as a whole, The Gambia's capital is compact. July 22 Square, formerly Independence Square, and before that colonial McCarthy Square, has half metre high grass around its edges and men playing cricket at its centre. A short walk along July 22 Drive – still called Independence Drive on its road signs more than 15 years after the July 22 coup d'état – takes me to the architecturally monstrous Arch 22 a stone's throw from the Atlantic. Designed by the architect of Dakar's more recent Monument to African Renaissance, he was clearly having a bad day at the studio. The arch stands over the highway south on eight classical columns, commemorating the overthrow of the country's democratically elected government in the early 1990s.

I'm asked to take the spiral staircase within one of the columns, since it is nearing closing time and the attendant has already locked up the lift. The columns in turn support a triangular pediment containing viewing platforms, an unused café, and a museum. A newspaper clipping from the day after the coup leads with the quote 'We will never introduce dictatorship in this country', yet the coup leader, President Yahya Jammeh – elected sometimes freely and fairly four times since – has claimed he will rule for a billion years.

I catch a battered *gelli-gelli* minibus along the River Gambia's estuary to Cape Point at Bakau, an attractive coastal town that has become an upper class suburb to Banjul: home to botanic gardens and the residence of the British High Commissioner. It even boasts a fire station, its engines donated by Avon Fire and Rescue Service. In the shady interior of the botanic gardens I'm able to imagine what this part of West Africa must once have been like; pools of still water among the tall tropical trees providing shelter for birds and large species of butterfly.

I stop in Bakau to pay a visit to the friendly consular officials of Guinea-Bissau and the sacred Kachikally crocodile pool. I'm escorted through a confusing layout of drab streets that surround the pool by the sort of people who fleeced Mungo Park two hundred years ago, as he headed inland from the River Gambia to another of West Africa's great rivers, the Niger.

From the small on site museum, that somehow results in a conversation about British circumcision practices, I'm led to the muddy banks of a small pond, the surface of which is blanketed with weed. A Nile crocodile about a metre in length is tempted onto the bank with a rotting fish carcass, while the pool's history as a place for ritual washing to improve fertility is explained to me. Instead of washing I head for Kartong, the last town in The Gambia, by taxi and *gelli-gelli*. I have travelled from roughly the country's northernmost point to its southernmost town, sticking into

Senegal like the stub of a book's badly torn out page, in two and a half hours.

It's not the tourist season, so much of the town is shut up, if the word town isn't an outrageous exaggeration for Kartong. Before returning to the Halahin Lodge three kilometres north, I fall in with a group of teenagers eager to teach me Zamma from a board scratched onto the tarmac road surface. It's a game as old as father time, played here using counters of pebbles and empty shells. It looks like drafts, and plays like drafts, though I still can't get my head around it, and the rules seem to change dependent upon how badly I am losing. I retire from my career as a Zamma master having been allowed to win one game.

I eat with the sun peeking through the dappled cloud and the waves pounding the beach within earshot. The atmosphere is pleasant, but I suddenly feel quite alone, and far from everybody I care for. I end up shedding a couple of tears to the sound of cicadas and evening bird calls.

I wait by the very quiet roadside outside the lodge for 20 minutes before the first *gelli-gelli* to go past squeezes me in between the seating and sliding door. I would like to stay in The Gambia for longer, but its small size means I've run out of coastline to follow. It has been relaxing to speak English for a long weekend, giving my mind a rest from worrying about language in addition to organising transport, lodgings, food, and negotiating for all of it, all the time. Being on my own, unassisted by a backup team, means I am reliant on my own wits every second, and I'm finding it can be exhausting.

A steady stream of shared taxis run from the border through the moist landscape of Casamance to a muddy junction at Diouloulou where I change vehicles. A soldier in fatigues stands warily on the back of a military pickup behind a machine gun the size of The Gambia, covering the vehicles approaching the junction. It's a reminder I'm crossing a region of Senegal where rebels have fought the central government in Dakar for autonomy since the time Senegal gained independence from France in 1960. With the main road running south, those that stretch towards the coast have been ground to bare earth by successive rainy seasons, a lack of maintenance, and heavy vehicles like the minibus I find myself on.

The first coastal habitation after The Gambia is Kafountine, a village with a fish market rife with activity. Men dripping with seawater rush ahead of me to the smokers, with crates of freshly caught fish on their heads, through the haze and smell of charcoal. Pallets of dried fish stand like smaller versions of shipping containers ready for transport by road. The scales, guts, and bones are being fermented down to a rich brown peat, before being bagged, giving the whole area the rich slightly putrefying smell of Worcestershire sauce. Every bit of the fish is used, none of it is wasted.

The town has a large Rastafarian community, pushed to the very edge of the country by a Muslim majority that frowns upon the smoking of marijuana and worship of Ras Tafari, the man who became Ethiopian emperor Haile Selassie. Alpha, a fiftyish Rastafarian offers me a glass of peppermint tea, which we drink by his foot-powered sewing machine.

'There aren't a lot of tourists at the moment' he says, 'because of the time of year. They don't come until the dry season. Tourists have lots of money; they buy these African trousers and tops I make.' Behind him hang baggy-legged trousers made up of strips of five centimetre thick brightly coloured cloths. I eat mafé, a peanut vegetable stew, with his son.

'You don't smoke do you? I can see. Your face is clean,' he says, meaning my skin, eyes, and teeth lack the gummy brown marks of regular hashish users.

I follow the fish lorries as they jump around the dirt road and join the north-south highway, where the road conditions improve towards Ziguinchor, the capital of the Casamance region, and a town I cannot pronounce for any want of trying. I pass my first monkeys along the way, as well as a chameleon walking slowly across the road on the tips of its curved claws.

I have to go inland once more given the lack of road, let alone public transport, along the coast of mangrove roots of the Casamance river delta from Kafountine to Cap Skirring. Though Africa has almost no inlets in its coast, having a coastline shorter than that of Europe, the coastline from Senegal to Sierra Leone is the most folded of any part, with deltas blocking any real development of the region. In many ways, it remains the least developed region of Africa's coast. The land towards Ziguinchor is even flatter than that of The Gambia and northern Senegal, the waters of the Casamance River flooding the fields lining the road south to create the perfect conditions for rice cultivation.

That Ziguinchor is a transport hub for the Casamance region hides the fact it is really very small. By the river port at which the ferry from Dakar docks is a small garden to 'Africa's Titanic'. In September 2002 the *Le Joola* ferry rolled over during a storm off the Gambian coast, sinking in as little as five minutes. 1800 died; 300 more than on the Titanic. Only 64 survived, while 700 survived the Titanic. The *Le Joola* is thought to have been three times over capacity, not so much a telling problem as standard practice, though rules are being tightened and enforced in countries all along my route. Guards at the port entrance don't allow me to get any closer to the new ferry.

The difference in atmosphere from chaotic Dakar to sleepy Ziguinchor is all the more noticeable where the predominant religious buildings aren't the soaring minarets of independence-era mosques but the sad looking colonial cathedrals standing on the street corners of Ziguinchor's tiny heart. The scratchy voice of muezzins crying *Allaaah-ooh akbar* – God is great – over the peels of high-pitched reverberations from the microphones is replaced by silent church bells. Everything is closed on Sunday afternoon but the churches and cathedrals, leaving me nothing to do but hide from the rain, getting soaked a metre into the veranda of the DHL office where I seek shelter.

Moving through town after the rain reduces to a heavy drizzle I follow locals over the street furniture, the main roads of town flooded to the top of the kerbstones. A hawker takes the opportunity to show me some beautifully decorated masks. He tells me 'they are our passports. We don't have papers; each tribe has a different mask which they would present at the border.' Beading of various colours follows the shape of the eyes and nose. 'The green beads represent the vegetation, the yellow the sun, the red the blood of the independence battle, and the black our skin. The cowry' sitting above the nose like an Indian *bindi* 'is our early money.' In the earliest manifestation of the slave trade men were even exchanged for sacks of cowry shells.

So many storks rest in the trees nearby they resemble a string of fairy lights on a Christmas tree, their off-white feathers gleaming in the semi-darkness. They chatter incessantly, banging together their bills to replicate the sound of a sped up second hand on a clock, time a constant factor on my mind.

The shared taxi across the border to Bissau, the capital of Guinea-Bissau, is falling apart in all the right places. There isn't a surface that isn't cracked, torn, or held together with string. The road is good, and mostly devoid of other traffic, despite being the main road between Senegal and its neighbour. Much of the way we drive along greenery like the New Forest, only the rust-coloured earth breaking the illusion. The newly built toll booths, still unused, look completely out of place.

Guinea-Bissau – Guinea

There is no dignity without freedom...We prefer freedom
in poverty to opulence in slavery

Ahmed Sékou Touré, first president of Guinea

Bissau City sits where the confluence of the Gêba and
Corubal rivers meet the Atlantic, in an area that resembles the
Norwegian fjords, with the Atlantic pushing its fingers deep
inland. Securing its coast would be like successfully policing
the Norfolk Broads in the nineteenth century, so it's no real
surprise the region should be used by cartels pushing hard
drugs from their South American countries of production to
their European marketplace. International sanctions cut into
the country's budget, making it harder to police the
impossible to police.

Trucks carrying shipping containers line Bissau's muddy
main road to the port, where the *Hispania*, a tiny container
vessel is being loaded. The drivers sit beneath the extended
chassis in the shade, talking and drinking tea, not moving
closer to the port entrance for days at a time; the road almost
free of other traffic. Only a few metres further to shore from
the river estuary the water has silted up and returned to
mangrove, the sort of environment that is to be found all
along Guinea-Bissau's folded coastline.

The country has suffered from a series of coups since
independence from Portugal that has made its citizens poorer
than their northern neighbour; the city elegantly dilapidated,
like a museum to historic buildings. Yet street sweepers work
clearing the gutters as I walk from the small port up the main

road, to the burnt and pock-marked presidential palace. A Marxist monument: a tall column of concrete supporting a red star stands in front of the palace looking grubby and uncared for on a roundabout. Graffiti covers its lower flanks. The national flag still flies from a pole in the palace forecourt, a single step from the pavement like any other building in the city, with no railings to bar access. But the roof is collapsing in from fire, with loose tiles half burnt and ready to fall, and all the windows are put out. The mortar marks on the pastel pink and white walls are only hidden by the fresh green of the trees in front. Six hundred West African peacekeeping troops couldn't prevent rebel soldiers attacking the palace and killing the elected president in 1999.

Bissau has a southern European feeling, perhaps because Portugal kept tight control over the country until the fall of Portuguese dictator Salazar in 1975. Benches have survived the years of turbulence, and cafés spill out onto the rough lumps of concrete that once formed pavement. Away from Bissau's main road I find wide boulevards. Rock-filled mud roads run off the boulevards, giving a mix of pre-independence colonial buildings loaded with architectural detail, and shanty dwellings of corrugated tin roofing and rough tree-bole joists where people live on less than the loose change in my back pocket. Several shops use recycled gas cylinders as bollards. Expecting war in Guinea-Bissau, I mistake them for shell casings.

I prepare myself for potential problems when I'm approached by a group of soldiers outside the grass banks of the bastions of the Portuguese Fortaleza d'Amura. Old cannon and machine guns hang limply from the bastion's top, rusted with underuse and age. I catch a view of inside the fort from an open gateway, seeing a loose collection of derelict buildings hidden behind unkempt grasses. The soldiers want to say hello: there aren't many strangers in tiny Bissau, and almost no tourists.

With the milder temperatures that come with the setting sun people in the residential streets sit outside their houses on plastic patio chairs, talking with neighbours and watching children use the roads for games of football. The old presidential palace is in darkness, as is most of the rest of town, there being only a few working streetlights.

There is very little information about the existence of public transport south of the capital. I hear that there is none, and I might have to walk for three days, but am determined to head south, if only to see more of this intriguing country before having to detour along the inland highways to Guinea.

The vehicle's chassis scraps across large pieces of bedrock protruding the dirt road as it takes me to Bissau's *paragem*, a patch of open ground full of shared taxis and *transporte misto* minibuses. In contrast to the rest of the vehicle, the seats of my shared taxi to Buba, southeast among the mangroves and lagoons, are lined with leather. We traverse through low hills and lush forest dissected by paddy fields. The land must look much as it did when the road was laid decades ago; the only housing we pass thatched roundhouses. It is the beginning of the bush meat trade too, with a vervet monkey hanging dead from a road sign for sale.

Buba was one of the small towns I would find myself in for very little reason other than it is where public transport took me. It is a single road town with serene lagoon-side location and simple tourist accommodation built for an influx that probably never arrived. The serenity belies the country's recent volatility. Around the failing concrete pier the only sound to be heard is that of a dugout canoe drifting towards the centre of the lagoon before stretching its tether taught and drifting back towards the bank as bright red winged birds dart through the trees.

I leave Buba for the country's southern border on a day I wouldn't forget and didn't wish to remember. On Buba's single road I follow two brothers into the back of a series of minibuses. The last is crowded, with additional central seating made from giant tins with 'USA vegetable oil vitamin A fortified' written on their sides. The cramped conditions stop me sliding about, my shoulders tight against others as I hold onto my backpack with a finger.

As the elder brother tries to organise onward transport he buys a large bowl of rice and sauce, handing me one of three spoons and a bag of water, despite having only known me for a few minutes. He must be close to adulthood, his younger brother perhaps twelve.

From a small glade outside of Québo I am eventually able to clamber onto the back of a motorbike, my backpack strapped down behind me with lengths of rubber cut from old tyre inner tubes. I join a convoy of another eight bikes travelling all of about 20 metres before having to climb off my bike at the border post for exit formalities.

The road through the no man's land that exists before the distant Guinean border formalities doesn't really take the form of a road but a complex BMX track of muddy rises, sharp turns, and deep puddles marked with the tyre tracks of previous bikes. Some puddles are so large my driver calls them 'small lagoons' as he warns me to raise my feet up to keep them dry, though the water is so deep I can't stop the water rising to my ankles. Beside the lagoons on muddy banks, a constant stream of butterflies launch themselves out of our path while colourful fish dart out of our way in the clear water.

As the vegetation closes in around the narrowing track, the only coastal north-south road to Guinea, the tall grasses whip my legs, arms and face. The grasses become forest, tree roots creating another obstacle set to overturn the heavy bike, and I keep my hands firmly around the chrome fittings. The path turns into an exercise in ignoring muscle fatigue and attempting to avoid extortion.

Pointing at the visa I collected in Bissau does little to persuade the men using the rickety table and chairs inside a low hut. I am told to handover enough cash to pay for a very decent hotel room, the first time in 40 days that I have been asked with anything more than vague hope. Every one of the passengers is handing over something, and my early refusal only leads to the uniformed men demanding I show them the contents of my backpack. Item by item, I pull out my kit, hoping it will be enough to satisfy their interest. Though they want every item re-moved, and examine each one as I do so – going as far as tasting my stash of salt – they retain some respect and place each item on the table out of the dirt. They take nothing but the money they demanded from the beginning. Had I my own transport I would have continued to refuse, but in the middle of the forest I don't know where, I fear my only transport abandoning me.

There is a similar hut a short distance further along the forest path. We drive around a string stretching across the road before coming to a halt. An angry official rushes from the hut, already shouting in French.

'What the hell do you think you are doing driving around the border like that?' he shouts at the drivers. Seeing me he goes on 'Do you want foreigners to think there is no law in Guinea! Do you want that? Do you want foreigners thinking that? No! Now, off you go!'

I see none of the scenery up to the next post, my mind preoccupied with my clash with authority. I don't have any memory of what the path is like, other than that we remain under the cover of trees. It is at this hut that my visa is studied for a few moments and actually stamped. I have entered Guinea, finally.

Though I have reached my sixth country, my journey through the mud-drenched lanes between Québo and Boké hasn't ended. As we skid over the surface the path widens, but is otherwise in no way improved as the bikes pull up at the end of the path beside the Kogon River.

The Kogon is incredibly beautiful, much like the calm natural scenes around Buba, and crossing the river with only the splashing of the paddle breaking the natural sounds of the forest is unforgettable. The bikes are loaded onto dugouts, lying precariously on their sides in threes, while I and the other passengers are pointed to another. We crouch in single file over the dirty hull, my legs screaming after the hours I've already spent on the bike, as small ribbons of river water run from nose to stern. The man-powered crossing is lengthened as the piroguers fight the upstream current before allowing the bow to be caught by the flow and taken without further struggle to the opposite bank, creating a U-shaped wake that is the only short-lived evidence I am ever here.

I force myself back onto the bike, between backpack and driver, my muscles tight, for the steep incline away from the river into an interminable ride on continuously rough paths that stretch my mental and physical strength to breaking.

Among a scattering of buildings several hours later the path widens into a road. The driver and I dismount in search of food. I groan as a mural on the side of a bar points to my destination, Boké, being 53 km away. I am not sure whether I can stand the bike for that long, my legs now continually locking and cramping, and I'm too fatigued to hold my body in the right position for riding. But knowing there is a definitive end I begin to relax, and start to enjoy the journey once more. The trees open out into beautiful hilly country-side, the odd palm standing tall, forests lining the more distance hills of Guinea's highlands. My grip on the bike's mud-splatted chrome-plated surfaces lessens and I am able to hold branches out of the face of my driver. I lend him my sunglasses, squashed out of shape after the day's ordeals, to stop the dust catching in his eyes.

I let out a small whoop of joy as the bike's wheels kick out at smooth tarmac for the first time for the last five kilometres to Boké. I manage a smile as the bike's speed increases, the wind hacking through my dusty hair and forcing tears from my eyes. It has taken seven hours to reach a point that cannot be more that 100 km from where I began the day's journey. I look a wreck. My legs are splattered with dried mud to the knee and I struggle to walk. My shoes ooze liquid at every step and have turned the dark ruddy brown of the dirt roads. My feet have been wet since the first lagoon dunking. My face has a thick layer of red dust clumping under my eyes where the wind-induced tears have dragged it down. My hands are covered in the black river mud of the Kogon canoe crossing. I am dirty, tired, and desperate for a wash even if it is from a bucket rather than a showerhead.

I spend the next day in Boké, an old trading post and the biggest town in the area, to give my body a chance of recovery. After a long sleep my muscles ache only minimally and I am able to take a walk about town and into the countryside for views of the pristine forest that still holds populations of chimpanzee. In the shanty-built chop bars of the town I find tea and regain my self-esteem and confidence, beginning to lose my new found fear of authority that sees me subconsciously tighten whenever anyone in uniform passes by.

Towards evening there is a sudden flurry of activity as everyone tries to get under cover before a storm hits, which is longer than the night's electricity holds out. With a deep rumble of thunder the rain starts, making the flat corrugated roof of the chop bar sing. The thunder and lightning seem closer, harsher, and more powerful than I am used to. The traffic all but disappears from the road. As suddenly as the storm begins, and with another deep rumble of thunder, the rain drops to a level where it can no longer be heard bouncing from the tin roof. The traffic resumes and the bare electric bulbs and stereo system spark back into life.

When I force myself to Boké's *gare routiere* the following morning it is pleasingly full of battered yellow and black taxis, mostly aging Renaults desperately in need of retirement. I claim the *premiere place* in transport to Boffa about three hours away, another colonial trading post, situated on the Atlantic. My money entitles me to roughly half the passenger seat while another four passengers share the rear seats. The road is good in places, but rough in most. Deep, wide potholes come close to covering the entire width of the road, risking the vehicle's suspension with every kilometre. The longest stretches of tarmac last for no more than 100 metres at a time.

A sudden downpour halfway through the 100 km journey reveals a lack of functioning windscreen wipers. The strength of the rain forces me to wind up the passenger window, rapidly increasing the intensity of the heat inside the vehicle, and ridding me of a significant amount of space. My centre of gravity shifts onto the bruised areas of my legs, and my back becomes twisted, inducing a shooting pain that runs up my spine.

In spite of its history as an Atlantic trading post Boffa is tiny and incredibly poor. The battered lodgings of the local mission provide a clean bed while I search for food among the sparse stalls of the main road until it becomes too dark to see; eating a supper of canned sardines and fresh baguette by candlelight, before washing in a bucket and slipping under my mosquito net to the sound of geckos fidgeting among the missing window panes.

I wake to the sound of the World Service coming from another room. It would be easy to linger beneath my net for the rest of the day, but gathering my kit together I'm soon drinking a mug of tea from a building made from vertical planks of wood beside a vehicle slowly filling for Dubréka. A continuous ribbon of tarmac runs to the town along the coast, though at a fuel stop I have to leave my place in the back for a stretch.

'You're tired?' asks the driver.

'Yes' I reply, 'My legs are.'

'It's all those women in the back, squashing you with their massive arses! Don't worry we'll soon be in Dubréka.'

I ask him to stop me a few kilometres south of Dubréka, beside the river Soumba, where I relax after a hard few days. The river is the nearest I come to running water for a week, and the best bath I have had yet in Africa. I'm the cleanest I have been in days, with the grit beneath my nails gone, and feeling completely refreshed. I only get out when I'm in serious danger of dissolving into the water. But it's impossible to feel clean for more than five minutes with the salt spray caught by the wind from the lapping waves of the ocean, the sand grains clinging to the sweat, sunscreen and insect repellent, the dusty red soil and city pollution of places like Conakry.

The road to Conakry consists mainly of potholed mud and stones, with traffic more appropriate to the M6 around Birmingham, the result of Chinese led road reconstruction works. There may be a million Chinese in Africa, a tiny percentage of the continent's total population, in roles of leadership like managers in construction work. From the maze of roads and overpasses, I see the gleaming metalwork of the new Conakry Express train waiting at a simple concrete platform. I walk along the ocean road of the spit of land sticking out into the Atlantic that forms Conakry's historic centre. The railings and balustrading of the corniche are rusting, cracked, often broken; the road some-times not fairing any better. A taxi driver stops to add his own waters to the Atlantic. The waves steadily carve out sections of the road beyond the rock defences with regular breaths. There are no beaches; just rocks and rubbish. From what I see of Conakry, the city is filthy dirty, dirt poor, and expensive. Almost everything has to be imported, the country lacking any manufacturing base beyond brewing the local lager. Away from the rat infested rocks, rubbish is piled into small mounds along the roadside and ignored. A pile sits just outside the hospital gates, empty saline bottles and syringes sticking out amid other detritus of hospital treatment. It's a demonstration of a country starting again from scratch.

In a historical quirk it is the former Portuguese colony, Guinea-Bissau, which is a member of the French-engineered West African Franc zone. In contrast, Guinea, the former French colony has its own franc, the only French colony to vote for total independence instead of federation when France was trying to keep control of its colonies in the late 1950s.

Aside from the rubbish there isn't a lot to be seen in Conakry; so much of my journey being about experience rather than sights. The closed old cemetery of Boulbinet, probably locked since its last interment in 1946, looks picturesque from the hustle of the impromptu stalls which line its extensive walls. Destroyed in February 1996, the Palais des Nations, right on the tip of the spit of land, is more lively, with building work taking place behind the high sheet metal fencing that stops me getting any real views of the progress to date. Having been built to host a later cancelled 1984 Organisation of African Unity meeting, it became the presidential residency until army rebellion destroyed it along with Ahmed Sékou Touré's legacy and the country's political stability, for a further 25 years. The country's first demo-cratically elected president is only in his second year in office as I traverse the nation. Guinea is two years along the road to development, 50 years after voting against French federation.

For me, everyone I meet in Forécariah, south of Conakry, falls under the classification of poor, and some of the poorest people I have met. But to them, they are rich if they have clothes on their backs, food on the table, and their children in

48

school. Travelling through Guinea has brought home to me how much of what I take as necessity in Britain is actually a luxury hundreds of millions of people in Africa lack. People live, even after dark, with the barest essentials. It makes me wonder what is actually needed to ensure a thriving nation, and what isn't.

Waiting to leave the *gare routiere* in Forécariah a young girl moves steadily closer to where I stand, until eventually having the confidence to gently stroke my arm, intrigued by its skin colour and hair. She will only ever have seen a white man on the bad quality pirate DVDs of American programmes on show at the small omelette bar at the junction in town where I ate last night.

A tiny red Renault 295 takes me to the border crossing at Pamelap along a road with the now standard combination of good stretches wrecked by deep mud-filled potholes, a sight so usual in Guinea that I almost forget to make any mention of them in my diary.

A scrum develops around me as I struggle out of the vehicle at the border, shouts of 'I have one place to Freetown, one place!' filling the air around me. Others offer to exchange money, or more comically, show me small shards of broken glass that they hope I will mistake for uncut diamonds. There's little doubt I'm about to enter Sierra Leone.

Sierra Leone

He stood quietly for a while breathing in the heavy smell of
the sea…he could hear nothing from the water but the water
itself, slapping against the jetties. The magic of the place
never failed him: here he kept his foothold on the very edge
of a strange continent

Graham Greene, *The Heart of the Matter*

I have no immediate idea where Guinean formalities end and
those of Sierra Leone begin. I am dealt with kindly and
quickly, my experiences crossing between Guinea-Bissau and
Guinea only a memory. There is no obvious demarcation
between the nations, a sign declaring *corruption slows
development* where I might expect one reading *welcome to
Salone,* the name Sierra Leoneans give to their country.
Below it, a round-faced military policeman may or may not
be asking me for a bribe.

'Morale is very low here,' he says looking over my
passport. 'Anything you can leave would make us happier.'

The man inside the immigration department building is
very cheery, clearly not suffering any drop in morale.

'You are from Great Britain. *Great* Britain. Not *small*
Britain, *Great* Britain. I had a lecturer at my school who
always used to say he was from *Great* Britain. Welcome.'

A brand new highway, with markers every kilometre, runs
directly from the border to Freetown, but I choose to make
my first stop in Sierra Leone at Kambia, a few kilometres
from the border and 144 km from the capital. Almost
everyone I pass here greets me in some way. A group of

children beam after having shaken hands with me, their fingers sticky with the orange halves they have been sucking for the juice.

A very jolly man, a traditional West African patriarch, Ibrahim introduces himself as 'retired from urban planning, but not tired'. Having set up the hotel after returning from the United States he liked the tranquillity so much he moved in himself, now sharing the hut next to mine with his wife. He even manages to call me Ian, most people so far not even recognising it as a name, and assuming it to be some sort of prefix like Dr or Rev. He has his eyes set firmly on the future.

'We are hoping now with the new road going all the way to Freetown the area will develop more. People might want to see the country without the "safari" roads' he tells me. 'Next month they start on the water supply to Kambia, then they will do the electricity – it's all private power at the moment. The President is a real democrat. He cares about the welfare of the people.' Ibrahim goes on to tell me I am sharing my accommodation with the US ambassador, who stayed here only three nights ago. I ask if the guard armed with an AK47 is really necessary. 'Prevention is better than cure' he replies.

I am eager to be within sniffing distance of the Atlantic again and accept the last unpadded seat on a *poda-poda* minibus to Freetown. Like Conakry, Freetown stretches out into the choppy Atlantic on a peninsula of land. The new road is already scratched and badly patched in places by traffic that begins to snarl in Waterloo, the first town on the Freetown peninsula and now a Freetown suburb, about 60 km from the centre of the capital. The traffic gets gradually worse, as I swap vehicles on a Waterloo roadside helped by a woman officer from the Sierra Leone national police in perfectly starched uniform.

The traffic in central Freetown is about as bad as it can get, with vehicles barely moving, though mototaxis are able to weave through the still traffic, inching past wing mirrors.

Coaches jostle for space with trucks, carts, cars, taxis, the mototaxis and pedestrians pushed from the narrow pavement by market stalls. It is hectic, and purposeful.

I leave my vehicle and walk uphill through the bustling market, clothes hanging for sale from the chain-link fences of the parliament building on Tower Hill, beside stalls stacked high with well-thumbed books, and men selling small pieces of grilled beef served on torn sections of newspaper. Women haul enamel trays of fruit on their heads through the crowds. They are so heavy I struggle to raise one back onto the head of a woman I buy oranges from.

Views from Tower Hill show off Freetown's aging centre, ringed by painted corrugated tin shacks climbing the surrounding hills. Many of the buildings from the era of the British protectorate fare better than their 1970s tower block offspring, despite the 200 year age difference.

Culturally and historically, the centuries old cotton tree close to the institutions of state is the heart of the city. The tree became a symbol of the city when freed slaves from the American war of independence landed on the beaches of the peninsula to found the city on March 11th 1792, although the first 400 freed slaves arrived from London on 10th May 1787. I learn later that cotton trees are an integral part of every village, the home of the ancestral spirits, as well as the bats that hang from the capital's.

In sight of the cotton tree is the Sierra Leone Peace and Cultural Monument, a series of three dimensional murals and concrete statues painted in vivid colours that explain unifying moments within the country's history. The civil war was brought to an end in 2002, with peacekeepers able to leave the country four years later. Sierra Leone is now able to send peacekeepers to Somalia. In comparison, British troops remained in Bosnia 15 years after the conflict there. Society is so well rounded I find it hard to believe there has ever been a war. A guide of perhaps 18 leads me through the series of murals and into a narrow hall of remembrance.

'This hall was officially opened two days ago by the president of Sierra Leone, Mr Ernest Koroma' he tells me. 'I must apologise for the mistake in spelling on this plaque: it reads "golry" rather than "glory". It was imported from abroad. We need to send it back now.' After a pause in which I take in the bouquets of plastic flowers and the names of the dead in gold on black around the walls he goes on 'I have to tell you my father's name is listed on these walls. My mother died by the gun three years later'.

The bay's flat grey water faces old government wharf, echoing the sky. I climb the eroded tall basalt block steps where freed slaves first set foot on the land that came to be called Salone. Midway up the tarred road of Leicester Peak a family of rock breakers work. Fathers use sledge hammers to smash up larger rocks, while mothers and children use smaller hammers, surrounded by pools of gravel.

I walk on through the green grass and red dirt hills to Regent and Hill Station, with its old rail sign, before returning to government wharf by mototaxi, dipping around the other traffic past old Krio houses of cream painted hand-cut horizontal planks, the side of the lower storey open, an enclosed staircase fronting the road like a bulbous calloused nose.

My horoscope for the day is a mixed bag but suggests it's a good, if expensive, time to move on from Freetown: 'Travel will be favourable. You could be quite erratic regarding your personal relationship. Expect to pay more than anticipated for entertainment or other purchases'. To reach transport heading to the peninsula beaches of Kent, I'm directed through some of the roughest parts of the capital, tin shacks hidden from the rest of Freetown, Krio houses, open sewers; the areas foreigners are told to steer clear of. Plenty of people point me in the right direction; none suggest I'm doing anything odd by walking around here.

Kent has budget busting accommodation, and perhaps the most beautiful beach I have ever seen. Devoid of rubbish, empty of people, with yellow-orange sand, rock pools, and views on the one side of lush Banana Island and on the other of tree-lined hills running down to meet the sea. Throughout the night I can hear the reassuring sighs of the ocean breathing, and I'm pleased to be directly on the coast for day 50, even if I must depart from it immediately on leaving Kent to take transport south.

The shared taxi from the peninsula reeks of fuel so badly I'm concerned that the scrum for places might ignite the vapour while I'm being escorted by a badged transport official to the passenger seat, which I share with two others as well as the driver. The passenger in the shining vehicle that passes before we depart is less cramped. A crowd gathers as police officers appear at various points along the roadside. A pair of motorcycle outriders lead the way, followed by two pickup trucks ahead of the gleaming black limousine, its licence plate simply displaying *P1*. A sincere cheer rises from the crowd as the limousine slows, and a presidential hand waved through the lowered rear window.

Moyamba will never be on a tourist's list of places to visit, even when the final 35 km of potholed road is replaced. It would be like someone from Sierra Leone travelling to Britain in order to visit Milton Keynes. There is no sense of history, no reason to visit but for the concrete cows of Milton Keynes and an incomplete concrete clock tower in Moyamba topped with an angel launching itself over the town; people getting on with living in both towns. It is, however, a convenient place to stop for a night before continuing by minibus to Bo, the country's second city.

There is an atmosphere of jollity to Bo that Freetown lacked. It has a lived in feeling, while Freetown had a worked in feeling, everyone disappearing from its heart come nightfall in the early hours of evening. A town built around the export of diamonds, it has a large Lebanese community, if a lack of public transport. Many routes consist of a single road to a single coastal town, the road network sparking off from the country's central towns like the legs of a spider from its body.

A converted four-wheel drive vehicle takes me along one of these roads to the coast at Mattru Jong; standard seating facing front and three tightly-packed plain wooden benches filling the space in the back where I find a seat. The tar runs out as soon as we leave Bo. The unpadded wooden benches, the complete lack of anywhere to hold on, the rough metal sides of the vehicle, and a severely rutted road make me consider getting off well before Mattru Jong, though there is not any town of any size along the way. It's difficult to remain seated with all the bumps and jolts, and the slow speed means it becomes unbearably hot. Sitting side-on makes it feel more like a boat trip, and I am not a good sailor. I get seasick in well-filled baths. I keep the rust-coloured road in sight through the five or six wandering heads in front of me. I try to stretch tiring muscles by lifting myself from the bench; the constant bumps push me back against the bench and the vehicle's sides.

I am soon offered oranges, and handfuls of rice baked and combined with sugar. We also share the responsibility of supporting one another. A group effort is required to stop the middle bench and its passengers rolling onto me, an accident that would have shattered my shin bone.

With the journey stretching into its fourth hour some of the other passengers confirm our arrival at the coast. An old gentleman dressed in blazer and smart trousers leads me to the Pennywise Guesthouse, a lovely welcoming place with large rooms and dodgy-looking electrics, the fan directly wired into a plug socket. The bed is large enough for four or five, only serving to emphasise my solitude.

Over a mug of sweet tea in a nearby chop bar I start up a conversation with Mohammed, a medical student. He is soon talking of the war, doing so with a detachment that I find surprising.

'Mattru Jong used to be a good *good* place' he says. 'But during the war, here all the buildings were burnt. It used to be good.' The dilapidated, soot-covered stone buildings start to make sense, and as if to prove a point an amputee, the stump of his left arm neat at the wrist, walks past like any other shopper. The civil war was one of the bush, not of the towns. Its complex beginnings stemmed not from a desire for political power but for resources: Sierra Leone's diamond industry. With the support of Liberian rebels led by Charles Taylor, anti-government forces successfully overthrew the civilian government, and with it the country's peace. Amputation of hands and arms was a common way of ensuring the loyalty of the population.

I breakfast on rice and *saka-saka* leaf sauce, removing the small fish carcass which is returned to the pot, at the empty *poda-poda* park on the edge of Mattru Jong the next morning, to follow the single road with public transport back to Bo. Many of those waiting were in the vehicle with me yesterday and we're soon discussing my journey. On hearing that I will not be returning to England for another 10 months, one woman says, 'By August you will have studied a lot of Africa. Maybe you can write something.'

'Maybe' I reply.

Having the same driver as yesterday has the advantage of being given one of the front facing seats with padding, to my great relief. I'm eager to leave Mattru Jong, but not of leaving on the hard bruising benches I arrived on yesterday.

A short distance from town a group of school children start cheering from the roadside.

'You know what they are saying?' asks the large middle-aged woman next to me.

'I can guess. It's like being a pop star.'

'They are cheering the white man.'

As she falls asleep, her right thigh collapses onto mine, pinning me down. It's so heavy I can't push it off me.

A day later and I'm back in a *poda-poda* waiting for additional passengers for Potoru.

'If you had a private car' says the only other passenger at 9 am, 'you just go. Very quick. No waiting for people. You become *mobile*.' It takes the entire morning for the vehicle to fill.

As far as Bandajuma the road surprises me in being good level grey tarmac. Even when the vehicle runs over the end of the tarmac to bare earth it is well-maintained and drivable at speed. I disembark to meet a waiting mototaxi that takes me the 16 km to Kambamba village. I keep my backpack strapped to my shoulders, where it wobbles precariously, threatening to drag me from the bike as I head between the peaks of the hills. Its weight pulls me back on uphill sections and pushes me close to the driver as we head downhill.

It is then a short motorised inflatable ride across the Moa River to Tiwai Island Wildlife Sanctuary. I see various types of monkey without even leaving the camp: Diana monkey, sooty mangabey, maybe even a black-and-white colobus in the trees lining the clearing that contain tents protected by metal roofing for paying guests, and more traditionally structures housing the staff, kitchen, and unplugged alcohol fridge.

The forest is still dripping from an early morning rain shower as Mohammed guides me into the trees for a forest walk of the 10 by 20 km island. I add a sighting of red colobus to my list, as well as confirming sightings of the monkeys I have previously seen. No chimpanzees however, one of Tiwai's main draws, or the secretive and nocturnal pygmy hippopotamus.

The sights are spoilt by the suspicion someone had been through my stuff when I return to the camp clearing. Had I imagined it or had my papers on the table outside the tent moved beneath their weight. I think my guidebook might be the wrong way around in my day bag, having left it in the tent with my backpack.

I have an emergency stash of €50 missing from it. It is not so much the quantity that bothers me – though I could have done without losing it, as my cash reserves are running low. It is the cheek – not mugging me in the street, but taking from me when I have already spent a significant amount visiting the island. It is also the assumption I won't need the money to pay for my stay, or notice it has gone, and the assumption I can do without the money in the longer term. So often, on bad days, I feel like nothing more than a cash machine; with local hawkers pointing out their stores of soft cheese on the off chance I might be interested. I rummage about the various staff buildings as best I can, through the musty kitchen area, but the thief isn't as stupid as I am in leaving my money lying around. The anger burns inside me and leaving Tiwai early the next morning, back across the Moa River by inflatable, the bright sun sits just above the tree canopy, blinding me as I look back at the island with a confusion of feelings.

From Potoru I spend time in negotiating with the owner of a mototaxi for an acceptable price to take me to Zimmi, where another takes me on to Jendema; the only forms of transport I am able to find. The second driver is what a Sierra Leonean might call old, what I would call middle-aged. He weaves the bike slowly around the pond-like potholes of the dirt road saying 'it's nonsensical! ECOWAS' – the West African economic community – 'agreed to pay for this road the last time they met. The Liberians laugh at us. They have a new road from Waterside to Monrovia – you will see it.'

The road cuts through the hills to the border and I am reminded of the Quebo-Boké road. The memories become stronger as the pain starts to build in my upper thighs. Eventually I reach the point when I can't feel my legs any longer, and am unable to lift them from the foot rests to stop them ploughing through the unavoidable puddles. We use a boat-bridge, hardly changed from versions I have seen in films of Sierra Leone dating back to the 1950s pre-independence period, large floats supporting rubbed planks of wood, the bridge drawn across the river by men hauling against a thick wire at head height.

'You're British? You should come back and build us a bridge' says my driver dryly.

The Sierra Leonean immigration officers at the border ask for a receipt I don't have, having given it to the officers at the other end of the country.

'What can we do?' I say. 'I don't have the receipt. The immigration officer in Kambia has it.'

'Logic should have told you to keep the receipt.'

'I specifically asked, and he said "no, I must keep this". I trusted the official.'

'Give me US$40.'

'I don't have $20' I say, mishearing his request.

'I said $40.'

'If I don't have $20 then I don't have $40.'

'We do not take advantage of people here. See this sticker on the wall? "No to exploitation". You have exploited yourself by not having the receipt. Give me $10.'

The actual border between Sierra Leone and Liberia is a bridge over the River Mano. A man walking across it into Sierra Leone says to me 'you will enjoy Liberia. If you liked Sierra Leone, you will love Liberia.'

Liberia

The love of liberty brought us here

Official motto of the Republic of Liberia

My first impressions of Liberia are of contrast: the road sign for Waterside pierced multiple times by bullet holes fired from its northern neighbour distracting from the polite Liberian official dressed in a fresh khaki uniform.

'What are you doing here? Are you Peace Corps?'

'No, I'm a tourist.'

'A terrorist!'

'No, no. Tourist. I'm a tourist, heading for Robertsport.' Having got my visa at the embassy in Freetown with a made up letter of introduction from the convent in Monrovia that had the wrong dates included in it, I pass through Liberian immigration easily enough.

A shared taxi heading for Monrovia drops me at the junction with Robertsport, Liberia's northernmost coastal town, 43 km from the border along the well-maintained tar road my mototaxi driver in Sierra Leone told me I would see. The voracious tropical plants are already breaking through where tarmac and earth converges at the roadside. The road is so new it lacked road markings, though cats' eyes have been pinned to its centre.

The time it takes me to write up my notes for the day so far is how long it takes for a shared taxi driver to decide to make the day's last journey to Robertsport, the road from the junction a muddy and potholed 'gift of the American people' that gives occasional glimpses through the brush as it sidles up to the beauty of Lake Piso, Liberia's largest lake.

The view, on tiptoes, from the shared toilet of my lodgings is even more amazing, a colourfully flagged fishing vessel moored up beside the wooden shacks lining the banks of the lake, its men unloading fish. The view from the toilet far contrasts with the rooms, usually rented out by the hour, a huge bag of condoms sitting on the lone, otherwise empty shelf.

I'm led around the town for a quick tour before the light fades by Karl, a nomadic German hotelier and the only other European in town, who has given up on Liberia and is heading home just as everyone else is increasingly positive about the country's future.

'You see that camper van there? That's how I got here, driving down from Germany' he tells me, tapping grubby bare feet on the side of the wicker chair he's sitting on. I own a hotel just down the road, but there are no tourists in Liberia, so that…and other things…mean I'm going back home.' His van won't be going anywhere, the canvas roof torn, the tyres sagging limply like Karl's attitude. I ask him if he can tell me anything about the rest of Liberia.

'Er, I haven't travelled around much. At the beginning the men at the checkpoints were really forceful about taking bribes. I don't think it's as bad any longer.'

In Fante town, the buildings begin their metamorphosis from the concrete early twentieth century structures and plantation style houses with plush gardens to increasingly makeshift wooden shacks beyond the small airfield. More buildings sit across the runway, though a fluorescent orange windsock still dances in the breeze, hopefully expecting incoming aircraft. Large smokers dry the day's fish catch, stinging my eyes; flames dancing in the dusk. Some of the boats are massive, their keels cut from the trunk of a single cotton tree, the sides extended up with planking. Out of the water they rise high above me, the length of a couple of double decker buses.

Robertsport is an African town, in an African country. Liberia was never colonised, but created like Sierra Leone, as a place for freed and rescued slaves to reside on their home continent, a fact echoed by the country's motto. However, Liberia was not a barren space on the map of Africa, and only half a per cent of the modern population is able to trace its ancestry to the fight against trans-Atlantic slavery. For the ancestors of most, Liberia was already home. The continued clashes between the indigenous populations and the Americo-Liberian upper class were a trigger-point for the cycle of war that brought Liberia, and neighbouring Sierra Leone, to their knees.

A child of perhaps six sleeps on a wooden table opposite my bread, eggs, and tea, a common breakfast throughout West Africa. The table I eat off is covered in an old worn plastic cloth nailed in place, the nails rusted with age; the boy in nothing but white underwear. He seems serene against next door's roaring generator and the smash of Zamma pieces on wooden boards outside. A globule of mucus drops from one nostril at every breath. I doubt the children here, or anywhere in Africa, get the sleep they need; I doubt most get to be children for long each day. He wakes and takes the remaining slug of tea from my mug.

From beside the telecommunication masts on the top of the verdant hills overlooking town I look over a cannon with no markings or record of its history. Across the town there are large, elegantly constructed yet dilapidated buildings, structurally sound but decaying. The grand Tubman Centre for African Culture is also abandoned; a shell.

Three men struggle up the hill as I make my way down, their arms wrapped around heavy loads of firewood. I walk through the ruins of a two storey hotel, what must have been

63

the hotel, with views onto the crashing waves and fishermen dragging their nets onto the yellow-white sands. Everything had been taken from the hotel; its pipework, doorframes, fittings. All that remains is a roofless structure formed of concrete lintels. I walk around it slowly in the company of large orange-headed lizards that scuttle out of my path if I approach too closely.

I accidentally find myself in the middle of a *poro* secret society ritual in Kru town, an area of corrugated shanty dwelling close to the burning midday heat of the beach, while sitting on a bench out of the sun. Noise and commotion follows a man wearing traditional wax cloth about his waist instead of the usual denim, his bare torso smeared with white pigment. Carrying a cutlass – the nautical term still used in Liberia for machetes – he charges at another man. There is laughter, but also apprehension from those, like me, that are not society members. It's easy to revert back to images of the war when barely-dressed African soldiers wielded cutlasses in anger.

The confrontation is followed by further shouting, and rhythmic chanting. Men appear smeared in yellow pigment from head to toe; some with blue spirals across their bodies. Two more men appear, smeared with white, their eyes large. They carry a rough stretcher made from wrist-thick branches stretched above their heads. On the stretcher lies the rough mannequin of a man, whom they give drink before disappearing behind the houses, chanting all the while.

The road to Monrovia takes me quickly over bridges made by Pakistani engineers under the auspices of the United Nations Mission in Liberia (UNMIL), their battalion details on small metal plates tagged to the bridges with a nail. Crossing onto the capital's Bushrod Island we pass the UNMIL headquarters, tall white perimeter walls plastered with 'no photography' signs, topped with barbed wire, and watched by African sentries wearing blue flak jackets.

With my catholic upbringing the statues of the virgin Mary, and images of the Pope and unknown archbishops make me feel oddly at home in the guest rooms of St Teresa's convent. The solitude, given the constant and continual noise of Africa, disrupts my thoughts. One of the mesh windows among the guest rooms looks out towards the Ducor Palace Hotel, a cuboidal ruin at the summit of the highest point in the city. Like much else in the country, its name points to Liberia's early past, the Ducor contract the document that handed the land to the freed slaves.

A walk around the capital early in the afternoon reveals a city on its day of rest. Neatly dressed Monrovians shuffle into and out of the many churches on the incline of Broad Street, one of the city's main thoroughfares, towards the Ducor Palace. Many others are enjoying the coast around the capital, meaning the streets are unusually free of congestion. Historic monuments dot the centre, hidden among the still broken buildings; a pet monkey wanders the small circle of pavement allowed by its chain in a side street. I see a group of people in the upper floors of a building lacking its outer shell. Water drips onto an algae-lined patch of pavement below. Hand-painted banners advertise the leaders' debates that would be taking place in Monrovia City Hall in a few days' time before the presidential election runoff. The razor wire gives the most immediate sense of lawlessness, and I'm followed to the national museum by men hopeful of loose change.

The museum staff tell me the building used to house 6000 objects. Now there are a few hundred at best. A heavy eighteenth century table imported from England survives without its chairs, looted during the war with the rest of the missing collections.

The upper floor displays a series of photographs by Associated Press journalists dating to the end of the war,

65

around 2003. In streets I have already got to know are images of a female anti-Taylor militia fighter mid-scream as she brandishes an automatic weapon, the ground around her covered almost entirely with empty bullet casings; US helicopters cheered on by a crowd of civilians; people seeking shelter beside the UNHCR office; the hospital at Mamba Point taking in patients for the first time in years, a Médecins Sans Frontières 'no arms allowed' banner hoisted over an external wall; naked children washing in a rainstorm; all here, inches from where I am standing. It says something about Liberia's people that Monrovia is already so much a city, with functioning ATMs and workmen cutting ramps into the pavements of the new one way system on a Sunday afternoon.

I get a guided tour of the capital by a young *okada* mototaxi driver as we pass through the main streets of Monrovia on my way to the Côte d'Ivoire embassy to collect the next of my visas.

'That is our executive mansion. The front is on the other side, this is the back. The foundation stone was laid in the 1960s. It's bomb proof; for any sort of bomb. The current president abandoned it.' It's guarded by UN posts like squat children's dens, an elegant looking block epitomising sixties design. Behind the tall metal railings a large coat of arms hangs from the upper storeys: the sun rising above the Atlantic horizon, a tall ship reaching a land of palms beneath the flight of a dove carrying the Ducor contract in its beak. Africa's first female president, Ellen Johnson Sirleaf abandoned the mansion after an electrical fire in 2006. She transferred her office to the foreign ministry building nearby, and lives in her large Monrovia house, her government declaring rebuilding the mansion a low priority when there was so much else to do. She is still able to travel in style and safety though; a gleaming SUV roaring past me in a wail of sirens, the Liberian flag fluttering from the bonnet's right, the presidential seal from the left.

The international news has it as grey in England as it is in Monrovia, large banks of thunderous cloud gathering and dispersing, though I think I may have finally outlasted the rains that have followed me across West Africa.

The bush taxi passes a sign for Hannah's Cock Shop – a chicken farm – on its way to Buchanan 125 km down the coast. The road cuts through the endless neat lines of thin silver barked rubber trees rippling from the roadside between me and the Atlantic after the international airport at Roberts-field, nothing but UN aircraft on the tarmac beyond the low chain-link fence.

The Atlantic is brown in colour on Atlantic Street. The fishermen deposit their catches, large fish that would go for a fortune back home, at a couple of spots along the road, the life-blood of Buchanan in much the same way as fishing is the life-blood of coastal communities across the continent. I'm followed towards the beach, and small port, Liberia's second largest, by Traycee. She hangs around while I sit on the industrial tyres designed to prevent further land erosion asking such probing questions as:

1. Do you love me?
2. Do you have a fiancé?
3. Will you buy me food?
4. Will you buy me juice?
5. Will you buy me water?

I bump into Michael and Moses away from Traycee and the ocean on Roberts Street, named, like Robertsport and Robertsfield, after President Joseph Jenkins Roberts, the country's first president. Michael is young, blond and beard-ed; Moses middle-aged, black, with four broken teeth all that remains of his smile. I ask them why they are in Buchanan.

'Well, I-yon,' says Moses in his southern American drawl, 'we're on a fact finding mission.' My mind immediately jumps to the upcoming presidential election. 'We represent ministries in the United States who are going to build a *self-contained* village here: hospital, orphanage, school... We already have the land... Why are you here I-yon?'

'Oh, I'm doing my bit by spending my tourist dollars here.'

'Good, good. They need all the dollars they can get. But why Liberia, I-yon?' Moses asks.

'Well, I'm trying to circumnavigate Africa by publically available transport actually.'

'I think you've got angels up there circling' he says, pointing skyward.

The road through River Cess Town to Greenville is a loggers' road, a thin scar of rust-red dirt across the dark green face of the gently undulating landscape. I sit between the driver of the four-wheel drive vehicle and a Chief Inspector of the Liberian National Police, one of the most senior policemen in the country. The rest of the passengers sit on sacks of cargo on the open back, protected from the sun by a thin tarpaulin.

'Are y'all still aboard?' the driver shouts at routine intervals after a particularly punishing drop in the road surface, his accent thick and not unlike that of Moses.

After four hours of fighting the road, he is defeated by a deep pool of sludge that settles level with the tops of the tyres, the banks of the pool too steep to climb out of from a standstill. An apprentice leaps from the back to get to work collecting rocks and grit from the green verge, throwing them beneath the front wheels as I try to avoid toppling over in the sticky orange mud as I climb down from the cab.

'The road is bad' somebody says.

'You should have seen it during the rains. It was impassable' adds the Chief Inspector. 'Even the police vehicle, an American Ford, with force, couldn't pass.'

Splattered slightly in mud from the churning wheels, a large articulated lorry ploughs through the mud around our trapped vehicle, and the Chief Inspector gets us both aboard. Climbing the steps into the cab with my backpack, I find the controls all neatly labelled in German. If the road troughs were worrying from the height of a standard vehicle, they are rollercoaster scary more than two metres up in the cab as we cross the aging metal bridge across River Cess into a town of single storey buildings located haphazardly about the road.

The Chief Inspector is greeted respectfully by the town's policemen, occupying a small building beside a wooden flagpole from where they control the length of string that acts as the checkpoint into town. The most senior officer follows us to a chop bar where I get a mug of tea and some cake.

'Can I smoke?' he asks me.

'I guess so.'

'Smoking was banned indoors in Liberia last month' reports the Chief Inspector impassively.

'I'm sorry. I didn't realise' I reply, expecting the officer to stub out his cigarette.

'This man' he instead declares of me to the empty room, puffing deliberately at his cigarette 'is important man! I can see it in your fizziom, physiog, physiognomy?' he asks turning to me. 'You must know the word... As Chinua Achebe once said...' He goes quiet for a few seconds.

'I'm just a tourist' I answer, looking at the Chief Inspector for help.

'This man' the officer begins again, 'is come to check we are all doing things *right*. He travels with the Chies Inspecta. No white man would come all this way from his country just to *see* things.'

By darkness at seven, half an hour after the lone star flag is lowered from outside the police post, I'm almost certain no transport will leave the town tonight, and I'm led towards the only motel. I'm taken to a room containing nothing but an unmade mattress on the floor that carries the powerful aroma of dank sweat and sex.

I am woken early to find the Chief Inspector, my guarantor of transport that I have come to rely on, has already continued his journey to Greenville, leaving me on a bench beside the lone star flag.

The vehicle I get myself onto stinks so badly of petrol I have to breathe through my shirt, and the journey worsens as it breaks down three times in the first 45 minutes of travel. The last of these breakdowns looks to my untrained eye to be terminal. Ploughing through a particularly muddy furrow about as deep as the vehicle is tall there is a large crunch from the rear beneath my seat and we shudder to a halt. The left rear wheel is bent at an angle, the top of the wheel pointing away from the vehicle, the axle broken.

I am lucky to be quickly offered a seat in a passing pickup, its hugely inflated balloon tyres taking it easily around the broken vehicle. The road continues much as it did yesterday, a simple narrow path through the West African forest, our speed averaging no more than 35 kilometres an hour. Sharp braking swings the strong smelling carcasses of bush rat and monkey into my line of sight from where they hang on the outside of the passenger door.

It's dark well before we arrive into Greenville, a town destroyed during the civil war. Relying solely on the vehicle's headlights to cut through the darkness makes spotting the bumps difficult and judging their depth impossible. Ahead it's pitch black, a thunderstorm ensuring that not even the stars can brighten the way.

At Greenville the road that has roughly tracked the coastline of Liberia for two days ends. The timber from West Africa's last areas of primary rainforest is shipped out by sea. To reach the towns further along the coast my only option is a massive 200 km detour to Zwedru in the north-eastern corner of the country by mototaxi, heading inland about as far as it is possible to go in Liberia.

At the police checkpoint on the outskirts of Greenville Madam Captain Avis doesn't really understand the concept of a tourist, and needs my help to spell it for inclusion in her handwritten ledger. In daylight I can see that the worst stretches of the coastal road is the section leading into Greenville, where wooden planks have been thrown over the mud as makeshift pontoon bridges. Travelling by bike, without the concern of driving, gives me the freedom to observe the country without limit, hearing the sounds of nature and feeling the cool rush of air as we cut through the humidity at speed.

At the worst points of the road inland the mud is deep enough to have trapped a large lorry I'm told had been stuck, up to the wing mirrors, for a week. Had I arrived just a few days earlier, getting to Zwedru would probably have been impossible, and my circumnavigation would have ground to a halt. Moses would say my angels are working overtime.

Having reached Zwedru after several hours on the bike, the countryside unwilling to mark any distance with a change in landscape, I am leaving again within minutes, a four-wheel drive ready to depart for the far south-eastern corner of the country. As night falls, roughly four hours in, the road improves. Chinese-built bridges, barriers, and road signs line the perfectly smooth dirt waiting for its cap of tarmac. The rate of road improvement across the continent is astonishing, and I half expect the road to be complete before day break. Had I waited a few more years to start out on my journey it's very likely I would be able to complete the whole 40,000 km without using a single dirt road.

I only discover the name of Pleebo, where I spend the remains of the night, from a shop front in the Maryland County town the next morning, before finding a shared taxi for the last 30 km to Harper, the last town in Liberia.

At Bobby's teashop, a bar-like wooden structure painted bright blue I meet Maggie, a British-Malawian working with Ivorian refugees in Liberia. She directs me towards the beach at the southernmost point of town, Cape Palmas, along Maryland Avenue. It is the southernmost point of my journey until I reach Cameroon, and marks the beginning of the Gulf of Guinea. The path leads me through the historic heart of the town, among the monumental structures of the early twentieth century: the empty masonic lodge that towers above the road only a short distance from the presidential hideaway of William Tubman, now a squat housing twenty families. The contrasting hymns of different churches fill the air, including one sung to the tune of God Save the Queen.

At the beach a white guy arrives on a motorbike, introducing himself as Andrew, one of Maggie's co-workers. Sitting on a fallen tree trunk looking out over the small cove, with UN flights gaining height overhead from the small airport, he offers me weed and palm gin. It's relaxing to be able to speak without watching what I say. I tell him about other towns in the country; the isolation of Harper evident from my difficult journey from Buchanan; and of the calming breath of the waves, but the constant movement of his head tells me I've already lost him to the weed he's rolled into a cigarette.

When I meet Andrew and Maggie at Bobby's in the evening I wonder aloud why there were so many UN vehicles about, Egyptian soldiers driving the clean white all-terrain vehicles I've become used to seeing.

'Actually it's a lot quieter than usual' Andrew replies. 'Without the UN cars every day is a Sunday here. The military are still here, but the UNHCR etc. have all headed to Monrovia; in case there's election violence here.'

Harper reminds me a lot of Robertsport. There is a similar dilapidated charm to the concrete buildings; the same combination of sky, sea and sand; the same sense of otherworldliness, as if these two small towns are the only ones to exist; a sense that the true Liberia lies here.

It's possible the atmosphere has changed overnight, there being a pre-election nervous tension in the morning, though it might be my own concern for my border crossing. The constant radio talk-shows have been discussing the need for a peaceful election in homes and cars for days.

A mototaxi takes me to Pedebo, the driver shouting over the engine noise, 'Are you going to France?' It's a phrase Liberians have used to describe the former French colony of Côte d'Ivoire since at least the 1930s when Graham Greene records its use. I cross into Côte d'Ivoire by dugout canoe, a single immigration official on either bank of the River Cavally. It's probably my quietest and easiest border crossing so far in Africa. On the Liberian side, having asked me if I'm an undercover journalist, Thomas Collins gives me the mobile number of his sister Gertrude in Middlesex.

'When you get back to Britain will you phone her and tell her I am stationed here? She doesn't know I've been moved down here.'

'I will' I say, 'but can she wait another 11 months?'

Côte d'Ivoire

To the east of the Grain Coast – in maps – lies the Ivory
Coast, now a misnomer. Hardly a tusk has been exported
from it for the last score of years; the animals having been
driven away by the "hot mouthed weapon"

Richard F Burton, *Wanderings in West Africa*

Richard F Burton wrote those words in 1863, 122 years
before Ivory Coast would abandon the name in favour of Côte
d'Ivoire, and in doing so becoming the first of only two
nations to have United Nations membership under a non-
English moniker. The other isn't France.

The local women are still checking the progress of their
breakfast cake baking on open coals, the fire's smoke
combining with the cooling early morning haze, as I take a
shared taxi from the wooden shacks of the dusty river bank
along equally dusty roads. The unmade surface evolves
through to bad potholes that slow the taxi's speed until the
evolution is complete with aging tarmac as I reach San Pedro,
heading due east rather than in a southerly direction for the
first time. Gratifyingly, I am ignored at the manifold police
checkpoints along the way; and it's calming to feel part of the
furniture again, with children using me as a climbing frame,
and baggage jamming my feet into a tight corner of the
vehicle.

A haze sits over the forest that stretches across from
Liberia, the trees breathing a heavy sigh of relief in the falling
temperatures of evening. Beyond the River San Pedro the
forest stops dead, facing off a large milling operation running

to the water's edge from the outskirts of town. Vast heaps of standardised orange wood lengths line the road ready for loading and transportation, amid the sweet smell of sawdust and the distant roar of electrically powered circular saws. After the simplicity of life in Liberia the contrast with San Pedro causes me sensory nausea. As the centrally administered electricity supply, television, air conditioning and piped water continues across the bridge, its barriers rusted to oblivion, perhaps the forest will be given over to neat rows of palm oil, the perfectly regimented lines of mature rubber trees, or the decades old coconut plantations dripping in orchids that I have observed along much of this area of the coast.

The coconut palms lead along the coast to Sassandra, which I reach quickly, perched precariously on a foldaway seat behind a waist-high carved wooden mortar bowl and beside the sliding side door of the minibus, diesel exhaust stinging my eyes and producing long black stains on my shirt and arms. The apprentices hang from the window on the outside of the vehicle, repositioning the door every time it jerks out of its runner.

The village climbs the dark green hills behind ocean beaches lined with ranks of colourful pirogues swarming with fishermen. Away from the calls of 'le blanche' – the town used to the attention of French tourists – the western end of the long Ébrié Lagoon stretches just inland for most of the country's length. Locally grown coupé-decalé music, a deep bass rumbling under repetitive riffs that urge movement, plays from a stereo in a restaurant on an empty hill opposite the town. The unusual sight of working street lights creates small orange orbs of light as another day fades into night and I consider the next stage of my journey.

'You know someone in Grand Lahou?' I'm asked by a waiter.

'No.' I reply. 'I've just come to see; to experience.' He smiles uneasily.

'No African would ever go to another country just to see. An African will only go to another country to make money' he responds.

Grand Lahou provides me with a rest stop before arrival in the commercial capital, and the means with which to visit Lahou Plage, separated from the mainland by Ébrié Lagoon. From the dugout canoe the Atlantic breakers roll through a gap in the sandbank, sending odd currents rippling into the lagoon about the canoe. We bump the sandbank before a familiar row of buildings, small huts made from sheets of plaited palm fronds, dried and crackling in the light ocean wind, creeping over the crest of the bank into the distance. I sit on a tree trunk beneath shelter where the fishermen of the village mend their nets, allowing the lagoon atmosphere to envelope around me before I return to the mainland for lodgings.

The owner-manager of the hotel talks to me, the only guest, over dinner. On hearing I'm trained as a scientist he takes me for a sociologist and tells me about the region's tribes, stretching to Ghana, where he has lived, all the way to Nigeria. He sees Ghana as a golden land.

'The streets are so clean. There is no crime, the politicians care for the people and development. Here they say "if you fight and *die* for me, then I will help"; I'm joking, but that is my opinion. During the recent war,' the former president's attempt to cling to power in spite of democratic mandate that ended with UN military intervention shortly before my journey began, 'the Gbagbo rebels demanded, not asked, *demanded* free lodgings …they came and smashed in all the doors looking for stuff to take.'

He gives me a free breakfast the following morning, including fruit from his orchard, in celebration of 'tourists coming back here after the war'. He then hails a passing friend to take me the *gare routiere*.

A rattling coach takes me on to Abidjan, Côte d'Ivoire's biggest city and economic capital. It was the political capital until 1983, when the title was transferred inland to Yamoussoukro. Côte d'Ivoire, my ninth country, is the first country I cross that doesn't have a coastal capital, a demonstration of how Africa has been built from the outside in by colonial powers, the poorest of Africa's nations found deep in the interior, without direct access to the sea lanes of the coast.

Abidjan's centre, a smart sophisticated skyline of towers, lies about Ébrié lagoon with the look of a western capital set in the tropics. The atmosphere on the long straight avenue of trees lining the thoroughfare of Boulevard de la République is heightened by the chattering of thousands of fruit bats among the high branches, overwhelming the sounds of the traffic and street hawkers below. At one end of the boulevard UN vehicles stand guard outside key installations, while at the other is the modern construction of the catholic cathedral. Inside the architecture is staggering. The floor sweeps down to the altar, pews looking like those in an old school room, while the ceiling rears up above the altar to a towering crucifix outside. Behind and to either side of the altar, walls formed of bright storytelling stained glass are ignited by the sunlight.

I stumble in during mass to the sound of a choir so good I think I must be listening to a recording until I locate the singers at one side of the altar among the organ pipes. I find myself returning to my youth: kneeling, sitting and rising in unison with the congregation. It has been a long time since a church has so inspired me. The sign of peace seems to really mean something, with slow considered handshakes, perhaps because of the Fête de la Paix public holiday.

With much of the city closed for the holiday, I walk through the quieter-than-usual central streets passing the time by examining the scruffy stacks of French language novels on the stalls that remain open. The national museum is also closed; though I'm told by the curator it's because of the war, with staff in the middle of recataloging the exhibits that survived the loss of law and order. Buildings in the vicinity show similar signs of damage, with windows smashed and missing from the upper storeys of glazed towers.

I end up in the Deux Plateux district, an area of bookstores selling the latest imported European paperbacks, rather than stalls of dusty hand-me-downs, hypermarkets and takeaway pizzerias offering free motorbike home delivery. The traffic-free side streets are lined with the clipped grass verges of smaller embassies like that of Ghana, where I fill out an app-lication form in quadruplicate and squeeze a 48 hour transit visa out of the staffer behind the glass. A tourist visa is simply out of the question because I'm not applying from my country of residence.

Other suburbs of Abidjan, like where I find myself for onward connections to Grand Bassam, are less immediately attractive, as if poured from a single delivery of concrete, tower block pinnacles rising from the stop-start traffic of the grey streets.

The steady stream of locals means the fifty or so seats are soon filled and the bus is able to rumble into action, the engine noise quiet in comparison to the quack doctor loudly pitching the wonders of mysterious factory packed sachets while Abidjan rolls out on the other side of the unwashed windows; wide flyovers and monstrous central hypermarkets, interior decorating stores, the low slung buildings of a university, an airport heavily guarded by UN personnel, shacks of the poorest of the city's five million people combining with the lines of coconut palms three deep along the ocean road half an hour from Abidjan's central districts. The *au revoir Abidjan* sign doesn't come into view until we are entering Bassam, the road now lined with stalls selling carvings, large plant pots that will make their way to the gardens of the better suburbs, and wooden children's plaques depicting Smurfs and Disney characters cut by hand. The Atlantic looks invitingly blue.

From the dirty beaches at the eastern end of town, where children defecate without cover in front of distant fishing vessels coming in from the surf, the Atlantic seems angrier, white water roaring on the beaches from the deep ocean. The sun also seems in a particularly fierce mood, one that makes my walk around Bassam's shadeless colonial heart a draining experience. The old buildings stand with different stories to tell, some derelict and slowly crumbing, tropical foliage squeezing through the wooden planks barring entry, others still in use, as shops displaying the bright colours of drapes of wax cloth in otherwise empty rooms beneath handmade signs resting on plaster pilasters, saying things like *Hôtel Golf Bis*.

To reach the New Bassam area of the city, inland across the lagoon I've followed all the way from Sassandra, I cross the aging Pont de la Victorie bridge north, its decorative ironwork failing as much as that on the bridge across the River San Pedro. Clumps of water lily float slowly eastward with the windborne current. Old Bassam is a European city, with a similar feeling to Saint-Louis in Senegal; the place where the first French explorer and colonial administrator to Côte d'Ivoire, Marcel Treich-Laplène, died in 1890. New Bassam is where Africa takes over from Europe, bustling market stalls of school bags and artisan ironmongery re-placing the discreet restaurants across the lagoon, and from where I continue my journey.

It feels as if the beaches should run the entire 30 km to the cluster of villages around Assinie, the hotels so close to the ocean that some have already fallen into the sea, their staircases collapsed, massive cracks running up the remains of the two storey structures. The strength of the waves is also evident in the neighbouring buildings, where sandbags are being used unsuccessfully to stop the open-fronted bar and dining room disappearing entirely beneath the encroaching waves.

The blonde beaches are the playground of rich Abidjan residents looking for a weekend away from the city, taking advantages of the pristine beach gardens and à la carte menus of perfectly decorated restaurants set up to cater for them. The tracks of quad-bikes run parallel to the waves as straight and continuous as the rows of palms separating the ocean beaches from those of the lagoon around a burnt-out hotel complex.

I swap the beaches of Assinie for the banks of the River Bia, running through the gardens that contain flower beds spelling out the town name: Aboisso, a convenient stop before the border, where I'm able to buy a couple of shirts to replace my flagging stock of three, and use fireflies as my only light back towards the hotel on the hill overlooking the *gare routiere.*

The easy walk downhill next morning to the loose collection of battered cars around the Oil Libya petrol station, forming the town's only true gateway, leads to a comfortable journey to the towns of Noé and Elubo, either side of the border between Côte d'Ivoire and Ghana.

Ghana – Togo – Benin

Accra is one of the five West Coast towns that look well from the sea. The others don't look well from anywhere

Mary Kingsley, *Travels in West Africa*

The clock begins ticking on my journey through Ghana, the 48 hours I'm permitted to cross its 560 km of coastline running down from the moment immigration takes a head shot with a webcam and I hand over the arrivals card, a much smarter version of a form I first filled out five years ago. My plan of taking a leisurely path along the country's Atlantic coast via the changing architecture of over twenty castles built by Portugal, Denmark, Sweden, the Nether-lands and Britain impossible. Instead, a few steps away from the border I climb into a minibus direct to Accra; new, clean and with comfy seating, entirely unlike the *tro-tros* I had previously squeezed into in Ghana.

The road to the capital is as good as any I've travelled on, no different to the roads back home, the hassle-free nonchalance of Ghanaians extending to their road network, bumping the coast as I travel east. Towns I had dreamed of visiting, including Elmina and Winneba, jut perpendicularly towards the Atlantic. At Adioke I only manage to catch a glimpse of the town's squat stone fort before it has meshed among the other images flashing by the vehicle as it speeds on.

It's 133 km to the deep water port of Takoradi, and another 215 to Accra. As my head starts to droop I think that staying at the Hotel Messiah – 'a glimpse of heaven' – outside

Takoradi would have been a miraculous idea had I more time to linger. The urbanisation associated with the capital starts about 40 km out, along with an increase in traffic. It takes another 45 minutes or so in heavy, slow-moving traffic to reach rest.

Accra seems cleaner than it did during my earlier visit, public rubbish bins lining the streets of newly constructed banks, and if anything, the road leading out of Accra is smoother than the one with which I enter. I head directly for Afloa and the border, 27 hours still on the clock, following the coastal highway via Tema, 32 km away. The *tro-tro* begins its passage by passing many of Accra's sights, including the new seat of government at Flagstaff House, designed to recall the shape of a chieftaincy stool; bypassing the older, poorer neighbourhoods of Jamestown and Ussher Town with its fort and stumpy lighthouse, and the slum housing around the stinking sewage-filled lagoon of the Korle Gonno slums I remember with such fondness from my previous visit.

Towards the border, 185 km from Tema, beyond the beaches of Ada Foah, the road turns to clay, the tarmac broken up for improvement works. The landscape turns to one of lagoons spotted with weed that turn out to be only knee high with water when fishermen wander through them. I stop the countdown at 30 hours and 20 minutes.

It would be entirely possible to travel between Togo's borders in less than a tenth of the time it took me to traverse Ghana, matching almost exactly the different in coastlines between the neighbours. Togo is minute; too small to even get the 't', 'g' and two 'o's of its name across it on the maps I am carrying.

Its capital, Lomé, lies within sight of the border. I walk the semicircular Boulevard du 13 Janvier past the old presidential palace and national assembly building to the beach and embrace the evening breeze. Sitting alone on a concrete bench so high off the ground my feet don't touch the sand I read the words 'one of the worst things you could do is walk on the beach alone, especially at night' from my guidebook. This spoils the atmosphere for me, and with the orange sun sinking over the border with Ghana I go in search of some food, just as the city's bats have the same idea.

Over the West African staple of fried fish I realise my rapid transit through Ghana may have screwed me over more than the 'slightly' I had originally thought, with the only Nigerian embassy readily providing travellers with visas being that in Accra. In need of additional support, I head to the *marché des féticheurs* first thing next morning.

I arrive at the rectangle of sandy ground as sapped of energy by the dazzling sun as the ground must be of water. Within the compound a dozen or so rickety stalls bear all manner of dried bits of carcass, much of it looking like unloved old stock ready for the clearance bin: elephant tails, the hair coarse; crocodile skins pinned to the ground to dry; whole monkey heads; a display of dried chameleons; gutted rats and birds; necklaces made from snake vertebrae, a larger live version shifting deliberately within some sacking. After a photo opportunity with a crocodile skull, and having noted down a recipe for skin moisturiser – active ingredient ground up whole chameleon – I'm told I can meet the Fetish, a mound of clay that rises out of the earth in the corner of a rickety hut with attributes including a simple face; the sort with which a young child would finish an image of its parents; otherworldly powers, and an erect penis. As I'm led inside the hut, a cross between a shed and a life-sized Christian nativity scene, my English-speaking guide simply refers to the mound as Fetish; others refer to him as Legba, an incarnation of a major Yoruba god.

As the son of Fetish, a sort of Fetish priest, a boy of about 15, rings a hand bell my guide tells me to repeat my name three times for good luck. I'm then shown a series of fetish charms, one for every possible scenario. There is a large flat conker-like ebony seed for good memory, another charm for luck in love, a small bound figure of wood ensuring safe travel, a clay head specialising in burglary prevention, and the figures of a king and queen designed to keep my family safe.

With my need for a Nigerian visa I opt for the charm of safe travels. The Fetish decides how much I will pay through a series of otherworldly negotiations. The son of Fetish translates the desire of Fetish through the pattern of cowry shells he casts to the ground, accidentally knocking the rock-hard erection every time he does so. Reading the pattern he turns to my translator, muttering words without emotion that are eventually passed on to me in English.

'The Fetish says you have very good luck. The son of Fetish ask if you should pay 25,000', roughly equivalent to purchasing Togo, 'but Fetish say no. You are lucky. He ask Fetish if you pay 20,000. Fetish say no. He ask if you should pay 18,000. Fetish say yes. But, if this is too much you can suggest a price to Fetish.'

'How about 5,000?' I ask. The son of Fetish throws the cowries, knocking his father's erect penis one final time.

'You are lucky' smiles my translator.

On the beach on the other side of town I try and remember what the guide has instructed me to do with the charm to ensure its protection.

'You must whisper into its mouth with your travel plans' he had said, failing to add 'without looking like a complete lunatic to anyone watching'. He had gone on 'then you must plug the mouth to stop the wish escaping. At the end of your journey you must remember to release the plug, so your wish can return to Fetish completed'.

Perhaps I didn't speak to my charm clearly or nicely enough. Almost immediately the fan in my grotty room catches alight, and I spend much of the next morning sitting on a deep sofa at the reception of the Nigerian embassy, waiting for a senior staff member to come out of a meeting.

When I finally make it into her office I hardly have time to admire the plushness of the carpet before I'm leaving again. She flicks through the pages of my passport casually as she says, 'I cannot issue you with a visa. You should have applied in your country of residence. This is the rules.' She flicks to a new page. 'You have been in Abidjan? Why didn't you apply in Abidjan?'

'Because Togo is closer to Nigeria.'

'No.'

'But surely they would have told me the same thing anyway.'

'I don't know.'

'You told me those were the rules.'

'But, maybe... I'm sorry. I cannot help you.'

Having no need to stay in Lomé any longer I take a short *zemi-john* mototaxi ride to the market-like *gare de Cotonou*, though Benin's main coastal city isn't my immediate destination. Leaving the capital, the bush taxi skirts the landward side of the *port autonome du Lomé*, the high breeze block walls covered with the roughly written warning *interdit du jardin*, no gardening.

It turns out, from my evening stroll in Agbodrafo, a village on the banks of Lac Togo and my day's destination, that it is much, much harder to pronounce than it is to walk around in 10 minutes. An ordinary African side street, uncared for, its last buildings a couple of better-looking chop bars, runs perpendicular to the lumbering lorries of the coastal Abidjan-Lagos corridor to the drying pirogues at the water's edge. The sun doesn't so much set as disappear behind the lake, causing the unbroken surface to take on a dull and uninviting air.

As the waters ignite again with morning I pass the two chop bars to the pirogues, swapping the Atlantic for a crossing of the lake to Togoville, a centre of voodoo practices like those I witnessed at Lomé's fetish market. The pirogue trip takes about 40 minutes, a twelve foot long central spine of a palm frond used to punt the narrow wooden boat across the water; the only real sounds that of the water dribbling from the frond as it is lifted from the lake bottom.

Togoville in turn has the deathly quiet of a village not quite sure what to do with itself, unsure whether to court or dissuade tourists from visiting. Climbing the steps from the shoreline I ignore the voodoo tours and strike out randomly on foot away from the market, eventually following an abandoned rail line in a large loop around the town. I encounter very few people until I return to the marketplace, though most of the stalls are empty in the lunchtime heat.

I'm squeezed into an old Peugeot heading for Cotonou, balanced over the handbrake with my knees tucked out of the way of the gear lever, breaking the journey at Aného, a town that sits firmly on the Abidjan-Lagos corridor. Access to the Atlantic is blocked by a thin tail of Lac Togo, and while the lake is a cold blue, the ocean, behind a deep orange sandbank, is invitingly aquamarine. The ocean's inaccessibility gives me the dreary sense of there being a long way still to journey, though Aného's Quartier Jericho must only be a couple of kilometres from the border post at Hilakondji.

Country number twelve has just over twice the coastline of Togo. I have onward transport before I am even stamped into Benin or have time to alter my watch, and while I am still 100 metres from leaving the no man's land between immigration facilities. Crossing the border I jump forward an hour, the first time I leave the Greenwich meridian on African soil, and a pleasing demonstration of just how far I have travelled; 6000 km in three months.

I jump into a bush taxi to Ouidah, sitting on top of the padded and unused handbrake. A modern archway welcomes me from the clean tarmac highway to a town that effortlessly combines Christian and traditional belief. Opposite the soaring grey-blue height of the catholic basilica is a small round windowless concrete hut roofed in thatch; the temple of Dangbé, the serpent god.

Inside, there's not much other than a knee-high concrete plinth ringing a pit that would make a perfect bench to rest on in the cool interior if it were not for the 50 coiled sleeping royal pythons, ancestors of the serpent deity. A temple custodian, a priest of Dangbé, grabs a favourite and shoves it into my hands before either of us can protest. A minute later and he's wrapped it around my neck, a strangely comforting feeling, like having a well-loved scarf across my shoulders, at least until the snake pushes its head and flicks its tongue towards my own, and then it's a lot like having a python around my neck. The skin is dry and smooth, as if lacquered. Beneath it I feel nothing but tough muscle perfectly adapted for crushing the rats and mice it feeds on. The custodian says the temple is 160 years old, and the snake eagerly exploring my shoulders 112.

Close to 300 years old, and Portuguese territory until 1961, a state within a state, is Fortaleza São João Baptista. Climbing the double stairway to the right of an open courtyard, it is the whitewashed walls of its rooms that interest me rather than the water stained copies of images hanging from them. With Ouidah the only port in Benin until the twentieth century, it was these walls that witnessed Benin's part in the Atlantic slave trade; the fort's gates the start of a four kilometre forced walk to the slave ships anchored offshore.

Following in the slaves' footsteps along the *route des esclaves* it seems appropriate to also walk. Locals and tourists alike pass by on motorbikes, the tyres digging deeply into the orange sand leaving snaking tracks, the route still the only path between the town and the Atlantic. The paint flaked snake swallowing its own tail and the arching body of a chameleon are two of many shrines and fetish monuments lining the distance. The tree of forgetfulness stands forlorn; slaves would circle the tree to forget their lives, their names, their families. The path ends at a second, modern gateway; a point of no return framing the ocean beyond, among the souvenir stalls laid out on the ground around it. The stallholders try to capture the attention of the few tourists as I follow a footpath along the coast to the Jubilee 2000 monument, a wall blocking sight of the ocean but for the Benin-shaped cut out.

'A-lle-*lu*-ia!' cries a woman facing inland, arms raised. 'A-lle-*lu*-ia! Jesus is Lord!'

I sit predominantly over the handbrake of the bush taxi for the 50 km journey to Cotonou's *ancien pont*, its old bridge; the rusting iron spanning the lagoon that links Lac Nokoué with the Atlantic. To one side of the bridge stand the ugly red and white horizontal stripes of the catholic cathedral's exterior, still sporting the banners of welcome from the visit of the Pope just a week before. To the other side stands the expensive Hôtel du Lac, followed by shanty dwellings running all the way to the sandbar at the mouth of the lagoon.

My first real task in Cotonou is to try for a Nigerian visa. A failure to do so limits my possibilities for the journey to giving up. The first task at the embassy is to nip around the corner and photocopy a few application forms for the staff. Then, with form filled out in duplicate, photos attached, and with copies of passport, Benin visa, yellow fever vaccination certificate, and a letter of introduction, I make it beyond the waiting room and into the clutches of the presiding officer, a man with so little time he carries out his interviews in the embassy foyer. It has taken me five days to get to this point. The officer looks through my sweat stained photocopies, pausing at my letter of introduction.

'Good; good' he says. 'Now I need a copy of the passport or driving licence of this person.'

'Really? Ah, okay' I say, 'but it might take some time.'

'No' is his response. 'It is easy. You phone them, get them to scan in the passport or driving licence, they email it to you, you print it off and bring it back *straight away*.'

'But they are busy people.'

'I'm a busy person too.'

I race to the only internet café I know in Cotonou and send off a pleading email to the writer of the letter, not so much a friend of a friend as an acquaintance of an acquaintance who has no reason to be helping me. Its times like this that I feel very alone. I am far from everyone I care about, and even if I were closer they could do nothing to help my situation bar claim Nigerian citizenship and make their way rapidly to the position of ambassador to Benin. Maybe Nigeria was going to be unlucky country 13.

With no immediate response to my email I have to revert to tourist mode, and I hail a minibus heading beyond the shoreline of Lac Nokoué. From the wooden jetty piroguers dig their paddles deep into the water, past fish traps and fishermen throwing spiralling nets, to Ganvié, a stilt village eight kilometres from shore. As unusual as it is for visitors, as a home to 30,000 Tofinu people whose ancestors were fed up of being chased around by slavers, Ganvié is like every other African town I have passed through. The sandwich women travel by boat, trays in front of them rather than balanced expertly on their heads; there are the stands of untaxed petrol smuggled in from Nigeria; the churches, schools and homes; the nightclub and waterways instead of lanes where local teenagers meet each evening.

In Cotonou, the teenagers linger about the beaches within sight of the Chinese-funded and Chinese-built convention centre richly named the Palais des Congrés. Liberia's Grain Coast, Côte d'Ivoire's Ivory Coast, and Ghana's Gold Coast all lead to these beaches, the Slave Coast. The memorial beside the convention centre is deserted, an air of despondency to it. A bronze statue depicts Liverpool, Virginia and the Slave Coast united by the trade of humans, and uniting in friendship at its end.

Among the government offices opposite I'm ordered away from the shaded bench I am sitting on by a soldier. After dark I can see nothing out to sea but the cargo vessels lining up for a berth in the port, each lit up like Oxford Street at Christmas.

I think I see the phrase 'abandon hope all ye who enter here' above the doors of the embassy as I enter, like a child on Christmas Eve.

'You have the additional information?' asks the presiding officer. 'Good; good. What is this? I need a mobile telephone number, not an office number. What if I want to contact this person out of hours?'

My heart sinks, aware how long the process has already taken. Failing to get the visa now will mean a further five days waiting. I race to an internet café in another panic, praying for an immediate response to my increasingly desperate and ridiculous requests. My eyes flick from the desktop clock to my email inbox and back.

I jog to the embassy despite the heat, greeting the gatekeeper like an old friend.

'Okay' says the presiding officer, 'that's it. You can go. Come back at four to collect.' Instantly my only problem becomes a lack of small change, and no cocktail stick to eat the cubes of fresh pineapple with which I celebrate.

Despite the presence of Nigeria's embassy and most of the government in Cotonou, Benin's capital is Porto Novo, situated on the northern shore of Lac Nokoué. A steady stream of bush taxis commute between the cities, as an early morning haze stretches towards the border, and Nigeria's former Yoruba kingdom of Oyo.

The kings of Porto Novo paid tribute to Oyo, never recovering their former power, even if King Toffa's palace remains. The Nissan of the present king, no longer with political power, is parked on the pavement outside, marked as unusual by its blacked out windows and number plate, reading *his majesty the king* beside the image of the cow tail fly-whisk regalia of traditional chieftains.

The palace compound is said to date back to the 1600s, the current incarnation formed of several connected quads lowered beneath ground level to collect rain water. The quads are surrounded by rooms for the king, his family, and the 108 queens King Toffa married. A *chambre noire* was reserved for the kings who lost wars with neighbouring tribes to commit ritual suicide.

Walking through the market I pass a *feticheurs* cart loaded with all manner of bones, horns, and skins and come to a tall structure resembling something between a medieval tower, termite mound and giant tree stump, and oddly described as the Chamber of Commerce and Industry. Hidden inside, just visible through gaps in a corrugated tin roof from a tight spiral staircase running through the centre of the structure, and far more intriguing than the display cases, is the original Yoruba shrine, inaccessible to the uninitiated.

At the opposite end of town next to the governor's palace is the king's sacred forest, which I am able to investigate more fully. It is a peaceful wood that reminds me of an English glade. Eagles call from above the canopy while smaller birds and butterflies dance happily in the shade, a layer of brown leaf mulch below the home of giant African millipedes. A sacred ikono tree has a central position in the forest, both a link between earth and heaven, and also the king's lynching post.

The ethnographic museum, inside an Afro-Brazilian house, a cultural crossover resulting from the trans-Atlantic slave trade, has a fantastic collection of masks from tribes including the Yoruba. Often more like headdresses than masks, some rise a foot or more above the top of the head. Bright and well laid out, the museum manages to show how masks were historically important, but also how they remain of relevance now. There is one depicting the head and cap of a colonising French soldier, and modern masks showing the importance of immunising children: a doctor in a white coat holding a large syringe to the arm of a toddler in its mother's arms. Another, more aged, either shows the importance of male strength and fertility, or the symptoms of elephantiasis: a man with a hugely swollen scrotum and out of scale penis. But it's in the basement I find the most interesting pieces: large communication drums, a Viking-like horned helmet studded with cowry shells that was used during marriage ceremonies, and the thin string of beads hung around children's belts as good luck charms that I've seen on otherwise naked toddlers throughout my journey.

Nigeria – Cameroon

If you land at Lomé, you drive first of all along the coast of
Togo and Dahomey, where the Atlantic surf pounds day and
night on the sands, beating right up to the first line of tall,
waving palm trees. Then you climb gently inland to the
rolling hills of Nigeria, lightly wooded in places, but for the
most part open and fertile. Crossing into the Cameroons there
is an abrupt change. You pass steeply up into a massive range
of mountains, through a narrow dense belt of forest, and on
still higher until you are above the tree-line… On all sides
this ocean of forest stretches for as far as you can see

Colin Turnbull, *The Forest People*

I reach the border with Nigeria, Africa's most populous, most
maligned, country on my 99th day of travel and International
Anti-Corruption Day, despite the immigration officer's best
efforts.

Among the chaotic roadside checkpoints desperate-looking
men without uniforms use homemade tyre stingers against the
flow of traffic coming from Benin, while two government
health workers, their uniforms a blinding white, argue with
touts to get me the 50 km to Badagri for the correct price of
300 Naira; or £1.

There is a similar series of checkpoints, manned huts
spaced out along the road, on the monotone outskirts of
Badagri.

'There is a problem…' says an officer, waving my passport
open at my visa.

'No; there is no problem. Please, there is no problem' prompt the other passengers, impatient to leave officialdom behind them. The taxi driver is shouting 'Go! Go!' ushering me away with a hand. The officer disagrees with the consensus that a problem isn't necessarily something we should concern ourselves with, and disappears on the back of a motorbike, still grasping my passport.

I stagger out of the vehicle with the driver shouting 'take your bag!' all the while, trying to glimpse the motorbike as the driver pulls away. From the grit of the roadside I can't see the motorbike, the officer, or where he might be holding my passport. Passers-by point down the road in the direction I have come, though I can see no obvious target for their pointing; no motorbike, no waving official. I cover the distance as quickly as I can in the heat with my backpack, stumbling over the slippery grit.

'There is a problem' repeats a second official, entrenched on a plastic patio chair in the shade of a hut, holding my passport open in his hand. 'The entry stamp should cover the visa; otherwise you could reuse it to enter the country; and it is a single entry visa. If your driver was still here I would tell him to take you back to the border. But you are a tourist and I don't want to cause trouble for you; though it might be too late for that.'

His colleagues buy me a bottle of water, seeing the state I am rapidly descending into, and pay for an *okada* motortaxi to take me the short distance into Badagri; the young driver having to dodge officialdom one final time in doing so.

Badagri, the very first town in Nigeria after the elongated border formalities, is separated from the Atlantic by a lagoon lined with attractive colonial-era buildings constructed with the profits from the sale of slaves, and many were directly involved with the trade. Some also have the words *Beware 419, this house is not for sale* neatly stencilled onto an external wall: warnings designed to stop fraudsters selling houses they have no right to sell. The barracoons – slave holding cells – of one of the buildings form the focus of the Seriki Abass Slave Museum. The simple brick rooms are now filled with heavy iron chains and wide mouthed drinking caldrons, a tiny window high in one wall. Here, in a humid room smaller than most children's modern bedrooms, with no washing or toilet facilities, 40 slaves would have lived for up to three months, before their ordeal truly began, before their health was examined in detail, and they were ferried across the lagoon to the Atlantic beaches for the ships heading to the Caribbean or Brazil.

The age of the ship has passed, and if you imagine London's M25 at its worst you get an inkling into the traffic into and out of Lagos on a Saturday morning. Often six columns of traffic develop on roads designed for three, vehicles ahead parting as they reach breakdowns and collisions. Perhaps that's why downtown Lagos is so quiet. It takes three hours for my aging yellow minibus, like the ugly older brother of a New York taxi, to cover the 50 km to the western extremity of a city struggling to hold in 14 million people: the populations of Togo and Benin combined; twice the population of Greater London. Though no longer Nigerian capital, Lagos is set to overtake Cairo as Africa's largest city.

In the 1920s Lagos was still a country town, large houses surrounded by even larger areas of well-manicured garden. The roads had yet to be sealed, though power lines hung between houses. Many, like those around the busy markets of the area around Tinubu Square have been knocked down, but some examples still linger behind the 1970s oil-boom sky-scrapers belonging to international petroleum producers. This is particularly true around Broad Street, in between its churches, Freedom Park – still bound by the high red brick perimeter walls of the colonial prison it was created from – the fast-food joints and the sinister concretion of the city's main maternity hospital.

The next day I head south, over Five Cowrie Creek, on a jumble of concrete elevated expressways around Falomo Bridge to Victoria Island, the exclusive suburb of Lagos that houses western embassies and the city's best hotels. To walk the pale and dirty sands of Bar Beach, one of Lagos' few Atlantic beaches, I have to pay a sanitation fee of 200 Niara. Through the unappetising stalls offering warm lager and hot pepper soup, the waters reflect the dull grey sky.

The melodrama of the sky doesn't lighten as I take a minibus run by de modern bus service international along good tarmac, an ordinary journey but for the bad accidents that appear *de rigueur* on Nigerian roads, the beggar that has coloured his vitiligo purple with a biro, and the stinging pollutants that burn my eyes. That the passenger beside me leads the vehicle in a long prayer before we depart is reminder enough of Nigeria's road dangers, I don't need to see a minibus like mine lying in a central drainage ditch between carriageways.

Nigeria's traffic means I don't reach Benin City until evening is closing in, and have to take my life in my hands to reach the gates of the national museum's Benin gallery, located on a roundabout surrounded by five lanes of swirling traffic with no crossing. Getting to the museum is almost as extraordinary as the intricate bronzes it displays. They come from the Oba – the king's – palace, where the intricate casts depicting palace functionaries and even Portuguese traders decorated the palace from the sixteenth to the nineteenth centuries, though the art of casting probably dates back a further two hundred years.

I get to see more of how the bronzes were created on Igun Street, better known as Brass Casters Street, where artisans continue the tradition. Away from the neatly laid brick paving and shiny replica brasses of the casters' storefronts, men melt down any brass they can get hold of, pouring the molten alloy over wax models of the cast encased in baked clay. Channels allow the wax to seep from the clay to be replaced by the metal. When the metal cools, the clay is broken away, revealing the cast. It's a time consuming process; the casts unbelievably fine. I see the broken halves of mango-shaped clay discards piled along the street.

A little further on, sections of the city's medieval walls rise above me, the steep grass banks made redundant by a modern road punched through them, the moat that together with the walls created a barrier 45 feet high, filled to ground level with landfill.

I then have an exhaustive and exhausting day of travel across the most dangerous region of the Niger Delta, to Aba, sitting in the front 'death seat' between the snuff-taking driver and a nun in white habit and wimple. It's another smoggy day, the sun and sky masked by pollution, my eyes already red, stinging and running at intervals. The sister keeps a running commentary of our progress, interspersing it with phrases like 'you are brave, very brave, for coming to this sort of country', as she points out a small village or the vast structure of the River Niger Bridge at Onitsha. I invent a friend that is to meet me in Aba to stop her worrying. The mightiest river in West Africa runs under the bridge as a single column of dull brown water, still to divide into the rivulets and creeks of the delta. The minibus struggles through a confusion of other vehicles around a go slow – a traffic jam – that lasts two hours.

Beyond the bridge we are able to increase our speed just enough for the tyre of a coach in front to explode, black smoke and fragments of rubber tumbling from the slewing vehicle. 'Very brave' mumbles the sister once more.

From Aba, it is another dull, eye stinging journey to Calabar, the last town before Cameroon. Marina Road runs the length of the Cross River into the Duke Town area of the city. The mud roads and shanty housing ensure I stay guard-ed, feeling unsafe, until the smiles and welcomes drop my guard; a description of my experiences in the country as a whole. The ever-present Nigerian smog hangs over the Cross River, the old churches, nearly the only buildings of stone, and the shanty dwellings around the grave of Mary Slessor, a missionary who lived with the Efik people promoting Christianity, women's rights and an end to twin infanticide.

It's a hot and steamy place, seemingly collecting above the city the humidity lost from my route by the loss of native forests in the delta. The old governor's residency, a pre-fabricated building shipped from Britain, manages a certain amount of coolness, with airflow channels built within the walls, and the doors and windows funnelling breezes through the rooms of exhibits focussing on Nigeria's history. Maps demonstrate the shift in borders over time, land moving from British to German control, from Nigerian to Biafran admin-istration.

The Republic of Biafra was declared in 1967, only seven years after Nigerian independence, by an alliance led by the Igbo tribe, disillusioned with their treatment by central gov-ernment. The state stretched from its capital, Enugu in the north, to Onitsha in the west, and Calabar in the east. In two and a half years of fighting, millions of civilians died. A huge Nigerian flag now flies over the city, ensuring no one mistakes where Calabar's sovereignty rests.

I have to be at the beach, a small dock on the Calabar bank of the Cross River, early the next morning. As a preacher delivers a lengthy sermon to the gathering crowds on the wharf, in front of Fakoship *Endurance*, via a wailing sound system, I'm given a chair behind the woman selling pre-stamped yellow fever vaccination certificates to wait out the preparations before boarding.

We head out to the mouth of the River Cross and into the Atlantic, as smooth as it probably ever is; the continuous barrage of distorting Nollywood movies on the big screen televisions more of a concern than the pirates lurking within the Bakassi Peninsula.

As I saw on the maps in Calabar's old residency museum, had history been different I would still be in Nigeria as *Endurance* docks at Limbe. The city has changed hands several times since its founding as Victoria in 1858, eventually becoming a part of independent Cameroon in the early 1960s.

Reaching Cameroon has become a major milestone for me. It means I have traversed Nigeria successfully, I have left West Africa for Central Africa, I am heading south again, and I can finally swap my Michelin *Africa North and West* map for the south and central Africa version. I am making progress.

Immigration formalities take place a short distance uphill from the jetty, inside a shipping container. It's empty but for a simple wooden desk and two chairs at its far end. I'm given one of the chairs as the chief of operations slowly notes the details of my visa onto the reverse of one of the scruffy pieces of paper that are the desk's only decoration.

'Those idiots in the Calabar consulate! They've issued you a visa with no number! The paperwork cannot be completed' he says, gazing through the open doors of the container to the window of life outside, an angular bus arriving to take passengers to the arrivals shed while baggage is transferred from ship to vehicle by a chain of hands.

'We'll send you back to Nigeria!' it's joked.

'No, it's not your fault' says the chief of operations eventually. 'I'm giving you the entry stamp. The paperwork will have to remain unfinished.' I leave the container the only passenger not required to pay additional fees.

The landscape from the bus between the jetty and the arrivals shed on the outskirts of the town reminds me of Surrey; grassy hills leading into dense woods, a wall-mounted pillar box lying at an angle beside the road, painted red and cast with the lettering E$_{II}$R.

I take a short stroll along the Atlantic coast from the Bay Hotel, an attractive Edwardian building slowly decaying, like Limbe itself, in search of an evening meal. An oil platform lies brightly lit offshore, in view of the seating associated with the open-air grills and bar, metres from beaching fishing boats. I eat a fish so fresh I think it could have been warm blooded rather than grilled through; the dull starchy taste of the banana side enlivened by a kick of chilli and a sweaty bottle of Guinness brewed in Lagos. As night fully cloaks the town, lights strung across the road for Christmas sparkle.

The route to the botanic gardens follows the Atlantic coast; tropical forest coming down to the wave-battered rocks. There's a brass band playing as I enter. With the instruments silenced, the gardens are peaceful enough to be able to hear the trickle of the shallow Limbe River running over rocks near the small Commonwealth war graves cemetery, the handful of headstones bearing the names of Africans that died in either the First or Second World War.

The nearby Limbe Wildlife Centre gives me the chance to see the 15 primate species that call Cameroon's coastal forests home, including western lowland and Cross River gorillas, chimpanzees, mangabeys, drills and mandrills. Most have habitats that stretch, like my route, somewhere towards Gabon and Congo. But first I travel a little way north, to Buea, nestled within the foothills of Mount Cameroon. When the cloud clears Mount Cameroon sits over Buea like a beached whale; stout, solid, massive.

Mount Cameroon was perhaps first sighted by outsiders as early as the sixth century BC, when the Carthaginian admiral Hanno travelled along the west coast of Africa by ship. His report survives, and contains the lines 'we saw the coast by night full of flames...by day, this turned out to be a very high mountain, which was called the Chariot of the Gods'. It's the highest mountain in West and Central Africa, and continues to regularly erupt, though it's quiet as I start out on the trek to the summit with my guide Samuel, and porter Emmanuel. I can see from his expression and by the questions he asks that Samuel doesn't think I'm strong enough to make it.

Maybe he's right. Despite the easy early hours of walking in the cool mountain air, past the wooden huts and cassava plots of local farmers, the atmosphere closes in as the farm plots disappear under the trees. The dirt path becomes steadily more difficult until beyond the treeline, at 1800 metres, it turns to steep unyielding rock that protrudes through the mosses with few obvious footholds. The constant climbing has my thighs burning, and I'm tempted to stay where we rest by the slender bole of the magic tree, said to have survived above the treeline for 500 years. I know I can't, and the sooner I trace my way through the steep path to hut two, at 2800 metres, the better.

The light is starting to fade as the path levels out to the narrow plateau, and I have just a few more paces to hut two, where I will be spending the night. It's cold even before the sun sinks behind the mountain's flank, and I add thermal baselayers and thick woollens to my clothing within the hut, its blue-grey walls daubed throughout with the charcoaled names of previous trekkers. With all natural light lost there isn't much to do but conjure up a quick meal and settle down to sleep. The extra bodies of Samuel and Emmanuel make for a cosy night. But 6 am doesn't come soon enough, the hard-wood platform we sleep on digs into my pelvis and shoulder blades, making it difficult to stay comfortable over the course of the night.

The path seems easier on day two, and by 9.30 I reach the flat, featureless summit of Fako peak 4090 metres above sea level, cloud swirling around us in drifts, the strong gusty wind dragging the heat from me and forcing me away from the highest point of my journey.

The first part of getting back down to sea level is skidding down the pure black scree made up of ash and pumice stones from the last serious eruptions a decade ago. It's exhilarating slipping and sliding free of my backpack over the loose ground barely in control; gravity working with me rather than against me for the first time on the trek. Samuel even lets me lead for the first time, singing the praises of my broken-up running shoes. By the time we reach a river of cooled lava from the 1999 eruption, strung out along the mountainside to within 200 metres of the Atlantic, the path becomes a flat but tricky walk over rocks that could easily turn an ankle.

I can't resist the chance to head back up for a short detour to the craters formed in the year 2000, the land all around them still black and barren, only a few plants having established themselves; tiny speckles of green amid an almost pure, unnatural, black.

It is only after hours of walking that the bare surface comes to be colonised by plains of clumpy tussock grass. The path disappears beneath their tall stems, narrow enough to make it difficult to put one foot in front of the other without tripping. It makes for a difficult end to the day, and I am just willing the night's camp to come into view after nine hours of walking.

Too soon it feels like I'm woken from my night's rest and climbing back out of my tent. Samuel sits by the fire he has kept alive all night.

'I am very glad to see you up' he says. 'I knew you were tired so I thought I would not wake you.'

When it becomes light enough to see where we are placing our feet we start out. Samuel says, 'The others didn't think you could make it. I said no. You are strong. I have seen it.' I can't help but smile at his change in heart, knowing how he tried to dissuade me from continuing during our first day together.

There is a lot more *up* than I am expecting, given I am descending the mountain. First we walk through low grass, much easier to walk through than the tussock. The path becomes easier still, and I'm able to admire views of Etinde – little mount Cameroon – in the distance.

We have to walk back around to the Buea side of the mountain through the forest, and the humidity of the trees after two days in the chill mountain climate makes for a shock. But by lunchtime, six hours on, I reach the beginning of the tarmac road, and half an hour after that I am back in the centre of Buea considering where and when my journey south should continue.

One of the first things Samuel said to me bounces around my head, as I watch young men trying to hawker the bits and pieces that young men all over Africa are trying to hawker. 'It is hard to get money here in Cameroon' he had said. 'There are no jobs so I became a guide. It is a rich country, but the president, the ministers, they embezzle the money some-where.' Paul Biya has been in power for twenty years, over-seeing one of the world's most corrupt regimes.

My legs are tight, and I'm probably up earlier than I should be for the journey to Douala by cramped bush taxi; the first Francophone city I encounter in Cameroon. Humid, 24 km from the Atlantic, its port – one of the largest in Africa – sits on the banks of the Wouri River, its walls opposite the up-market supermarkets and restaurants of Boulevard de la Liberté. I sit in a restaurant not too distant, half full with business travellers alone over Christmas; the fruit bats passing over the outdoor pool to and from their roosts come afternoon.

The taxi from the hotel to the bus company depot costs as much as the minibus ticket for the four hour journey to Kribi. One of the last passengers to board, I am perched on a fold-down seat between the driver and passenger seat, my feet wedged under the dashboard. It gives me a clear view of the route we travel, edging the mouth of the Sanaga River, through the hills, until finally stumbling upon the Atlantic on entering Kribi.

Its single through road leads from the beach through the centre of the village to waterfalls eight kilometres south at Lobé. I find the falls perfectly hidden behind the bars that have sprung up in front of them, along a precarious footpath. The waters, wide and low, drop over rocks resembling submerged elephants, straight into the Atlantic. They are more local bathhouse than tourist attraction, and it feels odd to be standing admiring the scene while men lather up and scrub down beside me.

Some distance further south, beyond the Chinese flags at the new deep water port development, the bush taxi arrives at Campo's main junction, the end of public transport in Cameroon. A hand-painted road sign points to Equatorial Guinea, the closed border crossing just a few kilometres further south, through the coastal forest. I can see uninviting, unavailable Equatorial Guinea from the beach, empty save for fishermen pottering about their boat just offshore and a couple of children chasing each other with a large stick.

As I seek out transport away from the border, other travellers are surprised by my direction of travel.

'Why do you not want to go to Equatorial Guinea?' they ask.

'It's difficult' I reply. 'The government doesn't like foreigners. They make it very hard for foreigners to visit. There is too much paperwork involved. Instead I will have to travel through Gabon.'

A small crowd slowly forms at the junction, the hand-painted road sign mocking me, waiting for the arrival of a white pickup we can see approaching on the iron-red road surface.

My back bangs against the vehicle's side as I sit balanced on a rear wheel arch. The loading of huge quantities of cargo closer to Kribi leaves me sitting on a large sack of yams. They are a surprisingly comfortable, though the ride is not. Every drunk in town seems to share the back of the pickup with me. My conversation with them starts innocuously enough.

'I'm Jacques. I'm a soldier at the barracks here in Campo. I'm here to protect you. You like Cameroon? You like Campo? There are no problems here, are there? No aggression? People leave you alone?' I only wish they did, for it soon becomes the verbal equivalent of a mob attack on a cornered target, Jacques doing nothing to stop it, eventually joining in. They shout aggressively in languages they know I don't understand, and try to catch my attention for a quick laugh, by calling, shouting, and waving their arms high above them as I face into the forest. They are drunk, cruel and stupid. Extra land seems to be dropped in where there wasn't any before, extending the journey as I will every mile to be the last.

Although a direct road between Kribi and the Gabonese border exists, public transport along it does not, meaning a long detour through the sporadic verdant hills of the interior to Yaoundé, 200 km inland. From Yaoundé, I am quickly on a nearly full minibus, the second of the day to Ebolowa, the town I wasn't able to reach any more directly, though it takes half an hour to leave Yaoundé's stop-start traffic.

I reach Ebolowa as night falls. My walk through the centre of town reveals some prosperity, and a definite bias for the country's leader. President Paul Biya Square is lined with photos of the president and his wife, but the flower beds look uncared for all the same.

Gabon – Republic of Congo – Democratic Republic of Congo

The Gabon is less a river than a magnificent estuary

Pierre Savorgnan de Brazza

Three days into the new year, an event that passes me by but for the drunken passengers the morning after on the pickup from Campo to Kribi, I am only the seventh person to enter Gabon using the country's main northern gateway. I'm asked why I didn't take a plane instead. The first six are Cameroonians. Gabon's foreign tourist numbers average 240,000 a year. London gets more in a week.

I break my long wait on the empty seats of the Bitam Express with a baguette filled with brand name *cow pâté*, waiting for the minibus to be loaded with disintegrating crates of leaky yellow tomatoes where the rear row of seats had been. Instead, the seats hang out into the road from the back of the vehicle; as myriad tiny insects begin searching the limits of the tomato crates for an escape.

A suited businessman who didn't have the foresight to spend the last two and a half hours on the empty seats of the minibus tries to convince the driver to bump me onto the next bus, but he's unsuccessful, my name already in the ledger.

Unusually, it's not me that is picked out for extra special treatment at the first of the checkpoints 10 minutes in, but three Gabonese in front lacking identification. The route takes us around the edges of Equatorial Guinea, nudging close to the border as it heads towards the Atlantic at Libreville 600 km away. In all, there are between 13 and 15 checkpoints along the route. I lose count from napping on the heap of bags next to me. At each one we have to climb out as armed soldiers circle the vehicle, our identities checked by torchlight after dark.

The minibus stops only once more, at the chop bars of Ndjolé for food, before arriving at Libreville's PK8 depot twelve hours on at 2.25 am. I transfer sleepily, glad of a waiting taxi, and direct the driver towards Mont Bouët, an area of the capital first surveyed by Europeans in 1839. Pierre Savorgnan de Brazza, an Italian-born Frenchman, acquired the land on the north bank of the Gabon river estuary by agreeing a treaty with the local King, 'Denis' Antchouwé Kowé Rapontchombo. It was the beginning of French Equatorial Africa. He made his way through the rainforests of Gabon's interior, founding Franceville, and eventually reaching the north bank of Malebo Pool on the River Congo. After 600 km and a 21 hour day, I'm rewarded with five hours sleep in a curtainless motel room.

I walk along the Atlantic coast as I had done during an earlier visit to Gabon, remembering Libreville's layout surprisingly well. The city seems cleaner and smarter than on my last trip, and friendlier too; the roads in better condition. It may say more about me than about the capital, for breaches in the sea defences still eat at the furthest lane of traffic four years on. The warehouses of early traders in Glass, south of the centre, remain too, a home to traders and small independent shops 150 years after Mary Kingsley.

Beneath the palms of the waterfront the concrete benches moulded with the words *VILLE DE LIBREVILLE* are being freshly painted the colour of tropical seas. The presidential palace, built in the 1970s, rises high from the roadside, the manned perimeter walls half-threatening and half try-hard. As a man who was in power since the break-up of Gondwana-land, former President El Hadj Omar Albert-Bernard Bongo almost bankrupted the country in the process of building his residence. In front of the palace, a folk art statue stands as a reminder that Libreville, like many of Africa's Atlantic cities, was created as a slave port: a slave stands between two posts, broken shackles hanging from raised arms.

I find early morning the best time to be on the move in Libreville. Traffic is less frenetic, and the morning cloud cover keeps the streets cool, while the humidity hasn't yet had a chance to rise. I am able to begin the process of organising visas for both Congos, using the next days of waiting to retrace my previous steps around the capital in search of a working ATM.

As Sunday comes around, streets usually heavy with traffic become empty. Libreville shuts up shop and heads for the beach. I follow middle-class Gabonese onto the boat across the Gabon estuary to Point Denis. From Port Môle, Libreville's tiny, aging port and fish processing centre, we clamber down to beaches lined with posh, weekend-only hotels with motorboat rentals and quad-bike rides. While the all-you-can-eat buffet – costing more than the price of my room at the catholic mission – is still going on I walk along the beaches to the point where the full force of the Atlantic meets the estuary. The ground is covered in the scrubland of untouched sand, lined with nothing but occasional fat tree boles washed ashore, escapees from the timber processing industry of Gabon's interior, and the marks left by nesting turtles.

In the opposite direction, the beaches lead towards the isolated second city of Port Gentil, and the last stretches of ocean considered the Gulf of Guinea. There are few coastal roads south of Libreville. In fact, there are none. Port Gentil lies isolated, its 4x4s redundant outside of its few surfaced roads, approachable only by sea and air. Instead, I turn inland, and to the psychic bush taxi drivers.

'You're going to Lambaréné?'

'How do you know that? I haven't said a word.'

I share the taxi with an elderly man and a mountain of supplies for Lambaréné's supermarkets squeezed into every spare centimetre of space, and several centimetres I'd rather my feet had. The pitted surface of Route Nationale 1 rounds the estuary before turning south. No one bats an eyelid when we cross the equator into the southern hemisphere, the point marked by a large billboard above the road.

From the north bank of the Ogooué River, the largest between the Niger and Congo, the vehicle makes straight for Lambaréné's Quartier Isaac. We travel beyond the low length of Adouma Bridge, across the markets of the Île Lambaréné, and the bridge to the left bank. While the Quartier Isaac is the most populous, the liveliest of the city's districts, the Ogooué's right bank at Lambaréné is the more famous, the site of the hospital of the Nobel peace prize winner Albert Schweitzer.

The Hospital Schweitzer is hidden from view by a tall palm forest until the very last moment. I first come across a small group of graves, including Schweitzer's own, large rectangular concrete structures uncared for in the tall snake-ridden grasses, separating the hospital from the leper colony the hospital was first set up to treat in the early part of the twentieth century, when Lambaréné was as difficult to reach as just about anywhere on Earth.

At the entrance, flags of several countries flutter. In the grounds, small, clean barrack-like blocks are reached by a series of wide dirt paths raked clear of rubbish. The place is calm, orderly, and well run, still relying on the services of foreign volunteers. Off to one side, beyond the hospital store, are the historic off-white blocks of the original hospital. Schweitzer's home, a large clapboard construction raised off the ground, is now a museum containing some of the doctor's belongings: his beloved piano out of tune and losing its ivory, letters from Eisenhower and Einstein.

There is a confusing array of options for onward transport from the Quartier Isaac, including the suggestion of boats using the waterways south. But road transport is the fastest way out of Lambaréné and to the outskirts of Mouila, a small town I remember for its absence of any reason to remember it. As my vehicle does a circuit of town it doesn't look like Mouila has changed in the intervening years since my first visit either. On a road separating the wooden shacks of the market from a grassy open space, deep open drains run beside concrete benches moulded with the town's name. The road surface turns to dirt, holding despite the rain, as the buildings peter out to forested rolls of hills. Thanks to the vehicle's high clearance and large tyres, the journey remains a pleasant one until Ndendé, a short drive from the border with the Republic of Congo.

It starts to rain again in the evening, as Ndendé stages an open-air concert of gospel music, and I suspect the short December-January Central African dry season may be over, meaning I need to get as far south as quickly as I can, to roads that don't turn to slush in the rain. There are significant road works going on in Ndendé; the roads stripped back, hand-cast concrete ditches and drains being lowered into position by cranes as others dry in the periodic bouts of sunshine.

The tracks around Ndendé are already softening by next morning when I'm beckoned to a green pickup, from where I wait in a small building off the main junction. The road to Congo soon comes closer to a country track than a trans-continental highway, only a little wider than a single lane.

While my passport receives its exit stamp from an unmarked building in Ndendé, it is checked again as the invisible border runs through the untouched countryside.

'And now you have to pay to cross the frontier' says the woman at the checkpoint. 'Ten thousand.'

'I don't have 10 thousand,' about £12, I reply, getting up from my chair and moving across the room to signal an end to the conversation.

'*Monsieur...*' she says, 'you must pay to cross the frontier.'

'No. I have a visa.'

'It's okay' says another officer intervening in the conversation for the first time. 'You can go.'

I make it about 200 metres into the tiny hamlet of Ngongo in Congolese territory; beyond the army, immigration, and police formalities; before being forced to stop. There is little to do but stare at the bare brick walls and concrete floor of the single store, hoping I won't need to make use of the only *auberge*, its rooms more like forgotten storerooms. A toddler screams as he is pushed towards me by the elderly women of Ngongo, never having seen a white person before, told by those around him I'm a spirit from another world. While everyone seems content with another lazy afternoon, I want to keep the journey's momentum going.

'Tomorrow. There will be transport at 5 am tomorrow' the shop owner assures me, resting beside me on the veranda. As the afternoon passes he has to rise more and more often to serve visitors to the shop, women and children that leave with a meal's worth of white rice or a single stock cube. The smell of wood smoke begins to wander slowly through the still air. The thin layer of humid cloud that has masked the sky for most of the day starts to darken to grey with evening. I consider the *auberge* again. A darker grey pickup arrives from nowhere, looking for custom, heading south; straight away.

The narrow country track that leads from Gabon, and cuts through Ngongo, continues into Congo, but considerably less well-maintained than on the opposite side of the border. It is both severely waterlogged from the recent rain and suffering from hard, protruding rocks that break its surface. I am wedged between the driver and his wife in the front of the vehicle, assured of their marital status by the severity of their arguments on how much to charge for fares.

I wasn't sure what to expect of Congo, but it wasn't the rounded grass covered hills that form out of Nyanga, my night's rest spot, and lead all the way to Dolisie, the road to Congo's third largest city only paved on its outskirts. There are few towns along the way, and I get the immediate sense that Congo is poorer and less urbanised than its northern neighbour. Larger than Gabon, its coastline stretches 169 km versus Gabon's 2000.

I break my journey among the swept streets of attractive under-utilised art deco buildings; the train station a prime example. With several days before the next train I head for the outskirts of town and faster transport to the coast.

The road to Pointe-Noire was inaugurated less than a month ago, the vendors of the *gare routiere* still wearing the free commemorative T-shirts from the day. On many of its winding hilly stretches there is still work being completed, Chinese contractors checking that lines are painted the correct distance from the edge of the tarmac, or directing black workers in orange jumpsuits and hard hats on the buttresses of the steep banking hills that run almost the entire distance to Pointe-Noire and the Atlantic.

Avenue du General Charles de Gaulle, which runs from the centre of Pointe-Noire to the Atlantic, has everything a traveller might need, except passage to the Democratic Republic of Congo, a necessity if I am to collect a visa for Angola, and the only way I will be able to stay close to the edge of the continent. Without such a passage I not only have to abandon the coast, but also surface transport. The closest border crossing with the DRC is between Brazzaville and Kinshasa, 550 km inland. Threats from Ninja anti-government rebels in the Pool region north of Dolisie means the only safe mode of transport to Brazzaville is via an African airline.

I spend most of the next day in some way involved in getting a 45 minute flight to the capital; trains covering the distance in 72 hours, and road transport somewhere between the two, barring holdups by rebels confusing themselves with Japanese martial arts experts carrying weaponry larger than they are.

The view from the plane echoes my experiences from the ground, with rows of low hills rippling inland, like the wrinkles on the sheets of an unmade bed. Trees nestle in the valleys, a darker green, like moss. Huts and buildings start to appear, models on a toy railway. A city never really appears before landing, the buildings get closer together, lining up to face the start of the street pattern in Poto-Poto, Brazzaville's poor district by the basilica of Saint Anne. It's striking for its bright green verdigris copper roof and angled walls of chocolate-coloured stone. The caretaker welcomes my interest but adds, 'You can take photos out here, but not of inside. This is Congo. You don't just go around taking photos.' I am desperate to ask why not, but instead push at the heavy arched doors decorated with religious iconography.

'Ah *monsieur*, you can't go inside. It's locked.'

'And what if I want to pray?'

'You can pray in the garden.'

In late 1880 Pierre Savorgnan de Brazza received a more positive welcome, signing treaties that saw the French tricolour flying over the River Congo's north bank. Months later, with ways of persuasion that were closer to that of Liberia's warlords than de Brazza, Henry Morton Stanley laid claim to the opposite bank for King Leopold II of Belgium, forever dividing people that share a waterway into the right and wrong banks.

De Brazza was never allowed to lie at rest, and he's been dug up more times than a central London thoroughfare. First interred in Paris after his death in Dakar, he was almost immediately transferred to Algiers by his widow. In 2006 he returned to Africa, and the city that bears his name, to rest in a publically-funded mausoleum, like something from Soviet Russia; the foundation stone laid by three patriarchs: President Omar Bongo of Gabon, accused of corruption and embezzlement of public funds; French President Jacque Chirac, convicted on charges of embezzlement and abuse of trust; and Denis Sassou Nguesso, President of the Republic of Congo, fighting accusations of embezzlement. The mostly empty building clad in Italian marble, and even emptier grounds, displays De Brazza's sarcophagus in the basement, beside printouts explaining his explorations through Gabon and Congo.

My own explorations have me catching a local minibus to Pont Djoué, on Brazzaville's outskirts, to see the result of Stanley's endeavours. It towers over Brazzaville with a population 10 times larger. The wide Congo rapids churn over the rocks, bringing to mind the chaos and corruption that go hand-in-hand with the high rise greyness of Kinshasa, sitting behind. As I stand by the railings overlooking the brown waters; watching both the natural and unnatural spectacles; men, women and children wash themselves and their clothes on the rocks below.

It feels like I should stay longer in Brazzaville. The low rise elegance of the city's mix of art deco survivors and modest modern towers calls to me. There is really nothing more to keep me. The only reason I can think of for not going to Kinshasa straight away is that it involves going to Kinshasa.

Brazzaville's 'le beach' river port is perhaps precisely the opposite of chaos. Everything has its place, and everyone except me has been here many times before and knows exactly where to go, and what to do, despite the lack of

117

obvious direction. By means I don't entirely recall, I identify a ticket office for the *canot rapide* speedboat service. Despite the name, it turns out using the *canot rapide* involves quite a lot of slow and confused. After some time, and having gained a handful of receipts for various exit taxes, I'm able to climb onto a speedboat for the 10 minute trip to the pontoon of Kinshasa's port a mile distant.

It lives up to the city's reputation of noise and confusion, and I am ushered from one person and one place to another before being lead to an overflowing immigration office. An officer in mufti fills out a form in a friendly but laborious manner in the heat of the room, filled with young black, apparently paperless men trying to enter the DRC. There is not a computer in sight; the form we complete is copied using a sheet of carbon paper. After 40 minutes the officer disappears for 30 more.

'I am sorry' he says on his return, 'but the chief is sending you back. He says your visa from Libreville is not valid, because you are not a resident of Gabon.'

I am taken back to the pontoon quickly, and there we wait for a long time, in full midday sun, having not eaten or drunk anything since early morning. I begin to sense a scam when I am not pushed onto the first of the steady stream of *canot rapide* heading back across the river. I don't know who is involved in the scam, seemingly everyone who talks to me. I don't know who I can trust. I am alone; and I feel alone. After much shifting of me and my backpack about the pontoon, without any demonstration of a desire to send me back across the river – lasting an hour, perhaps more, it felt like many days – the officer whispers 'give me 200' as he dashes away with the paperwork, in a way that makes me wonder whether I imagine him doing so.

From then on I don't know what's going on for the rest of the day. No one will talk to me for long enough to get a full story from them until much later – after another hour, maybe more – an English-speaking porter begins talking to me. He seems to think 'the situation' can be resolved, and I am finally escorted onto a speedboat. I am not sure if leaving my foothold in the DRC is a sensible thing to do, but I have little choice other than board. None of what I am told makes sense or connects with what I am told by others. The porter goes on, 'then in one, maybe two hours, when the chief is off duty you come back and we'll get you through'.

On Brazzaville beach the scam continues. I speak with yet another official, who tells me my single entry visa for the Republic of Congo is invalid, since I have left the country and am now returning. A colleague tries to surreptitiously hand him a sheet of empty visa stickers, and it looks like a simple matter of buying another. I don't even bother with French as I tell him I know my visa remains valid, my DRC visa untouched, and I am told to wait – kept waiting for another hour or more – with the official holding my passport, and the afternoon moving on as much as the other passengers for the *canot rapide* crossings. One of them approaches as I wait on a wooden pew.

'It is your first time to DRC? You give $200 in an envelope with your passport and you get the stamp. It's easy.'

'I don't have $200.'

'I'm sorry… You have three month visa? No? Then you go to the embassy on Monday and get it changed. Your single entry visa is finished.'

By now I feel like my crossing is more than spiralling out of control, with both sides of the river playing me. I know it, they know I know it, they don't care, and I can do nothing about it. If I get my passport back and cross again there is nothing to stop Kinshasa returning me once more, whether I have given them the $200 I don't have or anything else. Then I am back in Brazzaville for a third time, being told my visa is invalid for a second. It is a game I cannot win, but one I am being forced to play out to the end: whatever, whenever and wherever that is. The DRC is living up to its horrendous reputation, and I have no real desire to visit the country any longer. But the fact remains if I don't cross into the DRC and get hold of an Angolan visa at a consulate there, my journey south will hang more precariously than my current attempts to cross the Congo.

I am given back my passport and pointed towards the *canot rapide*, where I am waved through the various taxes. Other passengers look on, glad of the entertainment. On the other shore, across a choppier Congo and duller sky, to a country that had only 13 university graduates on independence in 1960, I am hustled off the pontoon, my passport taken, and rushed back onto the pontoon. My passport is handed to the captain of a departing speedboat, forcing me on board. I have to ask him if we are travelling to Brazzaville.

'Yes, because your papers are not correct' he says, putting the engine into gear. The boat drifts, the engine running on idle for a couple of minutes within shouting distance of Kinshasa. I wonder if this too is part of the game. The engine is thrust into reverse, the boat paddling back towards the pontoon when the captain shifts gears and the boat jumps towards Brazzaville.

There isn't much hanging around at Brazzaville now. Few passengers remain; everyone is getting ready to go home for the evening and want to be done with me as quickly as possible. The official who dealt with me earlier seems surprised to see me return. Shifting through the pages of my passport, he raises that of the DRC visa to me. It has the French *ANNULE ANNULE ANNULE* stamped across it. He in turn annuls my Congo exit stamp by hand with a biro.

I feel emotionally crippled. I am ready to lie down right now and not get up until morning. My options for my circumnavigation are limited, maybe limited to giving up. I already feel like I have failed. I set out with an aim of showing that travel in Africa could be trouble free; that Africa wasn't a dark continent with a central heart of darkness. I thought I could travel along its vast length of coastline without recourse to bribery or corrupt practices to keep me on track. It feels very bleak this evening, and it would be good to be anywhere, so long as it was anywhere but here.

'What hotel are you staying at?' asks the official.

'I don't have one – I thought I was going to Kinshasa. Yesterday I was at the Hôtel Siringo.'

'Okay. Go to the hotel tonight. Then tomorrow you go to the airport and leave. No Kinshasa. Kinshasa is finished.'

Namibia & Angola

The system by which Zaire works…is very simple. Every official you encounter will make life as unpleasant for you as he possibly can until you pay him to stop

Douglas Adams and Mark Carwardine,
Last Chance to See…

It doesn't seem like much has changed in the DRC since Douglas Adams' visit in the late 1980s other than the country's name. Once I stop thinking about the mess I'm in around midnight, I sleep well, through the night until the movement of brooms on stone, and the sound of radios that comes with early morning, and I remember the last words of the officer at the port yesterday.

Slumped over a breakfast cup of tea at a shack on the corner of a dusty road I start to consider that Encircle Africa could become *almost* the first solo and unassisted circum-navigation of Africa by public transport. Even walking down the pavement of the main streets around the basilica of Saint Anne feels like a battle. My confidence is shot though; my house of cards teetering. When it's all down on paper I realise I have just one option for continuing: 9 hours 50 minutes in the air, 15 hours 30 minutes with connection times between three flights; a total distance of 6502 km; the flight originating from Kinshasa.

By the time I clear the visa free immigration procedures at Windhoek Hosea Kutako International Airport after the last flight of the day, having travelled overnight via Johannesburg and Nairobi, the revolving baggage carousel has been turned off. Most of the bags have been collected, my fellow passengers gone. Three bags remain on the rubber paddles of the carousel. None belong to me, leaving me with only my small day bag and the contents of my pockets; a problem I haven't suffered with surface transport.

As one of the last passengers of the day to leave the airport, the only means of reaching Namibia's capital 45 km away is by chartering a taxi. Travelling along the clear well-maintained roads, passing regular signs for safari lodges and taxidermists, it takes me a while to work out where I think I am. The skies of southern Africa are not like those of West or Central Africa. They are big and blue. It turns out to be either Switzerland or New Zealand: the mix of German and English, the cleanliness, and the sudden sense of order. It doesn't stop a policeman receiving a folded low denomination note from the taxi driver in front.

I think for a moment things might be improving when the owner of the guesthouse undoes the padlock of the beer fridge behind reception, but he is only pulling out the condensation drenched cash box to give me my room key. In the room I lay out the possessions I currently have to hand: my diary, a finished French Agatha Christie novel, a new novel, camera, camera tripod, three new AA sized batteries, a map of Lüderitz picked up at the airport, a pencil, a pen running low on ink, torch, compass, wallet, and passport; together with a half-eaten packet of Moir's Tea Lovers biscuits, a bar of soap, toothbrush and toothpaste bought at a supermarket in town.

By morning my clothes have dried from their wash; though the feeling I am trapped in something I cannot get out of lingers. I keep reaching to get kit out of my missing backpack. Without a guidebook or sunscreen I roam the centre of Windhoek at random, hoping the clear southern African sky and drier heat don't burn my skin. There is a bewildering array of shops – shops with tempting glass-fronted displays –

lining the spotless, busy streets of banks, payphones and public art of the richest city I must have visited since Morocco, making the odd lurking religious hawker more bearable.

'How are you?'

'Not very well.'

'Not very well? I will pray for you. God won't make it a good day, but a brilliant day.'

'That would make a change.'

'Come in and we will pray…'

Instead I await news of my backpack visiting some of the city's historic sites, like the glaring whitewashed walls of the German built Alte Feste, or old fort, on Robert Mugabe Avenue, between Fidel Castro Street and Sam Nujoma Drive. A laminated printout on the door warns visitors to the national museum within that entrance is free and donations should not be given to staff. The only noise inside comes from the creaking floors of exhibits on Namibia's history, and hard fought independence battle. In the creak-free grounds of the botanic gardens, home to African millipedes and rock hyrax as well as a beautiful collection of natural flora, I stumble onto the grave of Chief Goab Xamseb, much as the Damara Culture and Heritage Forum stumbled on his grave in 2006, his resting place unknown for more than 20 years. Oral tradition has it that the chief was captured and beheaded by German colonial authorities for resisting colonisation in 1890, the year the Alte Feste barracks were constructed.

On Independence Avenue several people watch me with suspicion as I make use of a public payphone to contact the airline.

'Dr Packham? We have a forwarding note here that says the bag will be on the flight arriving twenty-past four. I'll send it to you straight away.'

*

When my taxi pulls into Monte Christo *combi* – minibus – depot all hell breaks loose. The vehicle is enveloped by touts trying to force hands through the crack of the open window, some climbing into the back seats while others yank open the boot to take possession of the backpack I've only just taken possession of again myself. It's a nervy experience as my driver organises a seat for me.

It takes until almost the very end of the long journey north, along straight roads and unchanging semi-desert landscape, for the road signs to list the remaining distance from my destination of Oshakati; so much so that I fear I misunderstood where the *combi* is heading. Most of the other passengers have already disembarked; the morning becoming afternoon, the afternoon giving way to evening as I stand within a few kilometres of the border with Angola.

Despite some dragging of feet I reach the Angolan consulate in Oshakati as its doors are opening the next morning. The staff are very helpful, and the additional information they ask me for – copies of bank statements and vaccination certificates – takes half an hour to sort out, rather than the several hours it would have taken further north. On returning to the counter I am warned that I am entering into an approval process only, one that sees applications sent to Luanda. There is no guarantee I will be granted a visa; my only hope for rescuing the circumnavigation and traversing Angola's coastline. It feels like the longshot it is, though I can feel the hope rising all the same; which could be very bad indeed.

I can find nothing else to do in Oshakati but spend time waiting in the hot reception area of the consulate watching a Portuguese language news channel, which is lucky, since it becomes something of a pastime over the next few days. A visit to the supermarket becomes an event I look forward to. The daily pages of notes in my diary are reduced to 'washed shorts'.

As I wait once more in the airless reception area of the consulate, glances in my direction from the staff increase my nervous shifting. By the time I'm called to the counter I am sure my application has been rejected.

'I'm afraid I have to tell you that Luanda has rejected your application. You must fly home and apply from London.'

'I'm sorry, what? I wasn't listening' I have to admit.

'I asked if you have your passport with you. If you give me your passport I can issue you with your visa.'

The consular staff seemed genuinely pleased to have been able to help me enter Angola, but the sense of having stood still, and of having spent another week in one place, with so far still to go, is weighing on my mind.

'It's a long way' admits the driver, taking me the 60 km to the border. 'We first have to go to Ondangwa. There was supposed to be a road straight from Oshakati…'

'But not yet?'

'Not yet' he replies, giving me a smile meaning 'somewhere along the line the money went missing'.

Namibian immigration procedures are efficient, paperless and unnerve me further.

'I give you the exit stamp' says the officer through the thick glass. 'If they refuse you entry into Angola, come back and see me. Ask for me, and I will give you re-entry. Ask for *me*.'

It's only at the open portholes of the Angolan post that the fun really starts, and I worry the Namibian official who spoke to me wasn't just being overly careful. I realise I should have asked his name.

'Where is your letter of introduction?' I'm asked.

'The consulate said I didn't need one' I reply.

'But we say we must see a letter of introduction.' The conversation continues in this vain for some time, before my passport is slipped into a trouser pocket. I don't know if this is the beginning of another scam, but I know I'm not interested in playing along. It's Angola here and now or bust. I'm not going to spend two hours standing by a chain-link fence in the sun waiting for a subtly phrased request for money to come my way; I'll return to Namibia now. At this moment I couldn't care less about my longer term goals, about my circumnavigation. I am about to ask for my passport when my thoughts are pre-empted and its handed to me complete with everything I need to enter Angola.

After a bit of discussion about the best way to get anywhere that isn't exactly where I am already, I convince several touts that Lubango might be a good place to start. It's a town that isn't coastal, but does have transport. I find where they are hiding some modern minibuses, and wait for the other seats to fill with the slow trickle of people that manage to find themselves on the other side of the border formalities.

At the bus station on the edge of Lubango, after hours of continuous, monotonous travel, the locals are very helpful despite my limited use of Portuguese, trying to get me a ticket for a bus bound for Luanda straight away. With all the tickets at three different coach companies sold out, they arrange for me to spend the night on an empty bus in one of the compounds, so that I'm in the right place when a new batch of tickets goes on sale at 4 am. It's not the most comfortable I have been, aligning myself so I can stretch across the aisle without collapsing on the floor, and it gets very cold even in the woollen sweatshirt I haven't used since Mount Cameroon. A mosquito buzzes my ear for what seems like the entire night.

The road north of Lubango is as bad as the road south. It is so pitted with holes it's like travelling over the cratered surface of the moon. The road becomes so bad that the bus makes frequent diversions from the raised surface to the level of the surrounding trees, choosing rutted tracks the colour of plaster instead. The Angolan countryside comes right up to the vehicle, dusty forest growing wild among isolated protrusions of rock. Burnt out tanks, remnants of Angola's long civil war, are some of the only signs of human impact on the land as the tatty bus brushes the edge of a minefield, marked out with fading red and white striped tape. It's so hot at the back of the bus over the engine compartment where I sit with my backpack that the candles I'm carrying melt into an unusable block of wax. Thirteen days after the annulment of my DRC visa, a convoluted odyssey across the continent sees me return to the coast tired, hungry, thirsty and with tight muscles burning with the need to stretch out; a second day without food and only minimal volumes of water; 1250 km after entering Angola; still heading in the wrong direction.

A hawker selling drinks outside the gates of the still crowded bus depot, out despite her only light being a candle, points me in the direction of a *pension* after telling me getting a taxi would be impossible. There are only a couple of hundred, newly imported, in a city with a population of three million.

'The *pensão*? The security is not good there' say a group of men I ask for further directions. I have been told this so often on the journey I don't believe it any longer; and I'm so tired I'm willing to take the risk. But one of the men arranges for me to stay with his younger brother, in his one room house. I suspect I have more stuff in my twenty kilogram backpack that he does in his whole house, secured by a thick steel door. Close to all the floor is taken up by a double mattress, a narrow corridor runs to a waterless toilet; a television set sits on a rickety table against a wall. It's cleaner, quieter, and more comfortable than many hotel rooms I have stayed in.

The Hotel Globo, where I end up after a long commute through the morning rush hour, has a few more creature comforts, like windows, running water and electricity; and at $60 a night is by far the cheapest hotel in the centre of Luanda, one of the most expensive cities in the world.

'The Angolan people – they are very lazy, they don't like having jobs, all these people' other Africans say in explanation, pointing down the streets. What I see is men armed with AK47s guarding the banks, the *compradors* fighting for custom for their minibuses, and the men in high visibility jackets excavating the hills above the Atlantic marginal in preparation for the next tower block. In truth, it is that Angola is still recovering from the civil war, and almost everything has to be imported, along the same horrendous roads I am encountering. I'm told one of the biggest expenses for multinational companies working in the country's oil industry is safe drinking water.

There is so much building work going on that by early afternoon I don't recognise the place, and find it difficult getting back to the hotel. While the cranes slowly climb the hills behind the shanty dwellings, along the marginal a swath of glass-fronted buildings jostle for space with colonial masterpieces towards the seven kilometre long spit of land called Ilha do Cabo. Square dirty 1970s blocks sit next to sixties space age design, the neoclassical 1956 Central Bank, and modern as yet unfinished glass structures, all overlooked by the low wide expanse of the sixteenth century fort of the oldest European city in sub-Saharan Africa.

The national Liberation Day holiday, commemorating the beginning of the independence struggle, falls on the day after I arrive in Luanda. Nothing opens but one or two of the more expensive restaurants on the Ilha do Cabo, catering for the expatriate workers; the multilane highway that the marginal has become in recent years is free of traffic. The only people on the streets are the security guards sitting on rickety chairs in the shade, listening to short wave radios outside the shuttered banks.

I linger in what shade I can find, like the small garden behind the pink governor's palace, a slow walk from the hotel. It's from the front of the governor's palace, on

Mutamba Square I take a *hiace* minibus – named after the Toyota model – to the São Paolo district, and another to the distant area of Kwanza. It takes two hours to get just a few kilometres from Luanda's business district. I'm taken to the place from where buses head north, a dusty side street like any of the other similar side streets, nothing to mark it out as special except perhaps the viscosity of the oil stains in the sand. There are no buses, which I am told have all departed for the day. Eager to be on my way, it's another blow. I haven't made it very far at all.

There is nothing more I can do until tomorrow's buses but search out sustenance down the gritty streets of the market, sometimes heavily strewn with plastic rubbish. I manage to get a luncheon meat sandwich from a teenager's snack stand with a pitiful level of Portuguese, only for the girl to call out 'thank you' and 'goodbye' as I walk away. I feel no animosity, though it's clear from the stares of astonishment that Kwanza is a place that white men don't usually go. Two young girls stroke my arms at a busy junction that seems to have been built over a landfill site, unwanted packaging mixing with the rich smell and dark colour of human faeces.

Seated directly behind the driver I can't see much of the route north. It's slow going, with the dust of the road surface seeping through the rattling, ill-fitting panes of window glass to give the air inside the bus a dry mustiness. Small soft-shelled cockroaches roam the coach's surfaces, my feet and legs. I find the journey strangely pleasing, satisfied to be notching up the kilometre count.

Northern Angola is the home of big baobabs, centuries old, though sadly not much tarmac. One hundred and seventy kilometres from the mouth of the Congo, at N'zeto, the bus rolls onto the smooth surface of a new road, more than nine hours into the journey – everywhere in Angola being very far from everywhere else – and rolls off the other side shortly after. It takes until 11 pm, fifteen hours after departing Luanda's outer reaches, to arrive at the right bit of road in Soyo for the bus to rumble to a stop. Opening up the baggage hold, a set of crockery clatters to the ground around the driver's feet. Ignoring the plates completely, he climbs deep inside the hold to drag out my backpack, thick with road dust. He looks at me and simply says 'Africa' with a shrug.

Wedged into Angola's northern corner between the Atlantic and the Congo estuary, Soyo is a shipping town with lots of import-export businesses, two banks, one supermarket, and the first children's playground I've seen for a long time. The town sprawls for some distance, the main roads paved, while those on the outskirts are surfaced with the thick sandy soil of coastline and river banks. On the southern bank of the Congo, the northern bank the end of DRC territory, Soyo is as far north as I can travel. Instead of relief at having covered all but a handful of the kilometres barred to me by the annulment of my DRC visa, I am just exhausted.

Refreshed with a couple of nights' sleep, and the most expensive sandwiches of my life, I endure the journey back to Luanda on the same rolling coach and awful roads, cutting through the stunning, unspoilt beauty of the north. Amid the rocky landscape, the Atlantic just out of sight, the bus rolls over quickly rebuilt bridges that are watched over by long disused tanks, and passes war graffiti carved into the bark of baobabs and the surfaces of isolated standing stones. We stop for a change of tyre beside minefields, and taped off areas so small they must indicate the position of a single mine. The warning tape around them, when not hidden by tall wispy grasses, is so old it has lost almost all its colour. It seems strange such beautiful land really could be deadly.

I clamber wearily down from the coach somewhere in Luanda's suburbs. At over 40 km across the city measures further than the DRC's entire Atlantic coastline. Unsure what to do, or where to find myself a bed or a taxi, I am adopted by another passenger. Laden down with bags and several small children she leads me to some sandy open ground – like the roads of Soyo – owned by the bus agency, where we spend the night. She goes as far as allowing me to sleep on a portion of the matting she has brought for her family to use. It's a cool night under the stars, a television in a protected corner shows the latest hit television shows from the US with Portuguese subtitles. The toilet facilities are less convivial.

Movement in the grounds starts early, with passengers leaving for early morning transport. With the first noticeable shift from darkness, ground that was crowded with sleeping figures last night is already empty. My luck changing, I find one of the few taxis in the city at the same instant I realise I have just a few minutes to reach an onward connection, departing from a different area of the city. I watch the dashboard clock as much as the traffic-free roads; a row of clean modern coaches with digital destination displays appearing as the minutes to departure tick by.

The televisions and white leatherette seating help mollify the road, tracing its seemingly endless route through the coastal towns strung out south of the capital. At Sumbe, one of the biggest, I have a prolonged sight of the Atlantic before the road twists inland; the breath of the ocean raising a heavy weight from my heart. The coach makes more permanent contact with the Atlantic at the port city of Lobito, the terminus for the Benguela railway, weaving through Angola's interior for 1400 km, to its eastern border with the DRC. We pass the simple straight lines of the newly renovated station, clean rail tracks once more running towards Benguela.

BENGUELA stands over the railway station in proud yellow letters beside perfect brickwork and the fluttering flags of a Chinese construction company, fencing still ringing its perimeter. Well-ordered streets, lacking the confusion of Luanda, orientate about historic squares lined with elegant buildings of varying styles, between art deco apartment blocks and gently aging colonial warehouses. As I feel the cool breeze of the Atlantic's Benguela current, the houses expand to mansions facing the coast. The small bare squares become large planted spaces that offer seating in the shade, and a home to the packs of dogs that are menaced by the stones of bored children.

With no public transport running along Angola's coast south of Benguela's hawker-lined beaches; ice-creams, nuts, and cheap souvenir trinkets sold without hassle from the paths lining the sand; my only option is to return to Lubango and extend the feeling that Angola has been one single long stretch of looping road. Asleep for most of the seven hour journey, on a hard plastic seat, the route is entirely absent from my memory, much like the keys to the well-proportioned rooms of the motel by the transport depot.

'No problem' says the owner with his smattering of English, in the spacious darkness of the foyer, the tall dark wood reception desk almost the only furnishing; 'do not worry, no key, no problem'. So much of my journey so far has relied on trusting strangers, I do not worry. I instead follow an avenue into the centre of town, all the while watched over by the brilliant white marble statue of Cristo Rei, a figure of Christ just visible from its hilltop position.

Namibia seems to remain equally distant however many vehicles I board and however far they take me towards Angola's southern border. I reach the gates that have *Namibia* welded onto them at 5.55, five minutes before they are closed for the evening, having received my tourist permit in the staff room, as immigration officers put on their hats and coats.

The warm black tarmac and comfortable *combi* minibus are welcome sights for me if not the metre long snake, the scales of which shimmer brown-blue-grey in the morning sun, which cannot get out of the way in time to avoid being struck by the vehicle, despite some of the only braking of the 10 hour journey to the coast at Swakopmund, along Namibia's empty road network. Approximately halfway down Namibia's 1600 km length, the town is surrounded by desert; the Skeleton Coast to the north, and Namib Desert to the south; limiting public transport to the national highways connecting with a spine of roads in the centre of the country around Windhoek.

At the northern end of Swakopmund I stumble upon the snake park, a small vivarium of southern African snakes and lizards. It's housed in the terminus station of the old Otavi railway, which ran from Tsumeb in Namibia's north to the mines on the outskirts of town, following closely the road from the border. The star attraction for me is a pen of chameleons that seem as interested in me as I do in them. As they display their colour changing abilities, the change so subtle I don't realise it's happened until the mottled brown has become a pale yellow, I hear an American lady cry 'that's a spitting cobra? It doesn't *look* like a spitting cobra!' followed by a sigh from the staff.

Writing up my notes on a bench, on coast lined with a mix of manicured lawn and flower beds, a local woman walking her small dog says to me 'tell her you love her'. A strong, cold wind picks at the pages, and at the canopies of cafés in buildings that wouldn't look out of place in Bavaria. German is as widely spoken as its colonial architecture is evident on the wide avenues; a result of Germany's short custodianship of the country and continued close links.

A German aid worker staying in the same hostel doesn't understand the reasons behind my journey.

'You're coming all this way to Africa without being able to *see* Africa? I've not been there, but the sand dunes at Sossusvlei are supposed to be amazing' she says over breakfast.

'But that's not the point of encircling Africa' I reply, a protective father. 'The idea is to stay as close to the coast as I can, using public transport. Sossusvlei is not on the coast, and I can't get there by public transport. And in any case I can't possibly see everything in Africa in one year. The Namib Desert alone is huge.'

Not only that, it starts right on the outskirts of town, dunes bubbling up along the road to Walvis Bay, 30 km further south. Compared to Swakopmund, it is not a pretty town. Pronounced closer to 'Wallfish Bay', and spelt at least eight different ways according to old documents I find in the museum, the town is named after the whales that inhabit the waters off its coast. Now its coastline is better known for the shipping containers that line the port, amid the winding tracks of a time when rail freight was preferred to road transportation. The port has existed since Bartolomeu Dias anchored in the bay in December 1488. Coming from the north, it's possible to catch a glimpse of a stone monument, etched with Portuguese caravels commemorating Dias' arrival, the first European to reach this point on the African coast.

Facing south from the port I can see desert dunes, and join the esplanade that follows the coast towards them. Gulls sit proud on the lampposts, their backs to the soft biscuit colour of the dunes, reflected in shallow lagoons. They watch fish they couldn't tackle leap clear of the smooth waves that push purple-red jellyfish the size of dinner plates to the esplanade rocks. The dunes stretch endlessly; the roads do not, with all *combis* leading to Windhoek.

The old battered red *combi*, tighter on space than its more common younger cousins, passes through a landscape of dry scrub. Goats feed behind the barbed wire that separates land from the monotony and heat of the straight black road, while snake eagles rest on the fence posts like totems. Windhoek's quiet Sunday afternoon is only broken by cracks of approaching thunder.

Other waiting passengers at Rhino Park attract my attention by calling me sir, a throwback to white rule by apartheid South Africa that only ended in 1990, with independence. I am third to claim a place on the next *combi* to Lüderitz, another isolated coastal town surrounded by desert. Getting there is simple:

1. Wait seven hours for the *combi* driver to sell all the available seats. Wander about Rhino Park aimlessly hoping for more passengers. Pay a visit to the petrol station next door, for something to so.

2. Head south for around 500 km, through a landscape of rocky hills, grasses and trees that contrasts with Namibia's desert scenery. Cross the Tropic of Capricorn, leaving the tropics for the comfortable temperatures of the southern hemisphere's summer. Stop at Asab, a village without functioning shop or petrol station, to allow a passenger to alight. Watch as he is greeted by relatives driving a four horse trap straight out of pre-industrialised Europe.

3. Turn west, and continue for almost 320 km, the land becoming increasingly arid as we approach the Atlantic coast, one of flat plains cut through with bridges spanning dry river beds, rivers of sand among burnt grasses. Wild horses, kudu – a donkey-like antelope, springbok, and a solitary ostrich all visible from the *combi*'s windows point to the presence of water somewhere nearby.

4. Stop, you've arrived. If you arrive after 10 pm you're too late. Lüderitz will be closed for the night. As my *combi* ends its journey at 12.45 there is no one about, and no lights anywhere. The other passengers soon disappear, collected by family. A lone taxi driver hoping for competition free fares, by enduring the chilly night shift, takes me to a succession of hotels firmly shut up until morning. It gets to the stage where I think I may have to find a doorway out of the harsh Atlantic wind; eventually finding a bed in the last hotel in town, opened up by a sleepy security guard.

5. Turn around and head in the opposite direction for 820 km. The hotel is decorated beautifully with all manner of taxidermy models worthy of Lomé's fetish market, but the charm does not extend to the town, which I find dreary and depressing during my initial scouting after a breakfast of *boerewor* sausages. The buildings displaying the German colonial architecture of the early nineteen hundreds have been converted into quick loans centres. The 10 year old waterfront complex is all but abandoned; the few open outlets hang on for dear life, the café with a desperate reading note in the window asking interested buyers to call Angela. 'Serious buyers only please' it adds.

By afternoon, having walked the length of the town in the blustery wind, from the tip of Shark Island to the old railway station, my views on Lüderitz have softened, matching the bright blue eyes of the hotel owner as I tell her I am using public transport to circumnavigate Africa, having begun in Morocco.

'Is it safe?' she asks, from behind the hotel reception desk, surrounded by a perimeter of electrified wire, and with a company security guard carrying a Kalashnikov around the car park like I might carry an umbrella. It's a question I would be asked frequently in southern Africa, with its obsession on crime.

'That's a good question. I've had no real problems so far. I like it because you get to talk to lots of people, and learn a lot more about their countries. You're looking at me as if I'm mad.'

A *padrão*, originally installed by Bartolomeu Dias stands idle on the coast to the south, but in reality the region south of Lüderitz is another closed region of Namibia's 1000 km coastline, the Sperrgebiet or Forbidden Zone, also called Diamond Area Number One, the centre of Namibia's diamond industry. An old enamel sign in the hotel breakfast room reads:

WARNING.
PENALTY £500. OR ONE YEAR'S IMPRISONMENT.
THE PUBLIC IS WARNED AGAINST
ENTERING THE PROHIBITED
DIAMOND AREA WITHOUT PERMITS.

The warnings remain; and the only population centre in the region is Oranjemund, a closed community of industry employees, run by Namdeb, the successor to The Consolidated Diamond Mines of South West Africa Ltd., makers of the sign. Sticking to public transport, and interested in not aggravating the bored armed guards that patrol the region, means I must head to Keetmanshoop inland.

The scenery is spectacular, views that remind me of the Alps, were they to be buried in sand, with only the tallest peaks of bare rock protruding through. The contrast between the arid landscape and the bounty of wildlife continues; the sharp eye markings of springbok, a larger gembok, a flock of ostrich leading chicks along the roadside fences, all ignoring the plentiful totem-like snake eagles, and raptors hovering effortlessly despite the blustering winds. The Arsenal mad driver of the *combi* asks me how much an air ticket to London would be.

'I don't know exactly, I've come overland from Morocco. Probably US$700.'

'US$700? In Namibian dollars that's…that's a lot' he says quietly.

Keetmanshoop majors as a grumpy small farming town, the largest town in the lower third of the country. For one of the only times on the trip I feel out of place, the obvious outsider; and a little wary. The sullenness, the heat, and the lack of things of interest all push me back into the hotel within an hour, and back at the Caltex petrol station, from where transport is organised, early the next morning.

Within five minutes I've found passage with an Etosha Transport engine pulling two trailers, that's parked on the other side of the road.

'Where exactly are you going?' asks the driver as he relieves himself by one of the man-sized wheels. 'To Ai-Ais? That's where the tourists head.'

'No, no' I say, 'I'm going to Grünau for a couple of days.'

'Grünau? 'You know it's five houses and two dogs...'

Through the windows of the high cab the scenery of the Great Karas mountains is spectacular, the weather hot.

'When it's hot in Keetmanshoop and Grünau it's hot, my friend' says the driver. 'And when it's cold, it's cold. One man sleeping rough died of cold last year in Grünau. The land here now is green because of the rainy season, but in the dry season you won't believe it, my friend – '

'Nothing?'

'Nothing. It's like a desert,' which I consider would be a good way of describing Namibia in general.

'Ah, I forgot the petrol station' jokes the driver, pulling up with the hiss of airbrakes, having taken me 160 km in under two hours. 'The only other thing in Grünau.' His description is accurate. Grünau makes small town Africa look big, yet within two minutes of leaving the petrol station's *akkommodasie* block the next morning, the sky a clean blue backdrop for a low ridge of mountains, I have organised onward transport with Peter taking a hire car into South Africa.

South Africa

the fairest Cape we saw in the whole circumference of the earth

Sailor aboard the *Golden Hinde*, the first English ship to circumnavigate the globe

Peter and I cross into South Africa at Vioolsdrif, 100 km from the Atlantic coast. As we travel south, the road straight and true, Namibia's low ridge of mountains develops into hills that look like boulders collected into giant piles, the brown hues of the landscape only broken by a strip of green on either side of the Orange River where raisins and mangos are grown.

I say goodbye to Peter as the road divides through Steinkopf, he continuing south along the Cape to Namibia route, the sort of name given to dull highways across the world, while I stop in hope of following a secondary road to the coast at Port Nolloth. I'm warmly welcomed by Letitia, the manager of self-catering accommodation on the edge of town, if not by others in Steinkopf. A small town of working class men, I'm asked for money three times in my first half an hour. I am greeted only once, by a student speaking Afrikaans and little English, like most of the town. There are few vehicles in the streets, and no public transport, locals relying on each other to get around.

'It's difficult to get to Port Nolloth and the coast' says Letitia. 'Plus, it's the end of the month; everyone's been paid so they're all paying bills, or shopping, or drinking.' Over the next couple of days she tries desperately hard to find me transport, but no one has the money or inclination to leave for even the nearest of towns. It's frustrating. I just want to get moving, to feel like the journey is continuing.

Acting as the town bus service, Letitia takes me, her three boys, mother, and a family friend not to Port Nolloth and the Atlantic but to Springbok, in her *bakkie* pickup I help jump-start. Her kindness keeps me a steady 100 km from the coast of Namaqualand, ancestral home of the Nama, surrounded by copper containing hills and structures dating back to the early days of smelting. Its capital, Springbok, centres on Voor-trekker Street and the *kopje*, a rocky hillock planted with quiver trees and a monument to the Anglo-Boer War of 1899-1902. Springbok is another Afrikaans town, and it means some change to my vocabulary, with *taxi* translating as minibus.

The only *taxi* to leave Springbok is following the highway to Cape Town, maintaining the steady 100 km distance from the Atlantic, and is fully booked. I didn't imagine public transport in South Africa would be the problem it was turning out to be; having assumed that South Africa's reputation as the continent's powerhouse would extend to its transport infrastructure too.

My only alternative is to *hike*, the Afrikaans for hitchhiking. South African hiking, with a fellow failed traveller, involves far more British-style hiking than I would like. We trek for several kilometres to the highway, my fellow traveller soon dumping his half-bag of potatoes by the side of the road. My shoulders are crying out for me to stop, as we take refuge beside the central reservation with other *hikers*, all black labourers heading for Cape Town, the two lanes largely free of traffic. The big SUVs of Afrikaners speed up, moving into the outer lane to avoid us, and I can't help but feel I would have more success if I wasn't surrounded by black faces. Each passing vehicle strikes as a personal slight.

It's the lorry drivers that pick us up, hissing to a halt two hundred metres distant; allowing as many to climb the ladder-like steps to the cab as will fit on the bunk behind their seats. The journey takes me out of Northern Cape Province and into the Western Cape, the scenery the dry, rocky emptiness of the past few days, beyond road signs for coastal towns with evocative names like Hondeklipbaai, Beeswater, Douse-The-Glim and Cheddar-In-The-Pantry. It makes me feel enormously close to Cape Town, my halfway point.

I climb down from the cab to the well-watered flowers of Vanrhynsdorp homes, the petals orange against green, following a sign for a campsite into a deserted back garden. The large single-storey houses are some of the oldest in the area; the Old Gaol dating to 1751, barely a century after the first European settlement on the cape, though the high modern walls prevent me learning more.

There are some cars I don't even bother to signal for a lift from, waggling an outstretched index finger: middle-aged white men in polished BMWs, SUVs containing their wives and children. So it's a surprise when exactly that – a white woman ferrying two children inside a polished SUV – pulls over beside my perch on the hot metal barrier, as I look down the road. I don't realise they are waiting for me until she releases the buckle of her seatbelt and steps out the vehicle carefully.

'I didn't think you would stop' I say.

'And I think my husband would kill me; so don't do anything to us,' Michelle jokes. Hearing about my journey she continues 'and you know about the crime statistics here in South Africa?' The country has the second highest assault and murder rate in the world; horrendous rape and carjacking statistics. As we discuss South Africa's problems we drive through mountain passes, scattering baboons into a belt of grapevines that lines the Olifants River, the vines irrigated through a series of shallow concrete canals winding down the mountainside below the road to Clanwilliam and its accommodation office.

'Hi. I know you're not the tourist office but I was wondering whether you knew anything about transport to Lambert's Bay. I'm looking to get back to the coast' I ask there.

'Yes,' replies the elegantly aging Afrikaans woman behind the counter, swallowing a portion of sandwich, and looking at me rather like a teacher looks at a stupid child. 'My husband normally takes people from Clanwilliam to Lambert's Bay and Lambert's Bay to Clanwilliam; for the cost of fuel, etc. I'll phone him. So you're going to the crayfish festival?'

'The er…'

'In that case we should see if we can book you some accommodation. They're all booked up for the festival in Lambert's Bay. We have their overflow here in Clanwilliam.'

It turns out her husband won't be making the trip to the coast for another couple of days, tied up like everyone else with the crayfish festival. Instead, she positions me in front of the town's petrol pumps and tells me to ask anyone stopping if they're heading in that direction.

Stephen glances up from the fuel cap of his bright yellow Citroën, dating back to the 1980s, perfectly matching his exuberance for life.

'Excuse me; you want a lift to Lambert's Bay? It would be a pleasure to take you there' he says, fourth generation British and sounding it, pouring water into the car's radiator. 'You'll have to forgive the car. These European imports don't like the Western Cape heat. So, anyway, tell me all the usual questions.'

'Well I came up with this mad idea to circumnavigate Africa by public transport – '

'What's mad about that?'

'I don't know. I don't really think it's mad. But a lot of people think I'm completely insane; my mum for one.'

'You'll have no trouble as a visitor in South Africa. Everyone will welcome you with open arms' he continues.

'The thing I've noticed already is that the cultures in South Africa are so different, even between Afrikaans and English, yet you're creating this amazing country.'

'We know we need each other' he replies. 'We may not like particular aspects of each other's personalities, but when the chips are down, we stand together.' I can hear a lump develop in his throat.

He takes me 25 km out of his way, through the wiry stalks of the *rooibos* fields, just pleased to spend time helping someone with whom he can have an interesting conversation. I catch the first glimpse of the Atlantic in South Africa as we crest a pass on the approach into Lambert's Bay.

'Oh', says Stephen, 'it's blue. It was red yesterday. There was an algal bloom, turning the entire bay a red colour. It's quite spectacular. Anyway, it's been good to share this 60 km of, what, 40,000 km with you' he says at the campsite, the sound of the waves just audible over a wind that makes putting up my tent almost impossible. 'I bet you're used to all this camping, being a boy scout or whatever.'

'Actually I was too shy to be a boy scout. My mum tried to persuade me, but I didn't want to meet strangers.'

'Too shy and you're doing this?'

A sign by the campsite office reads 'the residents of Lambert's Bay request you do not encourage 1) begging 2) crayfish smuggling 3) car washers'. By the fish canning factories, on empty streets, following the line of the bay, and leading to Bird Island Nature Reserve, men with buckets ask if they can wash my car. Bird Island, linked to the mainland by a concrete mole, is a space for South Africa's aquatic wildlife to exist undeterred by development and crayfish

145

smuggling. A home to Cape Gannets, the African Jackass penguin, and Cape fur seals the island was for decades a source of fertiliser, tons of bird droppings collected until the advent of artificial alternatives in the 1950s.

I wait two hours at the town's southern road junction without any transport joy, what few cars that pass me making their excuses. Arthur is the first to stop to talk to me, convincing me to stand at the beginning of a private gravel road that links the coast between Lambert's Bay and Eland's Bay, 30 km south. Black, a fourth generation British immigrant like Stephen, his family had been Cornish tin miners who relocated to South Africa for better opportunities. He asks me where in England Cornwall is located, before leaving me at the roadside in front of his church.

If anything, there is even less traffic here, a sign warning any oncoming vehicles that a permit is required to travel over its dusty surface. The only vehicle I see is a large minibus that turns ahead of me, towards the marquees of the crayfish festival.

On one approach the driver leans out of his window to inform me of the lack of traffic. He convinces me my best chance of transport is from the side of the highway I left at Clanwilliam, and offers to take me, going 100 km out of his way to do so. There I get a ride in a *bakkie* full of black labourers, the landscape that runs alongside us uninspiring. I feel a little apprehension, sharing no language, with more and more labourers, their clothes rough and patched, joining the vehicle on its way to Piketberg.

After a night's rest in Piketberg, a small predominantly white middle-class town in the mountains, like Clanwilliam, I follow Long Street for two kilometres back to the highway, a road I have found almost impossible to leave, joining two other *hikers*. An otherwise empty vehicle takes me to the northern outskirts of Malmesbury, almost exactly half the distance to Cape Town. Failing to get onward transport from here, I end up having to walk the two or three kilometres to the southern end of town, where I find an assortment of other *hikers*, most heading for Cape Town like me, lined up beside the junction where Malmesbury's roads join the highway. The first vehicle that stops doesn't have space for me, the back of the van – that from its strange shape I imagine must date from the 1960s – taken up with the gently quivering guts of at least one elephant.

I struggle to find any vehicles willing to stop, the minutes ticking into an hour. A whistle has me turn to see an aging hatchback pulled onto the verge, its hazard lights flashing. Dennis, hiding a faint stutter under a moustache, is already walking in my direction; seeking a destination from me. As we head towards Table Mountain, looking innocently menacing, dominating the landscape, he apologises for not speaking very much English, before mentioning he's already two hours late for a conference in the mother city. He drops me on the highway before his turn off, forcing me into a short illegal walk along the motorway barriers.

The Castle of Good Hope, a British fort of Dutch construction, adopts the standard star pattern of fortification of the early colonial period, sitting uncomfortably in the centre of the City Bowl area, surrounded by shifting vehicles rather than the waters of Table Bay. Table Mountain looms above the city from every position, a friendly monster, looking like a painted backdrop, a lapping layer of cloud rolling from its flat summit. The castle surprises me by having the apartheid-era flag flying, as well as the modern flag of the rainbow nation.

The mixed heritage of Cape Town means that the city was never really a strong advocate of apartheid: an Afrikaans word meaning separateness. In 1966 the national government redefined the city's District Six as a White Group Area. 60,000 people belonging to other racial groups were forcibly removed to the Cape Flats Township. Though their District Six houses were demolished, this prime real estate remains largely empty, the apartheid redevelopment plans shelved because of local pressure. But such treatment of non-white occupants dates to as early as 1901, when Africans in Britain's Cape Colony were resettled under the pretext of an outbreak of bubonic plague, brought to the country in straw for cavalry horses.

Other traditionally multicultural areas, such as Bo-Kaap, survived demolition by becoming townships; Bo-Kaap serving the Cape Malay community. Brightly coloured houses straddle Signal Hill, around the stumpy minarets of thick stone mosques, guarded by the daily firing of the noon day gun. The community date their settlement of the area to the time of the Dutch East India Company, a reminder that Cape Town is, and always has been, a European city. In Company's Gardens stands a pear tree planted by Jan van Riebeeck in 1652, after arriving at the Cape to develop a loading station for the company.

Though it was Chinese ships that first made use of fresh water sources in the area, the first to pay it serious attention was Vasco da Gama, searching out fresh food for his crew; not only African penguins and their eggs, but also seals – the Dutch for which is *robben*. The Cape fur seals still inhabit the coast around the city, darting under the bridges of the Victoria and Alfred Waterfront, and ahead of vessels travelling to Robben Island, the maximum security prison where Nelson Mandela spent 18 of 27 years imprisoned, their sleek bodies breaking clear of the still harbour water as the waves beat at the sea walls, watched over all the while by the shear mass of Table Mountain.

From the well-to-do frangipani scented roads around its lower station I take the Table Mountain Cableway to the summit of what is considered the world's oldest mountain. Six times older than the Himalayas, it rose from the seabed

600 million years ago, just as Omar Bongo was becoming President of Gabon. The first European to climb its steep sides and reach the 1085 metre summit, carved flat by glaciers, was António de Saldanha, who called it *Taboa do Cabo* – Table of the Cape. The indigenous Khoi San people had called it *Hoerikwaggo* – Mountain of the Sea. Coming to the end of my walk around the blustery summit, the views showing Robben Island's isolated position as the bay continues south, the cableway horn sounds to warn of high winds.

From Table Mountain the city merges with the Cape Flats Township and the peninsula towns of Muizenberg and Simon's Town, where a boardwalk leads to Foxy Beach, home to a colony of African penguins. They are the only penguins to breed in Africa, and take their other name of Jackass penguin from the braying mating call that resounds across the colony of underground nests that protect fledging chicks. Officially classified as endangered since 2010, the species future is not certain. Overfishing and habitat destruction leaves the population at five per cent of its former level, and there's a real risk these lovely creatures could be extinct by 2025.

The Chacma Baboons of Cape Point Nature Reserve seem to be having no such problems, young clinging to the fur of large troops of adults stalking the roadside. The land narrows to a rocky finger, reached by *The Flying Dutchman* funicular, overlooking Dias beach, the most south-westerly tip of the continent; described by Paul Theroux as 'the uttermost end of Africa'.

I return to Cape Town, for onward transport, via Chapman Peak Drive, a road that took seven years to force through the complex topography around Hout Bay. The Dutch named the bay *hout*, meaning wood, after the strong timber of the milkwood tree that was used to repair their ships, the only means they had of departing the South African coast.

My only way of getting to South Africa's southern coast is to travel to Caledon by the evening Intercape coach service, a journey of two and a half hours.

'You don't like the top deck?' asks a woman settling down into a seat. 'You're like me; but *you're* still young.'

'Yeah, but getting older all the time. And I've still got more than half a continent to go.' She looks at me quizzically, saying nothing for the rest of the journey. The setting sun silhouettes the mountains beautifully, but means my choice of bed for the night is limited.

In the tourist office the next morning, Veronica visibly scrunches up her nose when I tell her I stayed at the Parklands Hotel.

'Umm, it's not a hotel anymore you know...it's self-catering.' I feel like she wants to add 'it's for black folk'. However, she arranges onward transport for me, for later in the day.

Caledon is small, and after Cape Town, barren. The roads around the town take me through shopping streets filled with bargain stores, to suburban housing and the few surviving historic structures, museums to everyday life in the 1800s. The lives of middle-class Victorian Britons was much the same as their compatriots in Victorian South Africa, with the same styles of dark brown furniture, dark wallpapers, and portraits of the royal family on top of the upright piano.

By five to six I've convinced myself that my 5.15 lift to Hermanus, organised by Veronica earlier in the day, isn't going to arrive, or that I have somehow missed it, not knowing what vehicle I should be looking out for.

When the minibus does arrive there is nothing to distinguish it from any other, but for a small *special hire* sign resting on the dashboard, and a passenger list consisting wholly of nurses. The drive to Hermanus takes me back

150

towards Cape Town before turning to the coast, giving me the chance to see the splendour of the surrounding countryside that I missed arriving last night after dark. Anywhere else these views would be spectacular, but in South Africa they are ten-a-penny, every view worthy of a photograph.

'You're accommodation is opposite the police station, but you won't need that' says the tourist officer, countering every other reference to crime I have heard in the country.

I walk along the cliffs from the east to the west of town, among the *dassies* – rock hyrax – warily watching a man collecting shellfish on the rocky beaches of Walker Bay below them. The adults resemble large guinea pigs. The youngest, recently born pups, sit as still as the cliff edge rocks they are on, waiting for the return of their mothers, only noticeable when they make an eventual movement of their heads. A low thin layer of cloud breaks up over the water, creating a humid day. A small colony of seals basks on nearby offshore rocks; less islands than isolated protrusions thrusting through the sea; and swim in the rough waves. Teenagers alter the signs along the walk so that they read *KEEP HER ANUS CLEAN*.

My ride to L'Agulhas arrives early the next morning, a saloon driven by JC Smit. The road switches between the coast and inland roads, with JC pointing out rare black springbok and equally rare blue cranes feeding from the farmland grasses. Around Napier, away from the vine-yards, small concrete bungalows that remind me of the colourful houses of Bo-Kaap dot the hillside, replacements for townships, already ruined by the addition of corrugated shacks and open kitchens according to JC. The farms turn to burnt scrub, ash and dust catching in the breeze, like the coals of the bread oven that ignited the veld in a wild fire a year ago, the vegetation only slowly returning.

JC takes me as far as the cairn marking the cape, the rich southernmost point of the world's poorest continent, and the only meeting point of the Atlantic and Indian Oceans, before asking me how I'll leave L'Agulhas.

'It's not safe to hitchhike, five years ago it was fine, but not now; and there's nothing like that Baz Bus this way' he says.

Though the simple stone cairn and its brass plaque written in Afrikaans and English also highlights the separation of the Atlantic and Indian Oceans, I can't identify where one ends and the other begins. So much of my journey so far has been about the Atlantic it has often felt like an Atlantic trip, and it feels strange to be leaving such a constant companion.

The town that edges away from the cape is a friendly little town and rather attractive, with a few stores and a fish and chip shop where I buy lunch as an echo of my last meal in Gibraltar. I shun Atlantic cod for snoek, a local species of barracuda. Canned and shipped from South Africa during the Second World War to alleviate rationing, it was the snoek that was shunned, and used for dog food. 60 years of culinary advances hasn't improved it. The long needle-like bones that run through the flesh do nothing to improve its dry texture or absence of flavour.

Cape Agulhas must not only be Africa's southernmost point, but also its windiest. I scale the 31 metre tall 1849 lighthouse by almost vertical ladders. The wind on the exterior gallery around the lantern room is so strong I am pushed backwards and cling to the circular wall for security, facing out towards Antarctica. As darkness falls the lighthouse sends out its beam of light south across the cape, the graveyard of ships, and north over the town, making me realise that everywhere from Agulhas is north.

I have Hilary, owner of South Point Guesthouse, and Maureen of tourist information competing against one another to find me transport north. It is a friend of Maureen's that takes me the 34 km to Bredasdorp as a favour, saying nothing but 'it's a pleasure' as I drag my backpack from her ridiculously large vehicle.

South Africa's first *dorp* was founded in 1838 by Michiel van Breda, the first mayor of Cape Town. Inland from Cape Agulhas, it loses the coastal breeze that keeps the temperature down to sweater wearing weather, making it sweating weather. It's the sort of place where random people delay you in the street to find out a little about the stranger in town, and make you more welcome than they do some of the locals. I'm welcomed to a guesthouse by a madly barking Jack Russell terrier, and an elderly German granny with her feet up on a stool.

'I'm sorry about ze daug' she says, her birth accent still thick. 'He doesn't like ze black gaardener' she whispers.

Despite its inland location Bredasdorp houses a shipwreck museum, anchors and exhibits from lost ships dotted around maps showing hundreds of shipwreck locations along the coast. I find a letter relating to the wrecking of the French ship *Le Souvenance*. 'Among the wreckage we found the body of a man, which like a wild animal was covered from its feet to its head in hair, no longer than that of a cow' reported Mr Hugo to the French consul in Cape Town. A week later he wrote back reporting that the man had been identified as an orangutan, the ship having sailed from Sumatra.

'No. I'm sorry. You're crazy. You're crazy' says Barbara smiling, the owner of the guesthouse and daughter to the German pensioner I encountered earlier. 'You're very brave; I take my hat off to you. All the way from Morocco? And where's your next port of call?'

Chatting to the owner of a corner shop reveals transport only to Cape Town, so I must hitch a lift. For a country with such an expansive and beautiful coastline, it's continuing to be difficult to stay anywhere near it, the only public transport using the highways running between major towns like Cape Town and East London.

I learn to choose the spot where I extend my arm to hitch carefully. It must be on the outskirts of town beyond any major road junctions, so that the majority of vehicles approaching are heading in my direction. There must be space for the vehicle to pull over, and it should be on the flat or slight downhill, so it is easy to stop and start. There should preferably be a reason for the vehicle to be slowing too: such as the wide bend a kilometre or two from the centre of Bredasdorp that I find myself on.

I am not waiting long before I am offered a lift in the back of an enclosed *bakkie* to Swellendam. I sit on top of my rucksack, hoping I'm not snapping tent poles, sharing the space with the great smell of freshly cooked chicken and steak pies. The passage is hilly, the scenery mostly the late summer stubble of harvested wheat, the remains being grazed by small herds of merino sheep spotted with blue cranes.

From the surviving historic buildings of Swellendam I take a Translux coach towards Mossel Bay. A series of road works make the journey a slow one; ostrich feeding from the bushes by the roadside. I am left at the Caltex garage in Voorbaai, eight kilometres from Mossel Bay. A quick scout around reveals a minibus taxi filling up with returning shoppers.

Being such a new country, politically and economically, I suppose I was expecting South Africa to be a country of high-rise glass skyscrapers like those of Johannesburg, but it's actually incredibly historic, with even the smallest towns I travel through having national monuments, museums, and buildings dating back to early European settlement. Mossel Bay was first visited by Europeans in 1488, when Dias anchored in the bay, after rounding the Cape of Good Hope.

Within the grounds of the Dias museum, housing a replica of Dias' caravel that retraced his route from Portugal 500 years on in 1988, there is a wooden cross marking the first

Christian place of worship in Africa, all that remains of a chapel built in 1501. More remains of the post office tree, a multi-stemmed milkwood tree used by Portuguese crews to carry messages. The first message left reported the death of Dias in a storm off the Cape during his second voyage around the continent.

Before Dias' arrival the area was inhabited by the Khoi San, and they used a cave beneath Cape Saint Blaize lighthouse a short distance from the Dias museum as a midden, a rubbish dump. Large enough to engulf a modern house it's now home to a population of *dassies* so friendly a youngster comes within inches of hopping into my day bag without me noticing.

Sitting in the waiting room for the coach to Port Elizabeth is like being back in a West African embassy: little more than four walls, ceiling, and a floor formed from two different types of tile; nine plastic chairs, two empty crates and an old traffic cone. A beetle the size of my finger nail flies to the fluorescent strip lighting, stuns itself, and plummets to the tiled floor before starting the process again.

With darkness blanketing the coast I see very little as the coach follows the highway into Eastern Cape Province. It pulls into an empty Port Elizabeth car park perfectly on time, an hour before sunrise. My plan to wait on the town's outskirts until daylight is scuppered by a lack of any seating or shelter, and a harsh gusty wind that has me shivering. A circling taxi agrees to take me to the resort area of Summerstrand, where, as the sun rises, it's warm enough to sit out on the promenade looking out over the beaches of Nelson Mandela Bay, to wait for a hotel room to become available. In the middle distance a cloud of spray hangs above the water attracting Cape Gannets, like gulls hovering over the trawlers that sprawl Africa's fishing grounds, the arching backs and dorsal fins of dolphins breaking the surface.

There are two cities. There is the Port Elizabeth of the gothic town hall, lighthouse, and pyramid built 'to the memory of one of the most perfect human beings who has given her name to the Town below', Elizabeth Francis Donkin, wife of the acting governor of the Cape Colony, who died in 1818. Around the pyramid is Donkin Reserve, a renovated green space and sculpture garden donated to the new city by the governor.

A series of steps lead down to the second Port Elizabeth, a black city. It gives off a wariness that makes me keep a closer eye on my possessions in its busier streets. There is a lot of 1970s concrete, and an equally large number of discount stores, the cranes and metal work of the commercial port a constant sight from the city's coastal roads, the container ships failing to dissuade the dolphins of the bay from coming close, parallel to shore as the sky turns pink with evening.

I feel a nervousness I long thought I had dispensed with as I hail a passing minibus heading for the city's terminus, the main stand for long distance minibuses, beneath the flyovers of an area of the city in which no white South African would be seen dead; or more correctly, in the part of town in which white South Africans might well be found dead, and missing their wallets.

The Indian Ocean is like glass, the cargo vessels on it like models. The road to East London then moves inland, through rolling hills and the gateways of private safari lodges offering game viewing and hunting.

It takes me more than six months to travel from my parent's home in South London to East London. It's the most African city I have visited since leaving Angola, the Northern and Western Cape Provinces predominated by white South Africa. Unfortunately, this change in culture means dilapidation, rubbish-strewn streets, and water droplets falling steadily from air conditioning units on the sides of tired buildings. I feel like I stick out. I feel very rich, and very much a target, though everyone I encounter treats me with courtesy, if a little too courteously.

It's a journey of 220 km northeast from East London to Port Saint Johns, via Mthatha, along the winding roads of the wild coast. The Outspan Inn is just a little way from first beach, where the River Mzimvubu makes its slow meandering progress into the Indian Ocean. Birds feed on the sandbank that separates river from ocean. Just opposite, half covered in subtropical vegetation, the straight architectural lines of the ruined Cape Hermes Hotel stands idle, like the ruined hotel in Robertsport. A lanky grey coated vervet monkey rushes from the path and enters the bar, only disturbed by an oncoming vehicle. It has the greenery and cicadas of somewhere in West Africa, without the stickiness, and it is here I feel I have returned permanently to black Africa: potholes, noisy bars, mosquitoes, and an ease of public transport. There are few Afrikaners, and almost no British presence, but for a few aging hippies drawn to the laidback nature of the town. A muezzin calls *Allahu akbar* for the final time today, yet another reminder of West Africa.

Durban, in KwaZulu Natal, outstrips my expectations very quickly, though I think that says more about my expectations than about Durban. I find a sunny, cultured modern city of skyscrapers, lively market stalls and shops. Between them and the non-descript buildings of the centre, are some historic architectural gems, and gardens green despite the summer heat. It's clean and well-cared for. One of its historic buildings helps record Durban's past as a white city, creator of the 'Durban system', a forerunner to apartheid. The Native Administration Department, now the KwaMuhle Museum, was the building in which Durban's non-white population had to queue in order to receive the paperwork permitting them to work within the city's limits. Often they didn't receive permission, and had to leave the city within 72 hours or face

157

arrest. A vivid contemporary photograph shows councillors proudly standing in front of the last corrugated tin homes during the forced demolition of Durban's Clan Manor Township.

Durban is South Africa's family friendly beach resort. Beyond the miles of new promenade, and the clean yellow sands and rejuvenated beach scrub, the ocean swimmers and surfers behind the safety of shark nets watched over by lifeguards, the adventure parks and paddling pools, I walk through rows of old collapsing red brick warehouses, and modern luxury holiday lets that abut them, both as empty as each other.

The city takes its old name, Port Natal, from the arrival of Vasco da Gama's ships on Christmas Day in 1497. The Vasco da Gama clock, gifted to the city in 1969 by the Portuguese Club of Natal, to commemorate 500 years since the explorer's birth, reminds me that wherever I go on this journey, I am only here because others have come before me. The stopped clock, the centrepiece of a rusting, yet colourfully painted metal bandstand-like construction, sits near the entrance of the Port Natal Maritime Museum. Dipping through an art deco subway under a railway line to get there, I wander about a couple of old tugs, rest in the senior officers' mess room, and go down to the close atmosphere of engine rooms that look like they would be death traps in a puddle, let alone the open seas about the South African coast.

Nearby, facing the high court and important municipality buildings, an equestrian statue commemorates the actions of Dick King, who helped relieve the Boer siege of the British garrison by riding 1000 km in 10 days for reinforcements during skirmishes in 1842. Though the tented garrison is long gone, the low ramparts continue to ring the flower beds of Old Fort Gardens, the narrow paved pathways leading to a chapel, a former ammunition magazine surrounded by blast walls two and a half metres high.

The sticker, with a telephone number for an ambulance, on the minibus taxi to Richards Bay isn't particularly welcome, though another of a chimp with *Mr Mhamishani* written above it in pencil breaks some of the long monotony of waiting. The town's coastal location has seen heavy industry build up on the road to the port; shiny as yet unoxidised blocks of aluminium, shaped and stacked like egg boxes, transported directly to waiting vessels from the metal foundries at regular intervals. But what the town lacks in interest it more than makes up for with transportation. The depot, taxi city, a vast series of warehouses beside the town superstores is busy, with hundreds of minibuses lined up waiting their turn, destination signs hanging from the high roof space sponsored by a local mobile phone company. It takes two hours for the minibus to fill, the other passengers mostly shoppers with heavily-loaded plastic bags of food for the week ahead.

The weekend shopping frenzy continues into Monday morning. Not only are there locals standing by the roadside outside the supermarket waiting for friends to collect them and their shopping, but there are long patient queues for cash machines, and the market stallholders busily trying to attract buyers. Even so, it's much easier than I had feared to get towards the border with Mozambique at Kosi Bay.

Most of South Africa's immigration team is sitting on a bench in the shade; the man I disturb, behind the protective glass of the immigration office, taking his eyes from the morning's newspaper to take my passport.

Mozambique

The north of Mozambique was like another country, sharing a border with Tanzania and possessing an East African culture, with remote villages inland, ancient fishing communities on the coast, and some of the best artisans and carvers in Africa, the Makonde people. No one went there

Paul Theroux, *Dark Star Safari*

In contrast to the flat concrete expanse of the border, Mozambique is beautiful from the very beginning. A cloudless azure blue sky that I hadn't noticed in South Africa is only interrupted from stretching on forever by rounded green hills, which in turn are broken up by the white sands of the tracks that twist around and away from each other the 11 km to Porto d'Ouro. There is no public transport from the border; I hitch my backpack onto my shoulders for a long drag through the bright scrub hoping that I'll be able to follow the most direct of the tracks, cut into the sand by the heavy lorry tyres that use it.

Having the sun as my only companion lasts a few hundred metres at most, where I reach a brick lorry readjusting its lopsided load. Its driver is happy for me to join him in the cab, the large wheels rolling easily over the land's sandy blemishes that develop into Porto d'Ouro.

I have little need to recover my Portuguese, the beaches, bars and restaurants busy with holidaying South Africans. Even the makeshift wooden stalls, hanging with shark's teeth and crushed shell necklaces, display prices in South African rand as well as meticais nova família. In the early years of

Portuguese East Africa, the name by which Mozambique was most usually known before independence in 1975, 400 meticais were equal to a large elephant's tusk or 500 bands of cloth. Now, after a revaluation of 1000:1, 400 meticais are equivalent to less than £10, and gets me a traditional prawn curry and several chilled bottles of the local 2M lager.

I am packing up my tent to the sunrise and the breath of waves, before heading to the market for early morning transport, an old *chapa* minibus waiting half full. Locals are just about moving themselves, though the market stalls aren't yet set up as they would be in Angola.

The road is mostly composed from sand, though there are signs it was once more properly surfaced, since every so often we drive onto a ruined black strip full of holes harder to endure than the make-do sand surface. Crossing through Maputo Special Elephant Reserve in the hazy early morning cool, signs warn of the elephants' inclination to push vehicles onto their sides. Vervet monkeys send the branches of the trees lining the route slapping. Somewhere out in Maputo Bay, despite the cargo vessels reaching port, and Maputo's modern coastal skyline, dugong and bottlenose dolphins live. Maputo feels alive, Mozambique's long civil war forgotten.

I follow the crowd towards the end of the quay where I queue for a small diesel-powered boat to take me the short hop across the bay to the capital, beating the larger and slower vehicle ferry.

A large white fluffy cloud rises out of the bay as I sit in a quiet colonial-era garden, decorated with the curling ironwork of the period, listening to the cry of hornbills within sight of modernist towers lining streets named in honour of disgraced international leaders such as Robert Mugabe. Even so, it's clear Mozambique is trying to move on from its history. The ancient Portuguese fort, the collection of brass cannon I have come to expect lying in the grass mostly forgotten, is hosting a charity funded exhibition on albinism; while the ornate pistachio-coloured central railway station is near the end of its conversion into the city's destination for culture, as well as train travel to the interior.

With the railway lines running inland, like most of those I've encountered, another 4.30 am start sees me onto a former Hong Kong school bus heading for Imhambane; *no smoking* signs in Chinese and English. I see much less of the coast than I hoped I would, but when I do it's spectacular. Verdant islands sit a short distance from the mainland beaches, ranging among clear blue waters under a bright sun.

Imhambane is quiet, the bay it overlooks stunning. One of Mozambique's oldest settlements, it is a hotchpotch of wide tree-lined avenues, dusty side streets and a range of competing architectural styles that are undoubtedly only still standing because of a lack of money to knock them down and build something new.

On paper the half hour journey across the *baía* by Transmarítima ferry is the quickest way north. It's certainly the cheapest at 10 meticais. On the other side, at Maxixe, I'm talked into taking a *chapa* to Vilankulo, being told it will be quicker than the buses heading the same way.

By the time we rocket past the small professionally produced *Tropico del Capricorno* road sign another half an hour later I am one of only two passengers left with the driver and his *comprador* apprentice. We make a decidedly permanent stop at the transport depot in Massinga not long after, the muddy earth packed hard in front of a series of shops. I miss the roads of West Africa, following every sweep of the coast; the trunk roads here, like in South Africa, set back from the water's edge.

The vehicle doesn't leave Massinga again for nearly four hours, which I break examining the dusty stock of a Chinese-managed supermarket. When it does, it travels only as far as

163

the next street, the engine tone rippling through the minibus while the *comprador* attracts more custom than he knows what to do with. Most of the passengers use the *chapa* to reach their roadside villages; almost identical groups of rectangular mud-built thatched homes that front onto a clearing filled with drying clothes and fires that burn all day. They call out '*comprador*!' within a kilometre or two of joining those standing bent double at the sliding door, hanging over the first row of seats, five people sharing the space of three. The cramping of my legs feels like a penitence for having had it too easy recently.

Having poured with rain all night, low cloud still covers Vilankulo the next morning, perfect conditions for the giant land snails that linger outside my night's room. The vegetation between the town and the folded coastline drips loudly, creating small indentations on the muddy paths. Fishermen bail out their pirogues, anchored in the blue shallows, with scoops cut from plastic jerry cans. Locals in their Sunday best pour out of one or other of the churches clutching bundles of palm fronds, Easter only a week away.

On the clearing in front of the municipal market is another donated school bus, a sign for Beira in the front window, parked up and empty. In order to see more of the country I climb aboard a *chapa* for Imhassoro instead, a shorter journey in a vehicle held together by discoloured spot welds. The *comprador* gives me a good seat towards the back; only four of us share the padding shaped for three. The roof struts buckle as the cargo on top of it – including my backpack – thumps down after dips in the road, brought back to rest by the old cord it's held down with. My thoughts of 'surely it must be full by now' invariably leads to the vehicle stopping to squeeze another person on board.

Towards Imhassoro we pass a minefield marked out by red and white poles, stretching for a couple of hundred metres parallel to the road. Just behind I can see circular reed huts and people walking between them.

A gateway to the exclusive Bazaruto Archipelago there is a tourist friendly ambience to the few isolated buildings that seem to make up the town, with further isolated upmarket hotels lining the most scenic spots, some distance away in the on-off rain of an East African wet season. It keeps me tucked into the depths of the veranda of my room, looking at a naïvely painted image of the ocean until late afternoon, lizards in the open bathroom snatching at the mosquitoes and midges brought out by the rain.

When I finally make it to the wide, empty streets, leaping the deep open drains to the stalls coloured with souvenir boats and T-shirts, and beyond the half-built telecommunications mast, a heavy downpour catches up with me, forcing me beneath the thatch of an abandoned bar with three young women balancing plastic washing up bowls of freshly caught fish on their heads. Water splashes from the bowls as they walk, forming short lived stains on the wax cloth that drops down to their bare feet.

I reach the felled tree trunk that serves as a waiting room by pickup, and wait with four or five others for transport north, though there is hardly any traffic at all; a handful of private vehicles owned by rich Mozambicans with drivers uninterested in the money that comes with hitchhikers.

An hour into my wait a single decker bus appears, *Maxixe-Beira* written on a card in the front window. The seatbacks of the *Transportes Púlicos da Beira* bus are high and close, meaning I see very little of the journey. Some stretches of the single-lane road are so bad I am reminded of the Robben Island ferry, but these areas are rare. As the time gets towards sundown the cloud of mosquitoes trapped aboard becomes visible, and I become keener to reach Beira. It takes another hour with tiredness washing over me, rubbing my naked arms and legs continuously to stave off the mosquitoes, before I see the English *Beira Welcomes You* sign through the darkness, with the help of the headlights. The comparatively short journey lasts nine hours, my travels through Mozambique becoming a series of inland loops linking insignificant coastal towns. It's not only that the road network is far from perfect, but also that Mozambique is simply huge; the size of Madagascar; 2500 km from end to end, four times the length of the British Isles.

It's easy enough to get a taxi to a hotel, but harder to get a room. The conversation with the receptionist circles perilously close to a mental plughole.

'Good evening.'

'Good evening. Do you have a room?'

'Yes.'

'Okay, I'll take it.'

'Pay the money and you can have the key.'

'Can I pay tomorrow? I don't have enough money on me tonight.'

'Yes.'

'Good…Can I have the room then?'

'Pay the money and you can have the key…'

Maybe it's because I eventually get into the room and get some sleep, or because the sun manages to penetrate the cloud, but I take a liking to Beira. It has a tropical elegance and laid back feel, plenty of squares shaded by the occasional tree, great sweeping architectural wonders sitting next to petrol stations. The ocean is a mucky brown colour, receiving the heavy sediment of the waters of the Púngoe River, cut through by the wake of small cargo vessels traversing towards the port on the river's mouth. Nature doesn't do straight lines, except where the sea meets the sky; the pure unbroken horizon visible from an area of wasteland yet to have ocean view homes built over it, the home of boggy reeds, birds, and chirruping insects.

Much of northern Mozambique remains pristine, meaning very poor. My coach to Quilemane passes little but tall grasses and round reed huts in small clearings until the Zambezi bridge midway through the twelve hour journey. Its sections stretch beyond the river's current width, low despite the rain, but still as wide as the Thames at Westminster, flanked by rich brown silt.

The children of Quilemane protect their pristine school uniforms from the next morning's rain, while street cleaners in blue overalls remove debris from the gutters beside the old catholic cathedral with brush stick brooms, not paying the weather the slightest attention as they shuffle slowly along the road outside other uncared for crumbling buildings.

A memorial plaque inside the cathedral dates from 1853; the Portuguese script rich with the confidence typical of the nineteenth century. The building has been stripped of almost everything it could be stripped of, why and how the plaque survives, clinging to the plaster walls, a mystery. Only the chequered red and black tiles, and three gravestones set into them, remain; plaster mouldings split from the walls to reveal the red brick behind. The roof keeps the rain from entering, the side chapels and stairs leading to the wooden choir stall above the main entrance destroyed. Holes in the far wall show where the high altar would have stood. As I move deeper into the building I can hear the murmur of nearby voices and smell human habitation.

With the rain and the slow decay, the only objects that remain spotless are the white four-wheel drive vehicles of the many charities headquartered here, and the children's school uniforms. I dodge the street-wide puddles as best I can through the centre of town to its green spaces, decked out in lengths of cloth taking their colours from the national flag, to the new cathedral. From the outside it looks like the aging nuclear power stations that line the British coast. Inside, it is nearly as Spartan as the old cathedral, with little to show for it being Good Friday. Blocks of colourful stained glass filter the only natural light.

From my map Pebane looks like any other town on the coast of northern Mozambique, and like any other town in Mozambique's north, getting there is more difficult than it should be. Two days after leaving Quilemane I arrive at its single tarmac road, having overnighted in the grounds of the transport depot, eager not to miss the promise of a lift with a Pakistani named Khan, in the cab of his flatbed truck. The night passes slowly, the music from the onsite nightclub ending just shortly before I rise at 5 am.

Khan's apprentice is waiting for me in the narrow corridors of the building, and leads me to the roadside by the depot, where men are loading sacks of flour onto the truck. The sun tries to break through the clouds and mist over the vast green of Mozambique in the rains, the only sense of a modern world coming from telecommunications masts piercing through the tree canopy. We drive for hours, following the orange-pink strip across the green, passing only a handful of hamlets that barely break up the grasses of the roadside. The only sign I might be reaching my goal is the steady gradation of the clay road to sand, as Khan cuts through a copse dotted with market stalls, circling and following his own tyre tracks to talk to acquaintances and offload his cargo.

'Back in Pakistan I was an engineer' he tells me. 'I have lived in Mozambique for 16 years, driving trucks like this one. Now I go back to Pakistan. Blacks are good for two things only: drinking, and fucking.'

He takes me to a guesthouse where he has a regular room: a long breeze block building with four or five rooms, the reed roof dropping grit over the mattresses. Like much of Mozambique, it is friendly, green, and tired, though there is the orange glow of electric lights, and a plug socket in one corner, behind a layer of dusty cobwebs. I duck under the mosquito net onto the mattress having washed from a bucket in a partly-fenced courtyard beneath the stars, foregoing the meal Khan offers for sleep.

The women running the guesthouse find it hilarious that I would want to wash my grubby clothes myself, and offer to do it for me. While I wash my clothes, the women replace the palm fibre washing line with one made from commercial twine, and help clear the soap scum from my clothes before hanging them out to dry. They seem surprised that I thank them.

The sun is hot, and the sky studded with fat white balls of cotton. The smell of open fires that was all pervasive last night has faded. A homeless man sleeps on the concrete stoop of a building beside a stinking rubbish pile half my height. A path leads me to the river mouth, where children shift ripe coconuts from a pile on the mud to the back of a flatbed truck like Khan's.

I pass a naked man lathering up soap in a pool of clear water. My attempts to reach a white sand beach like those I can see in the distance fail, leaving me in front of the fetid smell of mangrove, small fat roots sticking vertically out of the thick mud, the buildings of Pebane not so much located on the coast as randomly positioned about it like hundreds and thousands sprinkled over a cupcake.

I seek shade in a wasteland of a public garden, the metal frame of a children's swing beside an overgrown climbing frame. The sound of the light breeze rustling the branches of the tree above the bench turns to the solid thud of something striking the ground nearby. A slender lime green snake maybe half a metre in length looks up at me, disappearing into the undergrowth with a rapid turn of speed as I reach for my camera.

As dusk settles over the coast Pebane adopts the smell of burning wood once more. Stalls along the only tarmac road sell the continent's staples: sardines, bread, and biscuits imported from Brazil. Bats leave their roost in the collapsed school building beside the guesthouse, momentarily caught in an electric light. The stars visibly sparkle through hazy white patches of Milky Way, so many it's impossible to count anything but the smallest area of sky.

I'm not waiting for long the next morning before there is a mad scramble to get on top of the cargo of a flatbed truck before the other 30 passengers, all desperate for the best sitting position. I singularly fail, and am left standing beside a tyre the same height as I am until someone offers me their hand. I'm forced to sit at the rear of the vehicle, no one willing to make space for me, and wedge myself into a space left between sacks of coconuts, part of a mixed cargo together with partially dried fish the size of whitebait still oozing oils.

The gritty covering of the damp ropes cut and gnaw at my hands as I hold on, fearful of falling at every jolt in the road. It's an insecure spot and I have to fight to keep my centre of balance in the right place: pushing into the other human cargo rather than over the flower beds of a passing house. With the passing hours, the acceleration of the vehicle pushes everyone towards the rear of the vehicle. It feels more and more like I'm being deliberately forced into the cloud of dust kicked up by the tyres. A light shower of rain distracts me from worrying about my exposure to the sun, and the pain of needing to constantly hold on to the rough ropes, but glues the dust to my skin, hair and clothing, so that half my body is monochrome orange.

The day passes on the top of the truck, what food and water we need thrown up to us in the hamlets we stop at. Most of the cargo is offloaded sometime after darkness settles, giving me the first chance during the journey to let go of the ropes and stand on a solid surface. As the ropes are slowly unknotted, the smell of drying fish rises from the vehicle. When the waterproof cover is raised from the cargo, fish oils run to the ground. Watching half-interested with the other passengers, I get talking to Eduardo, a 21 year old, the only one with any English. He thinks nothing of the dust stuck to me. He doesn't believe I would come to Mozambique just to visit, and thinks I must be 'investigating just one thing'.

Back on the truck's bed I investigate the liquid which seems to be oozing from my bag. I don't get the smell of fish from it, but don't manage to locate its source to an exploded bottle of shampoo until I am in a room for the night.

I am only looking lost for a couple of minutes before I am offered a seat *em frente* beside Emmanuel, an English-speaking primary school teacher, in the cab of an empty biscuit truck heading to Nampula. Quickly leaving manmade structures behind us, the scenery reverts to its natural spectacle: small mounds of rock sticking barnacle-like to the earth, clouds playing with the light.

I wake on the edge of Nampula, the driver mocking me gently in Portuguese for falling asleep for so long. Emmanuel directs me onto a *chapa* to the centre of the city, before going further and arranging a room in a *pensão*. I have my first proper meal in three days on the first floor veranda of one of the town's better restaurants, looking out over the dimly lit buildings and the shining vehicles of international agencies parked below.

Though Nampula is not a coastal city, it is the largest in the region, with piped water, and onward connections to the Isla de Moçambique from a depot behind the train station. With a seating capacity of 25, and an actual capacity edging over 35, the large minibus is almost ready to depart. Perched on one buttock in the gap between two seats for most of the three and a half hour journey, an English girl, a seat to herself, complains 'you're basically sitting on my lap' as soon as I squeeze in beside her.

Camping on the mainland, with views of Mozambique Island, I walk the four kilometre causeway, a single lane stretching over the shallow waters on angled concrete legs. The wind threatens to pull the buttons from my shirt and the camera from my pocket.

The island represents the early aim of Europeans: to take advantage of the continent's resources while barely touching the continental mass, using a string of islands around it, the fool's gold around a diamond. It was the capital of the Portuguese empire in East Africa until 1898, when it was transferred south, to Maputo.

The poverty, the torn clothes, and the children playing in the crumbling houses give the place a timeless feel. Grass grows through the quartz and black spiral paving, many of the benches are broken, and the public toilets locked, leaving locals to defecate on the slipway to the beach, beside the old customs pier. There is a relaxed atmosphere, helped by the lack of motor vehicles, which only circulate the wider roads around the edges of the island. The sky blanketed by cloud, the town slowly wakes up around me. Mansions fit easily among the reed houses; the massive leaning walls of the fort of São Sebastião at the northern tip of the island, as integral to the island as the ageless pirogues bobbing on the shore. Even the children seem somehow muted. On a tumbledown backstreet of stone buildings, which could describe any part of the island not made from reeds, a small girl approaches, holding a small piece of rectangular white plastic to her eye.

'Click' she says grinning widely, 'photo!'

I get into the otherwise temporarily closed fort under the guise of the island's first cultural festival. Workmen have yet to complete the Vodafone sponsored main stage, and finish carting patio chairs around the dusty central quad to the roughly taped off VIP area. I sneak about the decrepit, empty, mouldering rooms; lacking doors and windows, devoid of any furniture. Sparrows nest in the interior gloom. Odd lumps, bumps, and funnily-shaped rooms demonstrate the continued use and alteration of the fort since its construction in 1558. Crosses adorn the battlements, giving it the feeling of a long ignored crusader castle, grass growing by the cannon, skinks at home on the hot whitewashed surfaces. Ending my self-appointed tour I'm spotted by a security guard and ushered back to the main stage, where more Vodafone posters are being put in position.

The cloud breaks into feathers slowly, over the several days of my visit. A jet-ski, purple and scarlet, sits on a trailer incongruously in a historic tree-lined square, as incongruously as the foliage green bandstand at the square's centre. A bundle of bored children watch from over my shoulder as I write up my diary. I would normally find them bothersome; telling them to 'move on' like I've had to others already today. In my supreme sereneness I let them be, and allow them to study my map of Mozambique with me.

Transport to the junction town of Monapo is easy to find from the mainland end of the causeway. The driver lingers, circling the roads and the locals in their free red T-shirts from the cultural festival, about the causeway, before idling the engine in further waiting. It makes the journey to Monapo a slow one, but there I am able to jump straight onto the back of a modified pickup to Nacala. Wooden benches run down its sides, a rusting flat metal roof giving protection from sun and rain. The driver goes in search of additional custom, back towards Mozambique Island for so long that even the patience of the Mozambicans is tested and a passenger leans towards the vehicle's cab to shout 'Hey, are you driving all the way to Maputo first or what?'

Nacala is industrial, spread out. It feels like an eternity from the vague cluster of buildings that makes up its heart to where the *chapas* deposit their passengers. There is a single spot between the two where I am able to see the surrounding countryside clear of any buildings. I look north across an

173

inland fold in the coastline, the ocean as grey as the day's intermittent drizzle. A small cargo vessel ploughs the waters from the port.

Two minutes before my wake up time of 3.45 am I think I can hear rain; not just rain; a downpour. I come close to convincing myself not to bother getting up; but I do, pushing myself out to the road.

The *noonvitigang* emergency exit signs on the windows of the bus suggest it has been retired from a city route somewhere in South Africa, to travel hundreds of kilometres across the rough roads of northern Mozambique. It's cramped, with my legs jarring against the metal frame of the seat in front. Since entering Mozambique I have had an almost permanent feeling of being squashed, while the land itself seems artificially stretched beyond its borders and 2500 km coastline.

I manage to sleep for much of the 420 km to Pemba, the next town on the coast, more and more of the passing scenery on my journey through Mozambique missing from my memory as exhaustion sets in.

The sun begins to make it past the clouds as I reach the reception desk of the Pensão Baía and am shown to its cheapest room, at 2 pm. I like the room. I like the fact I have to walk past the DIY kitchens and through the washing up area. I like the fact I have to leave the building, descend a concrete flight of stairs, past turkeys and puppies, into the basement. I like the fact the window faces out onto a discarded toilet bowl and the front end of a car. There is a whimsical lack of care that draws me in. I don't like the large cockroach that walks across the bed when I move a pillow.

On a spit of land, Pemba is surrounded by ocean to the north and east. I walk through the shanty of the lower town that has developed beyond the bounds of the coast road – a lively community of mixed dwellings of new concrete, older stone, and even older reeds set uneasily on the shifting sands. As such a common sight I barely recall the chickens scratching through the monstrous piles of stinking rubbish, or the foul smells that come from the dark untreated sewage.

A municipal market created in the 1940s separates it from the upper town, a couple of rubble-strewn streets of well-constructed Portuguese buildings; a battered red post box cast with the word *Moçambique* protruding from the surface of a side road. At the tourist orientated Wimbe beach, on the southern edge of town, waves lap at the rocks that front the short widths of beach, but from the centre the ocean merely wobbles like jelly, the still conditions preventing waves from developing or doing more than ripple gently with the water's surface tension. A pirogue and two swimmers make use of the calm conditions. The land visible to the north looks as flat and peaceful as the ocean.

In the grogginess that comes with waking the *gubba, gubba, gubba* of the turkeys outside my room transliterates in my mind into *up! up! up!*, a subconscious recognition that I should continue my journey north.

There are 50 kilogram sacks of rice from Pakistan and India filling the floor space of the Pemba – Quissanga pickup, between the unpadded wooden benches, so I stretch my legs out horizontally on top. As the bus fills with a mixture of tourists and locals, I am wedged into a corner, the metal supports for the canvas awning knocking against my ribs. Sitting on the bench, the hard jolts of the road shift from a mild discomfort of early on to excruciating pain; my legs cramping and my muscles becoming bruised. The road becomes sandier the closer we get to Quissanga, reducing our speed further, to no more than 15 km an hour. I have difficulty standing on arriving eight hours later, having only travelled 220 km.

Within a couple of minutes of stretching my legs I can see that Quissanga is exactly the sort of place that will end up in a holiday brochure as representing the real Mozambique. Aside from the daily *chapa* departures towards Pemba, it cannot have changed much for a long time. Locals only leave to ferry the few tourists – none of which stay to visit the village – to the nearby islands, or to make a living by subsistence fishing of crabs, prawns and clams in the bay. Fresh water comes from communal pumps. There are no cars, meaning people are still able to wander the sandy paths and alleys – barely streets – between the reed pole houses as freely as the chickens. It feels like an abuse to take photographs. It's also the first time I notice the Swahili influence, an aging woman sitting on the front stoop of her home saying '*salaama muzungu*', the Kiswahili for 'welcome white man'. *Muzungu* was first used to describe someone who was constantly travelling, and had a desire to witness everything, like the earliest European visitors to Africa.

As I sit on the Y of a tree trunk on the shoreline I am welcomed again, by a friendly local speaking no English, and waving fiddler crabs leaving their burrows in the dark sandy loam between the mangrove roots.

In the hour and a half I am waiting at the junction 15 km from Quissanga, only five vehicles pass heading north. That's less than one every 15 minutes on the predominant arterial route in northern Mozambique. When playing cards around the still smoking ashes of a palm-fed fire with a group of teenagers gets boring, I manage to flag down a pickup, the driver agreeing to drop me off at Chai 240 km away.

The half bag of something that I'm sitting on is offloaded at the same point at which the good tarmac road becomes what I can only describe as awful. I'm flung clear of the metal floor constantly, my legs, back, and arms all striking different parts of its metalwork. The driver slows from his rocket-like pace only to buy dinner or pick up additional hitchhikers. I try sitting on my backpack, and using it as a back brace, my legs outstretched on the floor. The driver places a dikdik, an antelope resembling a small springbok, in the far corner, but it soon makes its way about the truck with the shaking of the vehicle, until its glazed eyes and slit throat get too close and I push it away with a foot, while ensuring I don't crush some live and trussed up chickens with the other.

'You speak Portuguese?' asks Emmanuel, a Tanzanian, as he climbs over the pickup's tailgate with his elderly father. I shake my head.

'Not really, I'm English.'

'Welcome to Mozambique. I speak low-level Portuguese, perhaps 60-70%. I speak high-level English: we must learn it at secondary school in Tanzania. At home with my father I speak Kiswahili', which literally translates as the language of the coastal people. His father, anywhere between 60 and 80 and in an immaculate if ill-fitting suit, crouches like everyone else, no provision made for his age despite the deep respect the elderly are afforded.

'*Hujambo baba, habari?*' I want to ask; *how are you sir?*; but I don't have the confidence as I look into his unchanging middle-distance stare.

The advantage of the vehicle's ridiculous speed is that I arrive in Chai in an improbably short amount of time; the driver refusing payment for the journey.

I am steered towards a set of rough benches outside of a grocery store by the long call of the English *hello*. The group of teachers that I shake hands with are drinking neat Rhino brand gin from the single shot sachets they are buying from the shop. They tell me that it was here in sleepy middle-of-nowhere Chai that the first shot of the war of independence was fired, FRELIMO fighters launching their first attack against Portuguese targets in the town on 24th September 1964, 11 years before the country finally won its independence. Though they are drunk to the extent that they struggle to speak clearly, after an hour or so they bring a passing lorry to a rapid halt, the air brakes singing and cab lurching forward, and I have transport to Moçimboa de Praia.

The road out of Chai is, if anything, worse than on its entry into Chai, the strong suspension struggling. It becomes increasingly hot in the cab. The driver turns to bottles of 2M lager for refreshment, while the smell of my damp-dry shorts slowly fills the cab. It takes several more hours to reach the town, with the driver only stopping to exchange the empty lager bottles rolling about the floor for full ones. It means I have been travelling for 15 hours, and I do little more than flop down on the bed of the cheapest *pensão* and sleep.

At 3.15 the next morning there is a knock at the door and a shout from the owner in Portuguese.

'It's time to travel to Tanzania!'

'I'm not going anywhere. I'm staying here today. I told you – Tanzania *domingo*.'

There is a cloudless sky, with the sun burning by 9 am. I walk downhill towards the ocean, the water's edge lined with market stalls and old warehouses. A thin strip of beach disappears entirely with the approaching tide, the shallows filled with children playing. Behind them well-trodden paths lead to the African village and the sometimes temporary-looking reed huts of the locals.

The owner knocks on my door the next morning at 2.20. I'm not really sleeping in any case, my stomach gurgling troublesomely. The pickup I climb onto sleepily drives around town for at least half an hour before turning north. As one of the first to board I take possession of the spare tyre, resting on it for the three hour journey, trying to keep my head out of the cold morning wind, rushing over the cab to the open back, as night turns to day.

After immigration procedures the pickup continues another four kilometres to the Rovuma River, the geographical border between Mozambique and Tanzania. I am punted across in a canoe by two boatmen, the water becoming so low they have to step into the water to push, and later drag the boat, the sand audibly scraping the bottom. It's beautifully picturesque, the river entering the ocean surrounded by vegetation, wading birds continuing their watch over the water from fallen trees despite our approach.

Tanzania – Kenya

By now we were used to being told how dangerous Africa was and we'd come to the conclusion that 90 per cent of what was said was bullshit

Ewan McGreggor, with Charlie Boorman,
Long Way Down

A *dalla-dalla*, the cleaner and newer Tanzanian version of Mozambique's *chapas*, takes me from the border to Mtwara, the first town of significance in country number 21 of my journey. I sense a vitality that was missing from northern Mozambique. At the collection of makeshift stalls that form the fish market, the Indian Ocean seems bluer, the sands whiter and cleaner, the sky clearer, the people at the market friendlier. Dhows zip up and down the coastline in the light breeze; their movement replicated by the steady stream of *dalla-dallas* leaving Mtwara early next morning.

The Iolos Line *dalla-dalla* covering the short distance to Lindi leaves within five minutes of my boarding. My legs are intertwined with a man facing me so, that if the vehicle accelerates too quickly I will end up with a severe groin injury. More importantly for the man opposite, if the vehicle brakes suddenly, a far more likely occurrence, *he* will end up with a severe groin injury.

Lindi seems less certain of itself, a confusion of colonial backwater and modern cosmopolitan centre. A woman entirely wrapped in black carries a wicker basket on her head as she sends a message on her mobile phone. The few tumbledown pre-independence buildings at its heart, away from the tiny

181

unused port, are owned by Indian and Arab traders, while the well-dressed middle-class meet at the teahouses of Uhuru – Independence – Avenue. Ordering a cup of tea, I am given what looks like a steaming cup of stagnant pond water, and the word dysentery comes to mind before the ginger of the spice blend comes through, and mixes perfectly with the black tea of the Kilimanjaro brand teabag.

I make it to Kilwa Masoko, called simply Masoko by locals, despite the ticket I bought last night looking like it belonged on a section of toilet roll. The *dalla-dalla* makes its usual slow progress, with every bus and coach in the country roaring by in a cloud of diesel smoke.

'In England no one really knows this place exists, I certainly didn't,' I tell Prisca, the area conservation officer, as we walk along the sloping road to the jetty at the edge of town. The speedboat she's called for from her office in the district headquarters hasn't arrived from the island of Kilwa Kisiwani. I am pleased, as it means Prisca and I will have to reach the island by dhow. We wade into the shallows, the waters crystal clear and perfectly warm; my normally enclosed feet looking ridiculously pale. The boatmen pull modern blue plastic ropes taught around me, and the lateen sail inflates with the wind.

Prisca begins my tour at the ruins of the so-called Malindi mosque and cemetery, dating from around the fifteenth century, when the Kilwa dynasty that based itself on the island was already in decline. The earliest buildings date as early as the ninth century, and stone-age archaeology has been discovered, representing 4000 years of continuous habitation. All the buildings of the palace complex are made from coral stone: fossilised coral. On the pebble beaches it's easy to find small examples, chalky lumps patterned with the imprints of ancient creatures, but Prisca tells me the stones used to build the palace were collected by divers. For conservation work it takes almost two weeks to collect a metric ton of the stone.

There must be hundreds of tons on site, joined by lime mortar made from crushing the stone.

The largest building on the island is the Portuguese fort, built three storeys high, during a short period of Portuguese colonisation in the early 1500s, and large enough to be visible from the jetty on the mainland. Later the fort became the responsibility of Arab and Omani rulers. We squeeze through a door in a much larger reconstructed entrance gate, solid brass studs protruding from the wood to prevent attack. The collapse of the massive west facing wall means I get a view of the mainland from the central grassed courtyard. On the three remaining sides, the walls soar above me, the stairs too dangerous to climb. Around us conservators mix lime mortar. Prisca leads me to several religious buildings including the Great Mosque, the arches beautifully cut like wood from the coral stone. Some of its domes have collapsed; revealing inset European blue and white pottery at its apex, placed there for decoration.

We wade back to the dhow, the rising tide reaching the top of my knees and threatening to wreck my passport. Prisca asks what I thought of the road to Kilwa.

'It was good' I say.

'Really? I came on it last week, and it was not good.'

'I came from the south, from Lindi.'

'Ah. The road from Dar is not so good.'

The early morning coach to Dar es Salaam spends as much time off the road as it does on it, with diversions around slowly progressing road works. I am glad the rain has held off for the last couple of days, with great waves of dried mud to either side of the road, the imprints of barefoot locals looking for all the world like those of early hominoids found not far away.

The blue smoke that the 60 seat coach has been billowing from its exhaust for the entire journey stops at Ikiwiri – literally meaning 'the white man died of despair'. After two hours I am told that if the problem with the engine cannot be fixed by the four men covered head to foot in treacle-like oil alternative transport will be provided.

I miss the first minibus replacement which is rounded up, not being quick enough to push to the door as it slows to a halt. About ten minutes later another arrives, better kitted out than the coach. Learning from my earlier failure, I barge everyone out of the way and climb on second. It's another three hours, and 150 km, to Dar along decent tarmac. There is no real warning that we are arriving – no slums, build-up, landfill sites, or chaos – like I usually find with the approach to large African cities.

I arrive just in time for the Union Day public holiday, celebrating the unification of Tanganyika with Zanzibar. I am one of the few who see the large presidential convoy make its way through the empty streets, led by a V-shaped formation of police outriders. I join Ocean Road, leading past the Moorish architecture of State House, just visible through its gardens and decorative high walls. The sound of a brass band carries from the gardens to the groups of policemen lingering in the shade outside. They greet me, and we exchange pleasantries, in a way that hasn't happened with policemen at any point on the journey so far. Dar lives up to its name as the haven of peace.

I get the sense the city is a relaxed one, a multicultural city at ease with itself, although the public holiday means there are a greater proportion of hustlers about. So many have already approached to sell me free maps that I have taken the standard line of firmly saying 'I don't want anything' as soon as one of them comes towards me. Around the elegant arabesque city hall it leads one to say 'if you don't want to talk to people, why don't you go back to your own country?'

'I am, just the long way. You don't want to talk to me, you want to sell me shit and I've already had 19 people do that to me this morning, and it's only half past ten.'

'Why don't you go to Nigeria or Somalia, and get yourself blown up?'

Within the grounds of the national museum, a structure of thick white walls and ornate doorways, and opposite a large sacred fig planted by the Germans in the early 1900s, is a memorial to the victims of the bombing at the US embassy on 7th August 1998, proving I won't need to visit Somalia to be at risk. I find the laminated English information sheet face down in the grass a few paces away. An armless statue depicting the pain of the victims' families is surrounded by twisted, rusted metal, a destroyed motorbike, and a panel of beaten up toughened glass.

I leave Dar, the former Tanzanian capital, since it was shifted inland to Dodoma in 1974 – though no one seems to have noticed – for another. Bagamoyo was the first capital of German East Africa, though the coast five kilometres south, at Kaole, along a bumpy stone-strewn road that I traverse by *pikipiki* mototaxi, has Swahili ruins dating from the thirteenth century. I'm most interested in the old port, a short walk from the mosques, and tombs marked with elegantly carved standing stones. It's nothing more than a mangrove shallow, with no buildings or jetty, nothing more than a sign nailed to a tree stating *old port*. But it was here that the explorers Richard F Burton, John Hanning Speke and Henry Morton Stanley arrived on the African mainland from Zanzibar, and David Livingstone left, dead.

The nineteenth century customs house in the old port in Bagamoyo is still in use, despite its partial collapse. On the foreshore, fishermen bring their catches to the market behind India Street, a row of crumbling colonial houses and elegantly restored Arab merchants' buildings.

There are a number of traditionally dressed Maasai, no one paying any attention to their kilts and wraps of red or blue checked cloth, their short swagger sticks, or their footwear made from exhausted tyre tread. They seem to blend in perfectly, in a country where everyone seems to be busy making money. Some run internet cafés, some cut hair, others sell pens or newspapers, and still more commute to city centre office blocks, while a very few bother tourists at the Zanzibar ferry terminal.

The two hour channel crossing on the *Sea Express I* is smooth. The ferry is crowded with Zanzibari's returning home amid the light splash of sea spray on the windows of the enclosed deck. I am surprised by the need to fill out an arrivals form for the 'United Republic of Tanzania', having come from there, the Revolutionary Government of Zanzibar maintaining a semblance of independence, with its own presidency and council of ministers, after unification with Tanganyika.

From the port I head first to the edge of Stone Town, the 'capital' of Nguja, the main island in Zanzibar's archipelago. In doing so in around 100 metres I realise just how small the place is, and return to Stone Town's heart via the ornate stone carvings of the municipality building, high court and post office. A short length of tunnel leads me to the coast opposite the old fort, built by Omanis after the Portuguese expulsion of 1699, the colour of baked sand, its four round corner towers linked together by thick walls around a grassy quad filled with souvenir stands.

The fort lies next to the largest building on the island, built in 1883 as an Omani mansion for the second sultan, Barghash bin Said. Wide wooden staircases wind upwards through doorways decorated in an Indian style for the four storeys of the *beit al-ajaib*, or House of Wonders, while verandas wrap around the building to catch the ocean breeze. A clapboard-faced clock tower rises from the roof, facing the mainland, added after the palace survived the shortest war in history. Anyone who nipped out for lunch on 27th August 1896 would have missed it. It lasted roughly 40 minutes before the new sultan surrendered his power struggle with the British and sought asylum in German East Africa. The lighthouse that stood in front of the palace, and the sultan's harem to its immediate left, weren't so lucky.

Towards dusk the Forodhani Gardens that now occupies the area in front of the *beit al-ajaib* comes alive. The children's playground is open, but most children, the boys at least, are swimming, take running dives into the shallows from a short pier, attempting tricks as they do so. Hawkers set up tables to peddle fresh juice from sugarcane crushed using what look like mangles; and Zanzibari pizzas are prepared to order in between stalls selling Mars bars and mugs of spiced tea. When the last of the natural light fades, lanterns are lit, casting an eerie light over the gardens.

Waiting for the torrential rain to reach a mere heavy drizzle the following morning, I meet up with some of the other guests of the Bandari Lodge over breakfast in the central atrium of the Swahili-style building. Arabesque windows and thick wooden beams distract me from the conversation taking place between David, a Kenyan dhow owner shipping 50 tons of cargo between here and Kenya, his silent young son, and a British teacher, Sarah, taking a holiday at the end of a volunteer placement in Moshi on mainland Tanzania. When David makes his excuses, Sarah tells me she went to see his boat yesterday in Stone Town's port.

'The lady at the customs gate wouldn't let me in without keeping my passport – and I wasn't interested in that. It's always the women that cause problems, like they need to prove their authority. Anyway, I told David to leave it, and he took me instead to the market. The boy was very sweet all day, sharing an orange with me etc., so at the end of the day I offered to buy him the pet dove he was after. Then, having hidden from view so David wasn't charged tourist prices for the dove, he asks me for money to stay here at the lodge for another night – saying that otherwise they'd have to stay on the boat, and the boy could get malaria…I wanted to point out that didn't seem to matter before he'd met me…'

The soul of Zanzibar seems to struggle against the modern need for tourists; the call of the muezzin in this conservative Muslim island drowned out by the frothing of milk in cafés catering for western tastes in coffee. Yet very quickly I am out of the tourist zone of Stone Town and into local Stone Town, where the mundane life of selling soap rather than overpriced curios goes on.

From the narrow alleys I spot the spire of the Anglican cathedral just as it begins raining once more. It was built to replace the largest slave market in East Africa, the slaves brought for sale here from Dar es Salaam and Bagamoyo, awaiting journeys to Oman and the Middle East. A disc of cream marble set into red in front of the altar represents the location of the whipping post at the centre of the market. To one side of the altar hangs a small crucifix carved from the wood of the Mvula tree in Zambia under which David Livingstone died and his heart was buried. The rest of him made a journey of several months to Westminster Abbey after resting in the cathedral.

In the cathedral hostel, a former hospital for freed slaves, holding cells remain in the basement. Like those on the west coast of Africa – the *maison des esclaves* on Gorée Island and the barracoons of Badagri in Nigeria – they are small and cramped, with low ceilings, very little light, and no facilities of any kind.

At breakfast the next morning I mention my plan to reach the far north of the island at Nungwi to Sarah.

'It's all big resorts up there' she says. 'And when the tide comes in, the beaches around them are cut off. I tried to get through one of the resorts to get back, but was chased away by Maasai warriors, and had to walk all the way back round! I met a British woman living on the island on the *dalla-dalla* there. She told me "local women don't like women like us.

Prostitution of local men by middle-aged white women on holiday on the island is rife," but I'm not middle-aged' she says cheerfully. 'I'm 71. I'm done with all that!'

A few twists and turns take me through the warren of alleyways to the main road, beside the municipality building and the *dalla-dalla* stand. Instead of the minibuses of mainland Tanzania, they are small pickups, a row of benches lining the open frame of an awning so low I have my stomach touching my knees to reach a seat on the 116 to Nungwi. Sitting facing out, I realise how content I am watching the road already travelled roll by. About three kilometres out of Stone Town we pass the ruins of Mtoni Palace, built during the reign of the first sultan of Zanzibar, after he abandoned the deserts of Oman for the fantastically wet weather of Africa's east coast.

It takes about two hours to reach Nungwi, the earth roads in the town in useable condition thanks to the lack of vehicles. On foot, I follow the sandy loam of the high street through the deep puddles to the empty beaches and turtle aquarium, where animals caught up in fishing nets are rehabilitated in a natural seawater lagoon, before being released to take their chances with the local fishermen for a second time. I'm happy to let my guide speak of life cycles and release weights as I watch the various species ring the pool, his enthusiasm for his local patch of wildlife taking me by surprise. 'I will stop there' he says. 'I could talk to you all day about turtles, but maybe you have somewhere else you are going today.'

I follow the tall grey walls of a resort through the short, tough scrub growing up around it, getting no nearer to the coast beyond. My scruffy appearance – old running shoes, shorts, and shirt I've been wearing since South Africa – doesn't stop a receptionist stationed behind a panel of glass set into the wall inviting me in, pointing towards the lobby. It's large, modern, and punishingly clean. I'm met by another member of staff, dressed in a modernised Indian mogul style, who allows me beyond the outdoor pool to a pier, stretching from the rocks into the shallow blue ocean, scattered with expensive furniture. I can't see any guests anywhere, making the signs warning that the beaches flood at high tide redundant.

Facing forward the landscape unfolds for me like a film reel on rewind: the slow-moving carts drawn by bony oxen shifted to one side by the island's subsistence farmers, the bored police half-heartedly manning their road blocks, the Mtoni Palace ruins coming into view. The clouds eventually break up enough to be able to see the blue sky beyond, a reassuring sight for the ferry ride to the island of Pemba, Zanzibar's smaller northern brother.

The 9 am service to Mkoani on the southern tip of Pemba doesn't leave Zanzibar until 10, having only arrived into view at 9.22. The second class compartment is already full from its channel hop across from Dar when I fight my way aboard and out of the rain, but a friendly seller of dried dates pushes me into an empty seat among a group of colourfully veiled women and their small children.

The journey to Pemba is longer than that from the mainland, the waters deeper and rougher, with no land to protect the ferry from the full force of the Indian Ocean. Maybe halfway through the four hours of plunging over the waves the grandmother next to me vomits quietly into a sick bag, hiding her face with her shawl of red and orange.

There are no immigration forms to worry about on arriving, and the customs shed is as abandoned as the rest of the port, so from outside its gates I follow a road uphill to what I guess must be Mkoani. A cluster of shops face the road, squalid and rundown single-storey homes behind, a couple of mosques only discernible from the piles of sandals at their open door-ways. Away from the buildings, the land comprises small banana groves and paddy fields. Most of the traffic that passes me is *dalla-dallas*, donkeys and cattle.

I take one of the *dalla-dallas* to Chake Chake. It's the most cosmopolitan, and largest, of Pemba's three towns, located roughly midway along the 60 km length of the island. Under the low board roof I get speaking to the local imam, a kufi prayer cap mounted on the crown of his head.

'Pemba is nice' he says 'but money – no. The people are poor. You speak Swahili?'

'No, no I don't. I've only just arrived, and soon enough I'll be in Kenya.'

'You should learn. Everyone here will speak to you in Swahili. You can learn slowly, very slowly.'

'*pole pole*' I reply, knowing the Kiswahili. The imam laughs.

'It's 18 miles from Mkaoni to Chake' he goes on. 'The same again to Wete.'

It takes nearly two hours to reach Chake through the wall of dark green created by the banana plants. As we approach, the driver makes an impromptu decision to the join the inaugural Pemba rally, and the countryside passes in a blur of leaves as I struggle to keep myself and my backpack in roughly the same place. I say goodbye to the imam at the overflow of stalls from the market, mostly selling electronic accessories and schoolbags, and use the need for a change of transport to investigate the ironmongery workshops lining the wide avenues of this part of town.

The *dalla-dalla* to Wete, in the island's north, drives past a brickworks, then a pale grey ox freckled with ginger spots; brickworks, another freckled cow, the bureau de change by the tourist lodge. Instead of beginning the two hour journey the driver has been circling for more custom, picking up a single additional passenger. Rain showers pass over; moving with greater speed than the *dalla-dalla* manages.

Wete's main street extends for some distance, from the dirty Soviet-style apartment blocks dating from the early years of the revolutionary government, to the seafront at State House, an altogether more impressive structure. A side road, orange with the rain, leads roughly north, the channel to the mainland visible through paddy fields and small villages in the hills. The overcast sky gives the water an anger it wouldn't otherwise possess, and I start to worry about my journey back to the mainland. Friendlier than Chake, everyone I pass whispers *karibu* – welcome – or *habari?* – how are things? – in greeting.

Wete lives up to its name in the wet season. I wake having had dreams of swimming breast stroke, the heavy rain falling since before dawn. A very soggy Sharook comes in as I eat my breakfast, his gap-toothed smile even broader than usual. Owner of the lodge I'm staying in, elderly Sharook has quickly become something of a personal assistant to me. I feel more comfortable in his home than I do in some friends' houses.

'Doctor, you are well this morning? I have just come from the port. There will be a boat to Tanga in two days' time, on Sunday. It will leave at nine in the morning. Tomorrow, when they start selling tickets I will go and purchase one for you. The ferry hasn't run for weeks. You are lucky!' His smile widens even further, his pink tongue visible through missing incisors.

I wake at 5.15 to the sound of the muezzin's call, and say goodbye to Sharook, walking the two minutes to the concrete jetty where I gather with other passengers, including several Maasai. The Al-Mukhtaar Express turns out to be less of an ocean-going ferry and more the type of vessel I might take on a pleasure cruise down the Thames on a summer's afternoon. Its long, narrow structure and canopy reminds me of Canaletto's paintings of the Thames, with twin outboard motors attached to the stern.

The sea is smooth during the slow manoeuvring away from the jetty. The landscape is full of the contrasting colours of the archipelago's islands: the blues of the shallow and deep water, the white sand of beaches, the greys and browns of bare bedrock protruding through the frothy white breakers, the dark greens of the forests hanging over them, and the insipid blue of the pale sky. Some of the islands are no bigger than houses, with roofs of vegetation fighting for light.

When the islands disappear the ocean gets boring. The waves start to knock against the wooden hull, and the brightly painted red and yellow benches become hard. The life jackets knotted tightly to the awning, swing with the boat's movement; 20 for the 100 passengers.

In open water, without any objects with which to make comparison, and against the waves, it feels as if our speed should be measured in metres per hour rather than kilometres an hour. It's only at the pace of the ocean that I ever truly learn how great a distance I am travelling.

As sea conditions worsen I close my eyes and try to forget the creeping boredom. I manage a half-sleep, desperate to open my eyes and look for land, but not wanting to endure the disappointment of failing to seeing any. Eventually, after five hours I spot land, a dark green line on the horizon that I think at first I've imagined into existence. It takes another hour to reach the path through the shipping containers of Tanga's port into town. It has taken me a week of travel to cover a distance that would have taken no more than half a day overland, or half an hour by air.

Maybe it's the fact I no longer feel like a dejected refugee, maybe it's being able to stand on ground that doesn't rock to and fro, the easy access to beer, or the presence of the sun above, but Tanga strikes me as the perfect place to sleep off the rest of the day before heading through the boring scenery on the way to Kenyan border.

*

The immigration officer issuing me with a visa on the Kenyan side of the border at Lunga Lunga is smartly dressed and quietly spoken. He flicks through the pages of my passport, smiling at the sight of so many entry stamps. The *ANNULE ANNULE ANNULE* of my failed DRC entry stops him dead.

'Why was this annulled?'

'Because I wouldn't pay the bribe I was asked for' I answer. He looks surprised.

'Are you sure?'

'Yes. He asked me for $200 despite already having a visa.'

He continues with the paperwork silently. Completing my visa and taking the fee he says, 'how much did you give me?'

'$50' I reply.

'And is that a bribe?'

I rarely notice a change in the character of a country from its neighbour as immediately as crossing its border, but there are obvious differences on entering Kenya. The road cuts through flat expanses of farmed grassland containing the first herds of cattle I remember seeing. Their herds make Kenya's Maasai some of the richest men in Africa. Signage along the road is spelt out in English rather than the Kiswahili that dominates in Tanzania.

The signs at the Kilindini harbour-front at Likoni tell *matatu* – minibus – passengers to alight and board the roll-on roll-off ferries making the constant crossing to Mombasa on foot. The driver of my minibus tells me to stay on board as the other passengers alight, and as he drives over the metal ramps to the open vehicle deck of the *MV Kwale* I see other signs warning passengers to be aware of pickpockets.

Mombasa is a nightmare of confusion; the rapid sounds and movements of the city combining into an overall envelope of white noise that attacks not only my hearing but all my senses. Changing my Tanzanian Shillings for Kenyan ones I am confronted by more types of public transport than even I thought existed, and in huge numbers. *Matatus*, tuktuks, coaches, taxis, motorbikes and pedal bikes all fight for space with pedestrians and goods' carts. It's impossible to walk in a straight line for more than two paces, making my path to the old town slow going.

Though it's the oldest part of the city, and takes on the street plan of a plateful of spaghetti like the medinas of Morocco, tall concrete apartment blocks dominate. Together with the narrow twisting alleyways between them they conspire to prevent the sun ever warming the stones at street level. Balconies and washing lines hang over the alleys; some only as wide as my shoulder span; making them more claustrophobic. It's difficult to know whether they are through roads, and I often stumble between the open drains to someone's front door by accident. I am soon disorientated in a scary block of modern slums.

At the nearest opportunity, a road wide enough to be properly surfaced, I leave the damp clay and paving of the alleys. The houses get more picturesque: wooden upper floors and balconies built on top of whitewashed stone ground floors. I follow the road, past *keep off the grass* signs in a small garden, to Fort Jesus, at the entrance to Mombasa harbour. It began life as a Portuguese garrison, before its capture by the Omanis, and later use by British tax officials. It's one of the largest forts on the African coast, and it takes me more than an hour to wander through the various rooms, entranced by the Portuguese graffiti of caravels and sea monsters rescued during conservation work.

'You are like Vasco da Gama all those years ago; going by sea' says Joseph grinning, as he hears of my journey so far. We share the back row of the express *matatu* service to Malindi. 'It's incredible. And then back in England you'll write a book' he says matter-of-factly, as if it's the most normal thing in the world to do.

The urbanisation of land around Mombasa continues for several kilometres, the monkeys with bright blue testicles using the high perimeter walls of exclusive resorts as paths between the remaining fruit trees. As land use turns from buildings to farms, the neat geometric patterns of palm oil plantations line the road, running into scrub and finally the trees of the Arabuko-Sokoke forest. Its spindly trees look tired from constantly battling against the encroachment of houses and farmland. Forming the largest and least fragmented area of indigenous coastal forest in East Africa, it once ran from Mozambique to Mogadishu. It now covers 420 km^2, roughly the same area covered by Barbados, and smaller than the New Forest.

I leave the Malindi express outside of Watamu, keen to get a closer look at the forest, and the ruins of Gede hidden among its trees. No written record of the Swahili civilisation at Gede has been discovered, and the ruins themselves were only rediscovered in the 1920s, meaning not even the experts are able to say who lived here or how the place was ruled, making the palace complex, with its sunken courtyards and monumental gateways, something of a mystery. What's clear is that Gede was ruled well. The ruins cover a wide area, enclosed by outer walls now little more than knee high. By the outer wall I hear the crackling of fallen leaves and turn to see the ginger and black fur, and naked rodents' tails, of golden-rumped elephant shrews hopping in escape at my turning; this forest their only home.

Having left Mombasa I realise how dirty the place is, with my skin covered in fine black particles of soot. The driver of the motortaxi that takes me to Watamu tells me the white-washed thatched mansions we negotiate our way around are all owned by Italians. The wind smashes the waves against the rocks around its tiny bay. The sand is so white and so fine, crunching under foot, that I have to remind myself it isn't snow.

The *matatu* never really leaves populated land on the short hour's ride to Malindi's transport depot, followed by a five minute ride on the back of a mototaxi across what could well be a landfill site, to my requested destination of the cheapest hotel in town.

I spend a good part of the morning heading up and down the same stretch of road, not having any idea where behind the tourist resorts the coast might lie. Using well-honed African logic I eventually find a tourist information centre hidden in an upstairs room at the back of an ordinary office complex. It takes me almost as long to find a staircase up to it.

I tentatively ask the three staff members if they know about the cross, or *padrão*, positioned by da Gama 513 years ago.

'Cross?' The three staff members have a discussion in Kiswahili, finally turning to me to say 'Do you mean the pillar?'

I'm given directions to its present location on a rocky outcrop, moved from its original position at the house of the sultan of Malindi, and variously altered so it now resembles a fat white traffic cone topped with a Greek cross.

Malindi was the last stop on the African coast for Portuguese caravels before making their way across the ocean to the Malabar Coast of India. As such, one of the first structures to be built by the Portuguese was a chapel. Both da Gama and Francis Xavier worshipped in the square white-washed coral stone building, the only aperture an arrow slit in one wall. Two of Xavier's sailors lie buried, alongside a British baronet, in the small graveyard.

The Tana Guesthouse turns out to be a two minute walk from where Simba Coaches leave for Lamu Island. We pass scrub and small settlements and the bus rapidly becomes an inferno despite the early hour. The heat becomes intolerable whenever the vehicle is brought to a halt and the air stops funnelling through the clattering window panes. Baboons skip across the road to break the monotony of the rattling compacted earth road; a large male chasing away a smaller younger interloper at a speed that matches that of the coach.

It takes five hours to reach the end of the mainland at Mokowe, where the easiest way onto Lamu is by speedboat. It's a relief to have the wind ripping at my hair and clothes through the wide blue waters of a channel lined with mangrove forest, until the last moments when the low structures of Lamu town come into view. It's attractive from the water, with a careworn charm that Mombasa lacked, and despite the steady influx of tourists I am still welcomed kindly, particularly by the elders of the community. That deliveries to the shops in the narrow alleys are made by donkey only adds to its historic feel; with only one road wide enough for vehicles, and barely any cars. The usual morning sounds of Muslim Africa: the muezzin calls and cock crows are replaced by that of the muezzin and donkeys braying in heat.

Though there are few cars, there are lots of dhow captains. Some knock on my guesthouse door before I've had time to shoe the cockroaches from the bathroom. When the power cuts out for a few minutes the heat and humidity becomes unbearable. Shirtless I drip with sweat, seeking out what little breeze there is by the window of my second storey room, before escaping outside to the noise of the streets. I'm approached again by a dhow captain beside the biscuit-coloured walls of the fort in the town's main square, built by the sultan of Pate to uphold the rule of his unpopular governance during the 1800s.

'Hello friend! You see: Lamu is very small. So it would be a good idea to go on that dhow trip now.'

Having spent plenty of time on dhows already I'm more interested in absorbing the atmosphere of the island by

198

trekking around its ridiculously narrow passages lined with plain shop fronts and the decorated doorways of the cool whitewashed walls of Swahili traders' homes, like the one containing the island's museum. At four in the afternoon I am the first visitor of the day, the ticket clerk needing to alter the date of her validating stamp. The thick white stone walls reduce the temperature inside, as does clever architecture that catches breezes and sends them about the large open rooms devoid of alcoves that could store up the heat.

In whichever direction I turn the alleyways end by spitting me out onto the water's edge, where new buildings are being constructed as readily as dhows are being repaired by hand on the mudflats below. As I face north I watch a layer of tiny crabs, some red-and-blue and some brown, sweep across the rapidly drying mud in the glare of the sun like a miniature version of the mainland's wildebeest migration. The donkeys shifting through the piles of gently smoking rubbish that lie everywhere are joined by a huge swooping Marabou stork and a pair of black and white ibis. I face north towards Pate Island and Somalia beyond that, knowing I have no choice but to leave Africa's coast. Following it further north would be like choosing to tread water in battery acid.

I return to the mainland at Mokowe not by speedboat but by public ferry, a large engine-powered dhow that chugs inelegantly through the still waters of the channel. Though I've a ticket direct to the capital, Nairobi, the coach makes it only five minutes down the road before stopping, the driver turning off the engine, and the two armed soldiers riding on it wandering off, though it takes one of the two other passengers to inform me that the coach isn't going any further. It begins to rain, to pour; the weather so often mimicking my mood. The only thing stopping me from approaching the driver, who is enjoying himself in a nearby café, is the fact he gets soaked to the skin walking the few paces to it.

'Hey; what's going on?' I cry, the rain having eased enough for the driver to leave the café.

'The bus has a bad engine. It cannot go. Another vehicle is coming to take you to Mombasa.'

'But I'm going to Nairobi…'

'Okay.'

The vehicle that arrives half an hour later, its windscreen cloudy with condensation and wipers working steadily, is a standard family car. I'm sat on a cushion in the boot with the bags and one of the soldiers, his AK47 making it difficult to close the boot lid. We're driven for about an hour at breakneck speed through the puddles to the village of Moko-topeni, where at a rough shack – the Simba Coaches Booking Office – we wait for another coach that is said to be arriving imminently.

From my aisle seat I manage to catch sight of a small flock of flamingos in the manmade shallows just outside Malindi, which we reach at nightfall. We reach Mombasa at nine, and arrive into Nairobi just after the 5 am time of our scheduled arrival. Suddenly finding myself at an altitude of 1500 metres, I can't stop myself from shivering.

Seven kilometres from the railway station in Nairobi's central business district I can't think of anything better to do on a lazy Sunday afternoon than visit Nairobi National Park. Almost as soon as I am through the main gate my super-market bought picnic lunch – a muffin, malted milks, two tangerines, and a bag of crisps – is stolen by a large baboon that calmly saunters over to me and snatched the bag from my hands. The wardens, dressed like sergeant majors, with khaki uniforms, swagger sticks and black berets, apologise for the snatch, claiming it to be 'part of the safari experience'.

The real safari experience comes as I climb into a large open-backed four-wheel drive with several expatriate men and women who can't find anything else to do on a Sunday in Nairobi. The most vocal is an Australian called Andrew.

'Wait, you can pick up a visa on arrival at the airport in Addis' he says, used to business travel, when I tell him part of the reason I'm in Nairobi is to pick up a visa for Ethiopia.

'But I'm not going to fly, and I can't get a visa at the land border.'

'You are lucky, the lions are in the tree' interrupts our driver, bringing the vehicle to a stop just a few hundred metres from the park's entrance gate. 'All day long people have been asking where the lions are; you are the first to see them.' A lioness and six month old cubs of both sexes rest on a horizontal tree branch that comes very close to hanging directly over the track we're on.

We see black rhino, three or four in the distance. Impala meander with ostrich closer to us, directing us towards herds of zebra, startled looking Kop's Haartibeest, disgruntled buffalo, and giraffe tugging at the tough leaves of bushes spotted around the savannah, all within sight of Nairobi's skyscrapers and probably my only chance to see these iconic African animals by public transport.

I join one of the wardens, now in her civilian clothes, in catching a *citi hoppa* bus back to the centre of Nairobi, taking an indirect route past the university and the edge of the improvement works taking place in Soweto West, a portion of the Kibera slum, one of the continent's largest. A concerted effort is replacing the corrugated tin lean-tos with small brick bungalows that share basic amenities.

The warden leaves me at the railway station. While she heads for another transport connection, I join Moi Avenue at the August 7 Memorial Gardens. The park sits on the site of the US embassy, destroyed on the date in 1998, at an almost identical time as the embassy in Dar es Salaam was attacked. A plaque names the 218 victims. More than 4000 were injured, the site located on a major city artery. The museum in the grounds is moving and thought-provoking, consisting mostly of images, accounts and some personal effects.

201

Though the embassy remained structurally solid, the neighbouring bank building was completely destroyed, trapping people under rubble seven storeys high. A Kenyan man, whose wife worked as a tea lady in the collapsed building, was interviewed on the news that day.

'She is still alive in there and they're trying to retrieve her. So I am still on the site waiting to see her retrieval' he said, in front of heavy machinery lit by floodlights. She became one of the 206 Kenyan victims.

In spite of its reputation for terrorism and violent crime I feel safe in Nairobi, the city centre having a cosmopolitan air often missing from other large African cities. There are some grand buildings, pleasantly planted gardens, and the most secure building in East Africa: the Ethiopian embassy.

Having been searched thoroughly I wait for over an hour in the consular section of the embassy, only to be told I cannot be given a visa because I don't have a Kenyan re-entry pass.

'I am not coming back into Kenya, I am not re-entering Kenya' I reply. My response doesn't alter the attitude of the woman at the desk, but convinces her to send me to see the 'woman at the end of the corridor', who turns out to be the head of the consular section. Many people come to see her, perhaps for her exotic tattoos, for she is no use as a consular official. She has a Greek cross tattoo centred on her forehead, and consecutive rings of a crenelated wall pattern ringing her neck as much as I'd like to. I wait some time, bypassed by various people and phone calls to explain my position again.

'Where is your re-entry pass?' she asks.

'I don't have one. I am not re-entering Kenya.' I still don't know what a re-entry pass is, or whether I should have one. 'I simply want to apply for a tourist visa.'

'Without a re-entry pass I cannot give you one. You are finished.'

'Potentially, yes' I reply, leaving.

My last hope for reaching Ethiopia overland, and not having to revert to flying into Addis Ababa as suggested by Andrew during the national park drive, is to try the Kenya Immigration Office around the corner, and see how readily a re-entry pass is offered.

Everyone is very nice, if slightly baffled, and I make my way up the chain of command to the Assistant Director of Immigration Services. Under the nodding, spectacled stare of a kindly female face, I explain my story again.

'We only give re-entry passes to residents of Kenya' she explains.

'There is no way I can get one?'

'No. You fly to your home country and apply for a visa there.'

'The thing is…I am on a long overland trip…'

'That's okay.'

'It is?'

'Yes. You cannot do what you are not permitted to do. You fly to your home country and apply for a visa from there.'

I feel like a well-used carpet: largely ignored, worn out, and walked over by everybody who sees me. Someone else is already entering the room before I've fully risen from my chair. I look back to the Kenya's days of corruption with something close to mourning. It feels like I have no energy in me, no more fight left, and still a long way to go.

Buses to the border post with Ethiopia at Moyale leave from the slums around Eastleigh, pronounced 'Issly', an unstable Nairobi district of Somali refugees that's been attacked by militants on more than one occasion. I'm unsure whether taking a taxi, rather than the solidly built *matatus* that look more like prison transport vehicles than minibuses, makes it a more or less dangerous journey.

'You should have asked straight away for the depot; us taxi drivers, we know where everything is' a taxi driver tells me as I struggle to know what to do.

'No you don't. My taxi driver last night didn't know where the hotel was. *I* had to direct *him*.'

'Maybe he was new to taxis.'

'He said he had been driving taxis for years. Anyway, I need to go to Eastleigh.'

'Where?'

'Issly.'

'No problem.'

The roads in Eastleigh are either potholed, thick with mud, under standing water, or all three. The roughest of rough-hewn market stalls litter the pavements in front of ware-houses. Stepping out of the taxi my feet sink up to the ankles into the liquefied ooze.

The coach, a sort of bus stuck over the axles of a flatbed truck, rolls slowly up the busy quagmire of Tenth Street, and it's not for 10 minutes that we break free of the ridiculous roads of Eastleigh. I move to the empty back row of the bus to stretch out my legs, and avoid my neighbour firing nail clippings at me, and using my left leg as a luggage rack. I am soon joined by a missionary, returning home to Addis Ababa, after three years living in London's Notting Hill.

'In the UK, the trains – you can go anywhere on the train' he says admiringly. 'Transport is a big problem in Africa.'

As if to prove it, a tyre change takes an hour and a half, and means we're still driving through the thick traffic of the foggy built-up areas of greater Nairobi when night falls several hours into the journey.

We pass Isiolo, close to the equator and Mount Kenya in the early hours, just before the tarmac road gives out. The driver's speed doesn't; intent on making up lost time. The journey from then on, for more than 12 hours, is like being repeatedly kicked and punched; I'm thrown through the air like a rag doll.

As a crisp sunrise cuts through the gloom I can see we're now in true savannah; Hemingway's green hills of Africa.

With the rains, the grasses are bright and tall. In the near distance a continuous landscape of low but steeply-sided wooded hills break up the ocean of grass until Marsabit, from where there is dry grassland as far as I can see. Women collect water in large orange jerry cans from a pool, also used by their donkeys and a herd of cattle, while camels nibble at the toughening vegetation that comes with the drier conditions of the north.

Passenger comfort is an optional extra no one has paid for. The road goes from unbelievably bad to intolerably bad, with loose rocks scattered over its surface, while a Chinese road building team works about half a kilometre to the right of the road. I am thrown about the back row more and more violently; the driver's only concern to get to Moyale as quickly as possible.

Eventually, exhausted, we reach the collection of buildings that comprise Kenyan Moyale. The first thing I do – before even my backpack is offloaded from the roof, is to book a ticket on a bus back to Nairobi for the next day. Air travel has made it too easy for officials to falsely impose borders to international airports. It means Ethiopia is a closed country for overland travellers heading north like me.

Moyale is nowhere near as grim as I had been led to believe, surrounded by rolling green hills and the rust-coloured roofs of corrugated metal on the Ethiopian side of the border. But it is not the sort of place I would choose to travel for 24 hours to reach, to spend 15 unnecessary hours before returning back the way I've come, like I do early the next morning.

The initial part of the journey is smoother than yesterday even though the vehicle is near identical. The driver doesn't see the need to break the land speed record. At the first stop, with a cup of stewed tea as refreshment, I get talking to a woman of about my age, one of the only Kenyans on the bus, the majority of passengers Ethiopians heading south.

'You work here?' she begins, pointing back to Moyale.

'No. I'm a tourist. I'm just travelling around the country.'

'It's good that you travel by road. It's the only way to really travel and see the country. Otherwise you will miss these beautiful hills.' It's as if she's channelling my reasons for attempting my journey and my thoughts of having to fly to the Ethiopian capital.

'I agree. I wanted to go to Addis but I couldn't get a visa.'

'It's very difficult to get an Ethiopia-Nairobi, Nairobi-Ethiopia visa,' she says. 'Many people try.'

'Now I will have to fly from Nairobi and collect one at the airport in Addis. No one will talk to me on the plane like they will here, and it's expensive.' It's ten times more expensive, two hours instead of 56. 'It's a long way.'

'It's a very long way' she says. 'I came here to see if I wanted a job, but I'll have to think twice now. What country are you from?'

'I'm from England.'

'You're British. So this is your country too.'

I smile. 'No, no. This is your country.'

'You helped us map this country. It's yours too. Welcome. It's your first time?'

'No. I visited Kenya ten years ago.'

'Ten years ago you must have been very young.'

'I was 17. Kenya's a lot better now, though perhaps the roads still need a bit of work.'

With the reduction in speed I am able to enjoy the grasses, low bushes and wooded hills, while herds of camel are led through the country. The fluffy, broken cloud allows the sun to do its best on the orange clay and shadows.

The tenth passport check comes about two minutes after the ninth, around midnight at Isiolo. As the bus returns to the tar I shut my eyes for a moment, opening them to find we're pulling into a wetter, muddier Tenth Street in Eastleigh than the one I left.

'You're going to?' prompts the immigration officer who calls me to the free Business Class/Diplomats desk he's working at in Jomo Kenyatta International Airport.

'Addis Ababa.'

'I'm from Moyale. It's on the way to Addis – if you go overland' he adds as an afterthought.

'Yes.' I say. 'I know. If only I could.'

Ethiopia, Somaliland & Djibouti

Patrick and I were coming now, fresh from the straggling, non-descript, tin and tarmac squalor of Addis Ababa

Evelyn Waugh, *Waugh in Abyssinia*

In contrast to the road on the Kenyan side of Moyale, the road from the border into Ethiopia is perfect tar, running for hundreds of ordinary kilometres to Hawassa. Even so, it's clear that although Ethiopia is culture rich, it's cash poor. Away from the few small towns south of Hawassa there are almost no signs of the twentieth century, let alone the twenty-first; and the contrast between towns and country is one of the most marked I have seen. A cluster of tiny round adobe homes might stand by the roadside, their thatched roofs recently replaced with the latest harvest of bright yellow grass, twisted to a point to keep the rain out. Skinny horses pull carts in the place of vans; better fed donkeys wander freely. Oxen drag wooden ploughs through the rich fertile soil while groups wrapped in hand stitched shawls use shallow pits on the field's edge as their main source of water. Vehicles are so infrequent along this stretch of road it's used as a footpath, old women and teenagers alike oblivious to the rapid approach of a minibus on their backs.

The sheet of cloud blanketing Hawassa prevents the light doing anything more than leaving the slightest sheen on the flat surface of the lake at one end of town, and on the three golden domes of the otherwise concrete Saint Gabriel Ethiopian Orthodox church at the other, like the layer of butter left on a warm knife. It has the feeling of a holiday town. Everyone here – the increasingly rich Ethiopian middle-class who can't quite stretch to trips to Kenya or Europe – relaxing and spending money on fine foods on the lakeside, before taking to the waters on short boat rides through the grassy reed beds in its shallows.

Marabou storks scavenge for scraps, rising to half my height and displaying twice my bravado, eager to snatch mishandled club sandwiches – capable of feeding a family for several days – over the fish scraps of the chop bars that thread the shore.

The lake's proximity to Addis Ababa means many of the families are from the capital, and most transport heads the 300 km north. Tall columnar cacti, and rounded sections of ancient prickly pears, act as fences to the fields strung along the road. As the altitude climbs from 1500 to 2300 metres above sea level I start to see roadside advertisements for Abyssinian wine. At Ziway, the minibus stops to allow some of the passengers to buy punnets of fresh strawberries, and for two grubby local children selling individual sticks of chewing gum to watch me with wide eyes.

Instead of continuing to the capital I leave the minibus at Bishoftu an hour away. Like Hawassa it's a resort town, with five small crater lakes dotted around the town. Without its lakes, Bishoftu is about as uninteresting as can be: a four-lane highway, one of the country's main arteries, cutting savagely through small town Ethiopia.

I spend most of the weekend asleep; so tired by the time I arrive that I subtract 14 from 15 and come out with an answer of three. With little else on offer I have to resort to a high end hotel to satisfy my appetite. It gives me the feeling that I am avoiding Africa rather than interacting with it. I worry what the smartly dressed waiters think of me.

The Monday morning queue of commuters heading for Addis at the dusty waste ground depot is politer than that for a

London bus. It has a quicker turn around too, with 40 people transported in five minutes.

We never really leave the urban sprawl spilling over from Addis Ababa, though the towns along the road are prefaced with signs of different names. It takes another half an hour to move through the traffic on the edge of the capital, where one of the first things I see is a man leading his goats across the overhead walkways above the road.

Ethiopia's capital is a hard place to like, but as a centre of world diplomacy – home to the African Union – the perfect place to collect more visas. In the grounds of the Somaliland Liaison Office, representing the autonomous north of Somalia, I am led to what was once a garage. An old sofa runs along the length of one wall, opposite a woman sitting at a desk in front of a computer. The plug hangs from the desk, its cord too short for the closest socket. Next to it sits a fax-ready phone, its wires entirely absent. The visa application process is short, completed by hand.

The piazza area of the city seems to be the beating heart of Ethiopian Addis, and contains its oldest buildings, dating back to the turn of the twentieth century. Meaning *new flower* in Amharic, the Ethiopian empire's new capital was founded in 1886, on a site chosen by Taytu Betul, wife of the emperor Menelik II. Two storey wooden structures with wide verandas and oddly shaped garrets overlook the filth and rotting fruit of chaotic streets jam-packed with minibuses and market stalls. The smell of rubbish and effluent on one road is so bad it is difficult to breathe. An apprentice working on the minibuses has large daubs of cotton wool stuffed up his nose to block out the stench.

An equestrian statue of Menelik II stands at the centre of the roundabout at Kiddist Giyorgis cathedral, built to celebrate victory over attempted Italian occupation 10 years after Addis Ababa's founding. The cathedral is in peaceful tree-covered surroundings despite the swirling traffic of the roundabout. Steady streams of worshippers approach the round building, bowing or kneeling before it and kissing its walls. So steady is the stream of people it would make a parish priest in England blush.

Menelik's mausoleum sits in grounds separated from the palace he built, now used as the prime minister's official residence. It's separated by a high wall manned by bored soldiers weighed down with automatic weapons. The thick grey stone walls of the mausoleum are distinctly un-Ethiopian, closer in style to an Italian basilica, the dynasty eager to demonstrate its sophistication in comparison to European powers.

The naïve paintings on the interior side of its central dome depict scenes from Menelik's rule, including his victory over Italy. Immediately below, hidden by thick curtains, is the mausoleum's holy of holies. Not content with its own alphabet and calendar, being seven years behind the rest of the world, Ethiopia celebrates its own form of Christianity, combining the old and new testaments with equal importance. Only accessible by the chief priest, the holy of holies contains a copy of the Ark of the Covenant: the box in which Moses and the Israelites carried the Ten Commandments through the desert. The Ethiopian national epic, the *Kebra Negast*, says the original ark was brought to the court of the Queen of Sheba in Ethiopia from King Solomon's court in Jerusalem by their son, Menelik. It's widely believed to rest in a monastery in Axum in the far north of the country. By contrast, Menelik II lies in the mausoleum basement in a large sarcophagus beside his family.

Haile Selassie, Ethiopia's last emperor, lies with his family in even larger sarcophagi in Kiddist Selassie – Holy Trinity – cathedral a short walk from the 1940s art deco parliament building. He was laid to rest here 25 years after his death, having spent the previous quarter century at the bottom of a toilet, following orders from the communist Derg regime that ruled after his overthrow.

Even so, monuments to Ethiopia's imperial past are everywhere. A statue at Arat Kilo celebrates Haile Selassie's triumphant return, five years to the day after he was forced to flee a more successful attempt at Italian annexation than the first against Menelik. A barley-twist concrete staircase, the upper steps supported with a metal prop, rises to nowhere from the grounds of the ethnological museum. Meant to mark Italy's conquest of the country, a lion, the symbol of the emperor, was added after the return to home rule.

Crossing one of the overhead walkways at Arat Kilo, I am quickly enveloped by the homeless children that bed down there, begging for change while another tries to unzip my day bag under the cover of a tray loaded with a couple of packs of travel issues and a stick of chewing gum. My long stay in Addis awaiting visas means I come to know every street corner that should be avoided.

Evelyn Waugh reached Dire Dawa from Addis by train, using the French-built line running to Djibouti. Though the area around the rail terminus in Addis – still called *la gare* – is busy, the line itself is not, undergoing a refit and forcing me onto an early morning coach.

A taxi takes me from my lodge in piazza to Meskel Square while the city is still asleep, early enough for the streets to be empty of vehicles. At this altitude the nights are cold, and I pass an entire street of homeless men wearing woollen hats and wrapped completely in blankets as they sleep. On Mahatma Ghandi Street donkeys struggle up the steep incline, heavily laden with loosely stacked hay. I pass three children on Theodorus Square playing football where the road meets the roundabout. A herd of cows are led to slaughter across the empty 14 lanes of Meskel Square, the herders using the light from mobile phone screens to see by.

I sleep for most of the journey, waking at intervals to find a few small non-descript towns and the endless monotonous hilly landscape of brown and green tones that I have already come to associate with Ethiopia.

Slap bang in the middle of the neatly planned European quarter of Dire Dawa, the station is ignored, transport limited to the minibuses and tuktuks that linger outside. At a much lower altitude than Addis Ababa, and edging the eastern desert that stretches into Somalia and Djibouti, the midday heat reflects off the grey road surface and ensures I soon retreat to the dark rooms of the Continental Hotel, where Evelyn Waugh stayed while reporting on the Italian invasion of the 1930s. It hasn't aged particularly well.

It was the rail line that made Dire Dawa, and without it functioning the town feels like it has lost its purpose. There's little to do but plan my next day's journey over a meal of *tibs* and *injera*. The damp spongy texture and slightly disconcerting sourness that comes from the *teff* flour, with which the flatbread is made, is a disappointment after all I have read. While Waugh described *injera* as 'wet grey bread', and Paul Theroux as a 'soggy doormat', I find it to be innocuous bordering on dull. It's food, plate, and cutlery in one, used to pick up the *tibs*: strips of beef cooked with onion and chilli that were a few moments before still part of the leg hanging in the butchery a few paces away. Hungry vultures soar overhead. Full vultures are too heavy with meat to fly very far, and after my meal I know exactly how they feel.

I share a tuktuk to the new bus station where a clean empty minibus fills quickly for the journey to Harar, climbing back into the cool air of the hills from Dire Dawa's valley location.

The first European to visit the city, birthplace of Haile Selassie, was Richard F Burton. I enter Harar through Buba Gate, one of the five gates that allow access into the streets of the walled city. The tourist friendly Italianate cobbles take me steeply downhill at first, giving a perfect view of the tiny stone and mud buildings that work their way back up hill to Feres Megela Square, the roads wide enough for a tuktuk to drive through, the narrow streets of the medieval city easy to navigate despite the promise of more than 600 alleyways.

In a bar on the square I arrange to meet a guide later in the day to take me to see the hyena men. I had imagined these men would feed the hyenas in the countryside far beyond the city's walls, but my guide stops me at a clearing with houses all around, shafts of light passing through ill-fitting doors and windows. Small children totter about, and a steady stream of foot traffic passes within metres of the animals, with neither man nor hyena showing any concern. My guide says the animals never attack humans.

The men call through the darkness to the spotted hyenas, although in reality routine means the animals are already lurking about in the shadows of the rubbish tip, flittering shadows that I catch with the corner of an eye. I am taken closer, the men patting and cuddling the hyenas like pet dogs. Most closely related to the mongoose, the animals are large, ugly creatures, with dark spots staining a rough grey mane. Thin strips of meat are brought out from a white butcher's bucket. The animals rise onto rear legs, snatching the meat from between the fingers of the men without needing to chew. Within a couple of minutes it's all over for another night.

I was expecting some sort of mysticism, a history, or allure to the nightly process. There is none. It's a bunch of teenagers in fake Adidas 3-stripes tops getting cheap thrills playing with some odd looking dogs, for which I have the pleasure of paying. It feels distinctly amateurish, even if it does have a historic precedence. Since the 1960s men from the town have fed the thin strips of meat to hyenas, a tradition that is thought to have begun during a famine in the late 1800s when feeding the animals ensured they didn't attack valuable livestock.

Throughout the night the hyenas' calls seem very close to my bed, always answered by the barks of panicked dogs. Then, in the early morning, I am woken by long chants drifting in and out of my consciousness from the nearby church Sunday services.

The road from Harar to Jijiga passes through the Valley of Marvels; the valley's hills made up of vertical shafts of rock that pierce the green of low shrubs like megalithic stones. They rest on and against each other in different states of freedom, some free rocks sitting on top of others waiting to be pushed off. Camels chew on the scrub around the rocks when the dirty white and multi-coloured layers of cloth of nomadic yurt-style dwellings come into view.

'Where are you from, by the way?' asks the man behind me, breaking my reverie of the landscape, as if we had been talking for hours.

'England.'

'England? It's unusual to see a foreigner on a public bus. There are many Europeans at the university, but they are not allowed to travel on the buses when volunteering in Jijiga. It's meant to be too dangerous. In fact this is my first time too! You use public transport often?' I smile, and nod.

Beyond Jijiga and a change of transport, from the smart new minibus to a dirty and broken school bus, the scenery flattens out, becoming brown and lifeless, save for low trees dotting the landscape.

The temperature seems to jump several degrees as soon as I cross the bridge over the dry Wajaale River from Ethiopia into Somaliland. A self-proclaimed independent state autonomous from Somalia in every sense but by the letter of international law; with a democratic government, functioning police and working tax system since its unilateral declaration of independence in 1991; Somaliland has enjoyed 20 years of peace entirely unrecognised by any international body other than Coca-Cola, which has a bottling plant on the outskirts of the *de facto* capital Hargeisa. Somalia, in contrast, is perhaps the only place where 'it is not safe for you to go there' is an accurate statement of fact.

I squash into the back of a bush taxi for the two hour ride to Hargeisa, my refusal to sit over the handbrake leading to a full on argument with the driver.

'I'm not going to sit on the hard fucking handbrake' I eventually shout in exasperation, thumping the plastic hidden under a thin cushion. I'm given the seat in the back instead. The man I swap with soon complains of his discomfort.

Hargeisa marks the easternmost point of my journey, and in celebration I stay at the Oriental Hotel, the oldest in the city, built in 1953, when Hargeisa was the capital of British Somaliland. The link with Britain remains strong, and many of Hargeisa's citizens speak good English. In its sweaty, covered courtyard restaurant I meet a teenager whose parents have just moved the family from Wimbledon. I find it difficult to walk for any length of time without stumbling into a conversation with someone about my home country or the crushing heat.

The streets are alive with colour, contrasting the dull browns of Ethiopia that I experienced waiting for visas in Addis Ababa; three days for Djibouti, another four for Sudan, two weeks waiting for permission to enter Egypt as a tourist. I walk beyond the individual glass cabinets of the goldsmiths' stalls, towards the money changers, sitting behind stacks of Somaliland Shillings as thick as house bricks and held together with rubber bands. With the largest denomination note valued at roughly 10 pence, most transactions over the cost of a mug of tea take place in US dollars, and the money changers do a steady trade in swapping their grimy bricks of Shillings into $8 of hard currency.

I doubt there are enough Somaliland Shillings in the central bank to pay for the camels for sale at the livestock market among the sheep and goats, a prime specimen going for $1000. I begin to feel a specimen myself, a crowd of 20 or so good natured but clingy children following me around the market tirelessly, ignoring the calls of the elders to leave me alone.

To escape, I return across the plastic-ridden Maroodi Jeex wadi, the wind casting sand into my eyes, to Independence Avenue. A red cast iron pillar box made in Stirlingshire stands on the street, torn open like a ripped toilet roll tube. A concrete model of a camouflaged tank stands as a memorial to the bombing of Hargeisa by the Mogadishu government prior to independence in 1991, along with the real fuselage of a MiG fighter jet that crashed while attacking the city. Further along the same street is the town hall, opened in celebration of the coronation of the Queen of England and British Somaliland on 2nd June 1953. It's one of the only buildings constructed of stone rather than concrete.

The hotel arranges for me to join a Toyota land cruiser heading for Zeila, on the border with Djibouti. I don't recall the four-wheel drive making use of the 50 km of tar that are supposed to exist as far as Borama, a town twinned with Henley-on-Thames. There's a surprising amount of space on the rear row of seats of the vehicle, and a surprising amount of wildlife visible in the dry scrubby landscape from its windows. The engine noise stops short of scaring away the dikdik and long-eared hares, or the eye-catching birds that dart between bushes on either side of earlier tyre tracks.

I can't find anywhere to wedge my head in order to sleep, eventually allowing it to drop limply, the driver continuing through the marginally cooler temperatures of the night after a shared meal on the roadside in a small hamlet.

With the break of day I begin to fear the Gulf of Aden, the strip of water connecting the ocean with the Red Sea, might not actually exist. The vehicle reaches Zeila's cluster of rugged buildings without having encountered it. I catch my first glimpse of it from behind the Somaliland Immigration Office. From the stifling heat of Zeila – where it feels like the air is on fire, and I perspire heavily even in the coastal breeze – the sea is grey, flat, uninteresting, and as uninviting as the army officers that man Djibouti's side of the border.

From the dusty road heading roughly north to Djibouti City, the country's capital, it looks as though someone has decided to use the desert as one giant landfill site. Camels graze on trees dripping in plastic bag blossom.

It takes 20 minutes and two different locations to get the price of a seat in a bush taxi down to an extortionate level that I can just about afford; everyone else on the vehicle paying four times less for the cramped sticky ride from the capital to Obock.

Lying across the Gulf of Tadjoura from Djibouti City, Obock is the end of public transport routes in Djibouti, and the end of my return to the very edge of the continent. North of Obock, the overland borders with Eritrea are closed, the only way into and out of the country by air. Suspicious of everyone, Eritrea has been ranked below North Korea for press freedom.

When the driver finally puts his foot to the accelerator the vehicle climbs through low mountains shunted together much like a brown image of Mars. Volcanic rocks rest uneasily on a ground with little vegetation. The road meets the curve of the gulf, following it for most of the six hour, 200 km ride.

By dusk I am on foot, racing the light to reach a hotel on a low hill overlooking the gulf, a hotel that looks increasingly deserted as I approach its perimeter. As I begin to fear, it's closed, if not deserted. One of the young security guards agrees to take me to another hotel; so far away I consider we may have crossed into Eritrea. I have to prevent myself from breaking down. The only thing stopping me from giving up on the day completely is the knowledge there is no backup

219

team to get me out. I'm entirely dependent on my own rapidly deteriorating mental and physical strength.

Come breakfast, after a night in the only other accommodation in town, it's 40°C in the shade. Even so, I follow the line of the Gulf of Tadjoura further north on foot, through Obock's shanty housing, prevented from continuing by tidal sandbanks. Rubbish strewn, poor, and only distinguishable from the rest of Obock by the rusting corrugated tin that makes up the shed-like structures, rather than concrete blocks. Walking as slowly as I can, I pour with perspiration. It drips down my nose in rhythmic pulses nearly as common as my heartbeat and the waves. I sit on the raised concrete seating of a basketball court catching the dry coastal breeze. I decide there is nothing I want more than to leave Djibouti as quickly as possible.

Mohammed, the son of the guesthouse owner, finds me. He talks on and off for some time, and I'm desperate for him to leave me alone, responding with single word answers. I gather from him that Djibouti's tourist industry shuts down for the hot and humid summer months from June to August that we're in. From my walk around town I can't imagine Obock changing much even in the cooler months. It not only has a frontier atmosphere – being the last town of any substance before Eritrea – but an end to civilisation feeling too. Trying to cheer me up, Mohammed keeps badgering me with questions, and finding out I'm heading to Sudan and Egypt he smiles wistfully.

'Ah, you're going on a long trip, like, like Phileas Fogg. You know? *Around the World in 80 Days*? I watched it on TV.'

I don't sleep for more than an hour at a time, conscious of the passing night and my continued wakefulness. Up and out of the guesthouse by half six, I have little to do but wait on a bench by the local store for the arrival of transport, at 9 am.

A few kilometres outside of Obock the land cruiser spills off the road and under a tree on the beach, to wait the arrival of the *quat*-carrying boat that will ferry me to the capital, though the tree's shade does nothing to lower the temperature. It's like nothing I've experienced before, and I can only compare it to being in a country-sized oven.

The speedboat from Djibouti City arrives, and the freshly picked mildly narcotic stems of *quat* unloaded, but I'm not yet allowed to replace them, the captain waiting for soldiers, who have requested a ride across the gulf, to arrive from their base in the mountains. I cannot complain, though I do, repeatedly, and the only thing I can think to hate more than Djibouti is the thought of ever having to come back.

The captain starts the outboard motor with a cord, smacking one of the soldiers in the mouth with the effort. A single flying fish sails across the surface of the water, startled by the engine, gliding tens of metres with such assurance I first mistake it for a low flying seabird. We're escorted into the capital's *port de pesce* by an inflatable manned by armed French sailors protecting one of their navy's destroyers, the sailors eyeing us suspiciously, as a cargo ship carrying live sheep leaves the port for Yemen. I move on quickly, desperate to leave, feeling completely exhausted. I get talking to a couple of Ethiopians heading home.

'Djibouti is crazy!' one says. 'All they do is chew great wads of *quat*. It's crazy.'

My return to Ethiopia confirms my opinion of it as a country tinted in shades of brown: a country of caramel, coffee, mocha, and chocolate tones; with a refreshingly cool climate. It might be dull in comparison to other destinations on the continent, but right now, that's exactly what I need.

It's almost a shock to see the bright leaf green of the short young crop of *teff* by the roadside, towards Dessie, after so many kilometres of russet ground. The fresh greens expand across the countryside, as far as woods of darker coloured pines that make way for low bushes and large fleshy cacti as I near the monastery of Hayk Stephanos. Running through the panel of greens are vast rivers of grey morasses, the rains having missed Ethiopia, the rainy days of Zanzibar a memory. Locals wash clothes in the shallow streams that remain, spreading them out to dry over nearby boulders.

Lengths of cloth matching the green, yellow and red of Ethiopia's national flag hang limply all around the main streets of Dessie in preparation for the Downfall of the Derg national holiday. It's thanks to the overthrow of the communist regime that Dessie is undergoing a building boom: Ethiopians returning from the diaspora with money in their pockets, and a taste for western housing. All the same, for the moment the tin shacks are still able to remind me of the Freetown peninsula.

It's a long journey from Dessie to Lalibela, climbing further through the mountainous highlands. It becomes something of a pilgrims' way, with monks sitting by the roadside in their heavy orthodox vestments, raising weighty metal crosses in the air as vehicles pass, hoping for enough donations to sustain them. I leave the bus to climb a short distance to a church, being hewn from the butter-yellow rocks of a crumbling cliff face, the path leading to it nothing more than the spoil that has been removed during its excavation. Large pillars of natural rock the circumference of Angolan baobabs are left to support the cavern's ceiling and a second storey which I clamber up to by a series of incidental footholds in the rock. Windows punched through the rock let the natural light filter into the bare and unfinished interior. For Ethiopia, this is nothing new, and Lalibela has 11 monolithic churches dating back to the twelfth century, cut from considerably harder stone than the soft chalk of the cliff.

From ground level I am underwhelmed, but as I take the steps down to the foot of the first of Lalibela's churches I begin to understand the sheer size of the structures and the complexity involved in hollowing out the solid rock. As I gaze across the site I'm watched by a monk, draped in a white cloak and wearing a green flat-topped hat, pissing behind a rock. Each of the churches has its monks, and its defined floor plan based around the hidden holy of holies. With bare feet it's possible to examine the intricate wall carvings while listening to the symbolism of each axe cut.

The symbolism is easiest to understand in Bete Giyorgis – the church of Saint George – its Greek cross design sinking deep into the pink stone below ground level. Legend has it that an order for the church was put in by Saint George himself, upset at not having been dedicated one of the earlier churches by King Lalibela, the town's legendary ruler. Guides laughingly show me the hoof prints of George's horse on the banks of the trench leading down to its entrance.

My coach winds up and around a further row of hills at close to walking pace, to stop the vehicle rolling on the tight regular turns of the road to Gondar. The castle compound there contains six castles belonging to the emperors; the town having taken its turn as the Ethiopian capital, like Lalibela. Built from 1632 onwards, for about 100 years, the castles have a distinctly European architectural style, planned and built with information obtained from Portuguese explorers to this corner of Africa in search of the Christian kingdom of Prester John. The dream of European kings was to unite against Islam and take back the Holy Land with his help.

My dreams are interrupted at 4.45 am by a distinctly English voice in the corridor outside my room returning from the toilet saying 'well, that was…horrid. Let's go.'

The accommodation's saving graces are its price – a mere handful of Somaliland Shillings – and its distance five minutes from minibuses to Metema. They are so easy to come by drivers are snatching, dragging, and manhandling potential passengers to their vehicles over the competition's, delaying the time in which any of them can depart.

From the passenger seat I'm able to see the sign just outside of Gondar giving the distance to Addis as 727 km. My minibus continues roughly west through yet more hills and mountains on a detour to Lake Tana. The source of the Blue Nile, the lake is home to several monasteries. White pelicans glide inches from the water's surface, while the water tumbles through to a hydroelectric dam that has reduced its noisy flow over the falls to a small portion of its former span. It is the sort of landscape I shouldn't be able to get tired of, but I have. The hazy green rises as far as the eye can see, broken infrequently by shear escarpments or jutting fingers of rock.

Sudan

Khartoum is as safe as Kensington Gardens

Major-General Charles Gordon

The image of Sudan as an unfriendly dust bowl are confounded by the existence of a plush and spacious new minibus waiting after immigration procedures – a visit to three separate unmarked buildings, spread across a compound, that includes a conversation with a guy who never takes his eyes from the wrestling on television. The minibus takes me as far as Gedaref, and the rail line to Port Sudan on the country's Red Sea coast, along a road no different from Ethiopia's flat ribbons of grey tarmac. The land levels out to meet it almost straight away, the earth remaining fertile all the while. It means I lose the cool of the hills, and the temperature takes a near instant leap, like going from a chilly spring day in England to a holiday on the surface of the sun. Simply sitting on the still minibus induces a sweat; and I am surrounded by a constantly moving swarm of flies, making me feel incredibly dirty, until we depart and pick up speed.

Gedaref looks to have come to an end as I reach my destination on the side of a busy street, only for more simple buildings to spring up; the sun bleaching the jalabiya robes of passing men a purity of white that forces my eyes involuntary squints. Years of isolationism means that many of the people I encounter only speak Arabic, but they are as keen to communicate as I am, and saying *Inglizi Inglizi* repeatedly brings smiles to their faces rather than the grimaces I had feared from the country's international reputation.

*

Immigration procedures at the border are only the start of the paperwork involved in travelling in Sudan. So while I have no reason to continue inland to Khartoum, the Sudanese authorities have a reason for me to visit the capital: alien nationals must register within three days of entering Sudanese territory, and complete sundry other forms including permits for travel, and photography, which makes me suspect it might be easier to claim asylum instead.

My hopes for a speedy entrance into Khartoum are dashed by a leave-when-full coach that remains rooted to the spot beside the defunct rail line in Gedaref for two hours. The woman in the neighbouring seat, elegantly dressed in red and gold sari and lots of clinking gold jewellery, offers me salted seeds that taste like popcorn. She shows no concern that I am both male and non-Muslim. Long musical extravaganzas – a warbling lead singer backed by a small Middle Eastern orchestra, watched on by an enthused audience – play on a flickering television screen mounted above the driver.

The road to Khartoum cuts through earth the colour of burnt sand, no longer fertile. On either side a lifeless series of twiggy bushes range in colour from brown to bleached coral via rust reds before disappearing entirely. The slow manoeuvring around the twists and turns of Ethiopia's road network is exchanged for long straight stretches. The single carriageway in either direction forces a continuous series of drifts into the opposite lane to overtake slower moving trucks laden down with everything the inhabitants of the capital might need.

What was supposed to be a four hour ride lasts longer than a working day, and I don't leave the coach on Khartoum's outskirts until early evening. With rush hour commuters swirling about me I realise how lost I could now be. Wishing I knew more than the most rudimentary Arabic I initially struggle to find anyone with enough English to help me

226

identify the correct minibus to UN Square, and the Al-Nakhil Hotel on Al-Sharif Al-Hindi Street.

The tiniest of rises, a solid lump of clay on a shortcut the driver knows, fatally stalls the engine of the minibus I end up on. The apprentice ensures I am led through the empty spaces between buildings to a depot and another minibus. Somewhere along the lines the instructions that have been handed from one passer-by to another to get me to UN Square for Al-Sharif Al-Hindi Street break down more terminally than the engine of the first minibus, and we pass Al-Sharif Al-Hindi Street without stopping. I see its name on a rare English language road sign on the opposite side of the road. The vehicle continues across the aging arched iron construction of Blue Nile Bridge before I am dropped off by the fluttering blue European Union flag of the Spanish Embassy.

'UN there,' says the apprentice waving me towards the embassy.

'What the - ?' I manage, climbing out, but the minibus is already swaying on its suspension an unreachable distance away.

Tired, confused, hungry, and drenched in perspiration even with the orange sun halfway down the sky, I approach the anti-blast barriers of the embassy forecourt and the armed security guards beyond. Their supervisor, a man with a kindly face and good English, tries as hard as I am to understand why I'm at the embassy he's guarding. Never mind getting to the Alien Registration Office before it closes at three; it becomes a race to find a room before the sun sets.

'I am trying to get to Al-Sharif Al-Hindi Street' I say again, exhausted from having to raise and lower by backpack, my speech rapid with worry.

'Al-Sharif Al-Hindi? What embassy do you want?' the supervisor asks.

'I don't want an embassy. Please, I want Al-Sharif Al-Hindi Street, for a hotel. I'm trying to get to the Al-Nikhil Hotel. I am lost. All I know is that I am in Khartoum.'

'You're in Bahri' says the supervisor: Khartoum North. 'Can I ask you a question?'

'Of course.' From the seriousness in which he asks this I'm expecting him to ask me out to dinner or invite me to a sister's wedding reception.

'Have you got money? Then you could take a taxi.'

He beckons a taxi from the passing traffic, handing a folded banknote of Sudanese pounds over to the driver, making sure he knows it's Al-Sharif Al-Hindi Street I'm after and not another embassy. If every day is as hard as this one, I am sunk, and my short, intense attraction to the country won't be able to recover.

I wake with the note I left myself beside the bed: 'To do – everything I was meant to do yesterday'. The Alien Registration Office lies miles outside the city centre, but the process involved in registering is quick if costly. In 40 minutes – less time than it takes me to reach the office – I have dispensed with money totalling $50, more than a dollar a minute and a serious drain on my cash supplies. There are no international ATMs, no credit card facilities outside of paying for rooms in five star hotels, and no working money transfer services. Yet another page of my full to bursting jumbo-sized passport is used up too.

I am then free to visit the Ministry of Humanitarian Affairs for a permit to travel outside of Khartoum. Despite the need for all foreigners to get a permit, no one in the relevant office of the ministry speaks English. A passing worker from another office acts as my fixer, leading me around the building and translating for me.

'Who registered for you?' she asks looking at my passport.

'I did.'

'You did? You went to the office alone and did it?' She seems surprised.

'Yes. This morning.'

'Who was your sponsor?'

How should I put phrase it to make it sound more official than it was? 'Some man at the Alien Registration Office. I didn't know I needed one until this morning.'

'You have the letter.'

'No, it's at the Alien Registration Office.'

'You have a copy?'

'No. I didn't know I needed one.'

'You have to have a sponsor, a guarantor to get a travel permit. See' she says pointing at the 'name of guarantor' section of the form, photocopied so many times it's warped and faded.

'Look,' I say. 'You give me two weeks to transit your country and then make it as difficult as possible for me to transit it in two weeks.'

'Where are you going?'

'Wadi Halfa. Then Egypt.'

'Come with me.' She leads me to an upstairs office, interrupting the work of a man shifting sheets of paper from one pile to another. They discuss my situation for a couple of minutes in Arabic, before turning to me.

'You are taking the train or bus?'

'I didn't think the train was running.'

'The bus is better.'

'Bus then.'

'You don't need a permit to go to Wadi Halfa.' My passport is returned and we leave the room.

'So can I stop off on the way?' I ask, coming down the flight of stairs. 'I'd like to see the pyramids at Meroe, Atbara perhaps, the World Heritage Site at Karima, maybe the ruins at Nuri if I have time, then Dongola. Ideally I'd like to visit Port Sudan and Suakin on the Red Sea coast too.'

'No. No stopping. Straight to Wadi Halfa.' It's almost as if the authorities don't want me here.

The truth is they probably don't. An independent traveller is just a pain. They insist on *seeing* things and interacting with people. No one in authority seems to think I might like to *visit* the country I am transiting through. My visa for transit rather than tourism, officially my only reason for being in Sudan is to reach Egypt. I am not a tourist. While the international community is suspicious and critical of the Sudanese government (former home of bin Laden, purveyor of genocide and crimes against humanity) the Sudanese government sees no reason not to be suspicious of the international community in return. It feels less like I am travelling than fulfilling a series of bureaucratic requirements, leap-frogging from inland capital to inland capital: Nairobi to Addis Ababa, Addis to Khartoum, then Khartoum to Egypt. All I can do is content myself with being beside some water, the Sudanese capital the point at which the White and Blue Niles unite.

The final piece of paperwork I need is a photography permit, though it's not so much permission to photograph as a warning to leave my camera firmly in my day bag at all times. I am not to image 'bridges, train stations, broadcasting and public utilities' nor 'slum areas, beggars and other defaming subjects' as if the existence of poverty might defame a state that routinely spends significantly more of its annual budget on war with its southern neighbour than it does on either health or education. The middle-class Sudanese I meet, always frightfully polite and immaculately turned out in contrast to my own rotting clothes, reply 'this is Sudan' with a shrug of their shoulders.

With nearly a week until the next ferry from Wadi Halfa to Egypt, each day in Khartoum stretches as languidly as the Blue Nile between Tuti Island and the national museum. Seeing it from the shade of trees, planted for exactly this reason perhaps 100 years ago, it can hardly be called a river at all. Despite the force with which the water of Lake Tana tumbled over the rocks at Blue Nile Falls, they move so sluggishly here I can barely see its direction of flow against the reeds growing in the silt.

The national museum opposite houses a superb collection of Nubian artefacts in its main hall. I shuffle quietly through the almost unbearable heat inside – ranks of air conditioning units silent on the walls, the staff sat motionless in front of large fans – so as not to interrupt the filming taking place. All the wonderful artefacts of everyday life do is emphasis that I will not be able to visit any of the sites they come from.

A large map painted on the wall near the entrance has been altered to include the new international border that came about with the independence of South Sudan. It also shows the disputed Hala'ib Triangle in Egypt's south-eastern corner as part of Sudan rather than Egyptian territory. The dispute dates back to the administration of the area during the period of the Anglo-Egyptian condominium over Sudan. Its continuance is the reason the Wadi Halfa ferry is the only legal border crossing from Sudan into Egypt, and why I cannot yet return to the coast.

The following day is cooler, hot but bearable thanks to a wind that has brought with it tons of sand, colouring the sky the same shade of brown as the Blue Nile. My eyes are sore by lunchtime, and photographing anything becomes impossible with or without regime authorisation. I feel like I spend the morning in a sandpit. When the wind drops at evening it dumps the sand over the city, clearing the skies, and providing an excellent livelihood for the car washers around UN Square.

I take lingering steps towards the ethnographical museum on the corner of the approach road to Blue Nile Bridge. My route along Atbara Street is blocked by military trucks and a throng of police, armed and wearing combat fatigues in the same blue camouflage as their transport. They watch a rooftop occupied by a dozen or so students of the university, protesting at increasing food prices, as a dog looks at a bone.

At the other end of Atbara Street, having taken a circuitous route around the protests, my eyes begin to water. There is very suddenly a peppery tingling in my nose.

'Is that – teargas?' I ask myself as a loud crack makes me duck involuntarily. It's followed by a metallic thud 100 metres in front of me in the middle of what I realise is an empty road. A blue-grey grenade bellows out a thick cloud of smoke. I turn and head back the way I have come, though I can't stop the gas affecting me, possibly the only person to be teargassed trying to enter a museum. There are lots more sirens and more falling grenades as I try and find a route back to UN Square that avoids the growing cordon; the museum closed.

Making it back to my room at the Al-Nikhil Hotel I discover someone has been inside my backpack. The wire lock that keeps the cloth inner closed has let someone squeeze a hand inside, though has stopped them pulling out any of my kit, now all askew inside. Either Kensington Gardens have taken a turn for the worse since I left London, or General Gordon's comments were no truer now than they were when he wrote them to the British garrison in Khartoum before dying with them when the besieged city fell to the Mahdi, Muhammad Ahmad, in 1885.

The British response to his death was an unusual one: they started building the single track rail line that links Khartoum to Wadi Halfa. Trains aren't going any further than Atbara, perhaps one third of the distance, but the main station in Bahri remains vital for transport to the Egyptian border. It is not the colonial structure I was expecting. Instead, it's a large Soviet-style hall, with acres of plastic seating, and no soul. The only activity is at the window of the Nile River Valley Transport Corporation, the organisation behind the Wadi

Halfa ferry, and the office of a coach company that gets people there at the next window. I join the queue behind a man buying tickets for most of Upper Egypt.

While in Bahri I follow the long, straight roads to Omdurman over Sambat Bridge, where I get a good view of the silt-laden reddish-brown Blue Nile converging with the clearer, lighter shades of the White Nile. I make my way past the tomb of the Mahdi, with its shiny piqued domes, and head south with a new friend.

'Hello! Hello friend! Give me some money. Look at my hand; look at my hand! Give me money. £7, £10, anything.'

'You've got a touch of vitiligo; it's harmless; look at Michael Jackson. Trust me – I'm a doctor. Now go away please.'

'Why do you tell me to go away, my friend?'

'Because all you want is money. I've been here long enough to know that.'

'I don't want money – '

'You just asked me for money.'

'I don't want money. I love your country. I go your country. Where your country? France? Germany? ...Spain? My friend, why you no speak no more? My friend. My friend? My friend!'

Alone, I join the bright orange metalwork of the White Nile Bridge back to Khartoum, my 12 km tour of the three cities about the convergence of the two Niles near complete as the military trucks roam the streets, their occupants looking vicious. I don't fancy being mistaken for an undercover journalist reporting on how the Arab Spring is inspiring protest in Sudan, but I can't shake the vehicles, everywhere I turn they seem to appear. But despite the constant presence of the authorities, the need to register and the limit on travel and photography, I haven't been stopped and had my identification checked once. I have been free to go anywhere I like – so long as it's in Khartoum.

233

The Republican Palace museum had previously been the orange sandstone of Khartoum's Anglican cathedral. Inside, the religious stained glass and plaques immortalising those who died keeping Sudan an Anglo-Egyptian condominium remain. If the poster displays around the museum walls are true, it was tough work, with almost constant revolt. Though General Gordon's body was never found, the rotting remains of his upright piano – the first to reach Sudan – takes pride of place among the diplomatic gifts given to Sudan's heads of state since.

I am asked eight times in 10 minutes to change money on my way from the museum. I have, in truth, very close to none, and it has been worrying me for days. Ready to leave the capital finally, I have $20 that needs to see me through the journey until I have access to a bank in Egypt. I am not sure how long the coach journey to Wadi Halfa should last, but it takes half an hour to leave the city behind and enter desert, broken up by twiggy plants and isolated breeze block buildings. The terrain becomes so flat and featureless it's no longer photographable until the road returns for a short distance to a considerably wider Nile, a thin strip of date palms fringing the sand and rubble beyond.

Only a few of the buildings in Wadi Halfa rise above one storey, and the search for a bed is simple: keep walking, preferably faster than everyone else on the succession of arriving coaches, until you reach a lodge that doesn't turn you away at the door with the shake of a head. Once installed in the El-Shaab Hotel, a rough construction lined with bed frames, which could be a walk-in chicken coup on days the ferry isn't running, there's not a lot to do other than gaze at the beautiful outcrops of rock that count as hills from the toilet and showers and wait for tomorrow to come. The only thing that differs between the two is that the showers have an extra hole in the concrete floor.

As the owner hunts down some special – for which read 'almost clean' – bedding for me, he starts to talk about Islam, a subject I have been considering more than usual since struggling through the Qur'an all week in Khartoum.

'For 35 years I was Muslim without thinking about what it meant' he says. 'Then I start to think about what it means. Jews, they follow the teaching of Moses, he is in the Qur'an. Christians follow Jesus – we call him Isa – he is in the Qur'an; and Muslims believe that the prophet Mohammed was brought the word of God by Gabriel and wrote it down. When Michael Armstrong' – he means Neil – 'went to the moon he heard a noise he did not recognise. Then, visiting Egypt he heard the same noise and rushed into the street asking "what's this? What's this sound?" And the locals told him it's the call to prayer. He says "wow, this is the sound I hear on the moon!" and he moves to Lebanon and becomes a Muslim!' Though it's true Armstrong moved to Lebanon, it was Lebanon, Ohio, and, for what it's worth, remained a Christian. Perhaps my friend knows this because he goes on: 'America system is not good. British is good. It has Islam system. Morocco, Mauritania, Senegal; they are Muslim but not Islam system'. I don't understand what he means. 'You should read the Qur'an' he says, 'to understand Islam better.'

'I am. Here,' I say showing him my copy, which he takes and flicks through slowly from back to front as if it were written in Arabic. 'This is not good' he says. 'Evil will come down on you if you don't understand it.'

'It's pretty easy to understand' I reply. He leaves my bedframe and I don't see him again.

At 5.30 in the evening it's still over 40°C. Having walked about 200 metres of the main street, eaten a meal of fatty meat and bread, and my first cup of *shai* – tea – in about a week, I have exhausted all New Wadi Halfa has to offer. Old Wadi Halfa lies somewhere under the swollen banks of the Nile in Lake Nasser, like most of ancient Nubia's settlements.

I climb beyond the piles of human faeces to the top of one of the outcrops of rock by the hotel, for views of the glimmering bright blue waters of the lake in one direction, and the town in the other. Already dazzled by the sun Wadi Halfa looks only part finished, with crumbling walls around empty yards.

Before I can leave the town for the lakeside port I must complete exit procedures, an hour and 10 minutes of my life so baffling I wish I *had* claimed asylum. There are a row of counters, some used, some not; some with larger crowds than others. I hand my passport to various harassed-looking officials, crowded by a harassed-looking populous, and wait for it to be returned before being pointed to the next official. In a corner a nurse gives yellow fever inoculations to those who need them while people push past into an office beyond. It is the only country I recall where I have to pay to enter, pay to stay, and pay to leave.

Procedures then continue in the warehouse ferry terminal building, the walls of which are lined with UNESCO information boards for all the sites I haven't been allowed to visit. I am given ticket number 114, though as it's written in Arabic I don't realise this for some time. I discover that when my number is called out over the loudspeaker system – in Arabic – it's my turn with another official. It's first come first served, meaning I have 113 people boarding the boat in front of me, and several hundred after.

While waiting for any noise that sounds like the Arabic for 114 I meet Ahmed, his friend Ahmed and other friend Ahmed. He has the beard and dress that would make a tabloid paper mark him out as a fundamentalist, though underneath I can see an attractive face. A teacher of Arabic and English, he asks me to search out the true, peace-loving Islam, and tell people back home, underestimating the ability of ordinary people to look beyond sensationalist headlines and seek understanding for themselves.

As the conversation develops he asks me to repeat an Arabic phrase phonetically word by word after him: '*lee illaah illallah Mohammed rasuul Allah.*'

Even with my limited Arabic I can guess its meaning: there is no god but Allah and Mohammed is his prophet. Ahmed is ecstatic that I have repeated it, smiling widely and tugging me to his breast. I fear perhaps I have accidently converted.

'When we get to Aswan we will get you some water, some long clothes' – he looks to my shorts – 'and we will brainwash you' he says.

'Sorry?'

'You will come and pray with us in Aswan, where you can get some long clothes and have water to ritually wash?'

'I, er…'

I'm given a sticker to say customs haven't bothered to check my backpack, before a bus takes us a couple of kilometres to the jetty where the *Sinai* is waiting. It's a much smaller ferry then I imagined, metal doors in its side open to the stream of passengers. The various pieces of paper I clutch in one hand – enough to keep an intern busy for a couple of weeks – are thrown to the deck, the crews' feet covered in their confetti. An interminable delay of some hours, as the crew fiddle with technical things, has me concerned we might not leave at all, and I long to be somewhere cold that speaks English – like England. Much longer and Ahmed would have me circumcised before I could say 'there is no god but Allah and Mohammed is his prophet' again.

The ropes are finally brought aboard and Wadi Halfa is soon a memory. As I watch the sand-coloured hills go by in the near distance on either side of the *Sinai* – Lake Nasser only five kilometres wide but stretching 510 km north, a third of it in Sudanese territory – it suddenly feels like the journey's final push, crossing the Tropic of Cancer into the temperate north, and I become emotional.

It feels like I speak to the entire ship as I watch the views from various decks and vantage points, until I can take no more and seek space on one of the lower deck's wooden benches to sleep out the night on board, squeezing myself into a space the length of a child. I would love to say I am sorry to see the back of Sudan, but I am not; my initial attraction vanquished quickly.

Egypt

There was nothing so much we desired as to be at some
distance from Cairo on our voyage

James Bruce,
*Travels to discover the source of the Nile, in the years
1768, 1769, 1770, 1771, 1772, and 1773*

Passengers jostle to remove their huge bags and reach dry
land, hot after the regular breezes of the ferry, before anyone
else. I join the snaking line of heavily laden passengers from
the *Sinai*'s concrete wharf up a steep slipway and into an
arrivals hall, where the customs officers shoo me through the
exit without checking my backpack, immigration having
taken place overnight, away from the noise of the lower deck
in the restaurant reserved for first class passengers. Though it
is routinely described as the Wadi Halfa – Aswan ferry we
stop short of Egypt's southernmost city, before the walls of
the dam synonymous with the city. Instead, I find a rank of
taxis and *servee* minibuses, ferrying passengers from the
bustling train station adjacent to the arrivals hall.

We drive across the Aswan High Dam, on the four-lane
highway it supports, the wide shimmering blue of Lake
Nasser on our left hand side and the lower, narrower flow of
the Nile to the right. The construction of the dam in the 1960s
used 17 times more stone than the largest of Giza's pyramids.
The creation of the lake behind its kilometre thick base – the
largest manmade lake in the world at the time – resulted in an
international mission to save 22 monuments from Egypt's
Nubian and medieval pasts. The Temple of Isis was cut into

blocks and moved 500 metres from Philae Island, so that it stands confidently on the edge of the lake at Aswan, rather than a couple of hundred metres beneath it.

Maybe I fall in love too easily, for, like my first day in Sudan, I am instantly attracted to Aswan. It has the corniches, cafés and greenery of a well-designed Mediterranean city, and the smoothest pavement I've seen since Cape Town. It feels modern and cosmopolitan after the dust and heat of Sudan, though it's equally hot. Campaign posters from the recent presidential election runoff abound, like the shops. Men walk around in trousers and shirts rather than jalabiya. Women are noticeable in the streets. The children in the poorer districts I stumble into are welcoming and interested.

I follow the Nile corniche south towards the Nubian Museum. Huge floating hotels, less than a tenth full in the low season of Egypt's scorching summer, line the river's banks. I have Aswan much to myself, and the thought that these boats could be full at the same time is a scary one. Islands connected by the wind caught in the lateen sails of feluccas act as stepping stones to West Aswan. The largest, Elephantine Island, is split between its five star resort, the Nubian village, and the ancient ruins at its southern end.

Instead of putting me in awe of the greatness of ancient Nubia, the Nubian Museum makes me melancholic for all that has been lost beneath Lake Nasser: stone-age sites, Kushite and Nubian kingdoms, Christian churches and tombs, ancient mosques, and the homes of 40,000 Nubians that were forcibly relocated. The only other museum visitors are a tour group that includes an argumentative Yorkshireman, and a Romanian woman, midway through disagreeing with one another.

'My father, before he died – god rest his soul – was the happiest man I knew. He never worried about money. He had a job for 40 years that he cycled to everyday. He only left the country once in 1942 when he was subscripted to fight in the

Second World War; we didn't even own the house, it was rented all his life. He died at 60-something the most contented man I've ever known.'

'When I was young, my father, he didn't own a bicycle and didn't have a job. He survived eating the fruit from the trees in his garden' the Romanian replies.

I was keen to follow the lead of James Bruce and avoid Cairo – a Nile rather than a coastal city – at all costs. However the few blank half pages I have remaining in my passport aren't enough to get me home, so I need to apply for a new passport via the British Embassy in Cairo, and delay my return to the coast by a few more days.

The 7 am express train I wake for especially either isn't running or doesn't exist. I am told to get the 10 am train, which arrives a little late at 12.15, after a luxury tourist train travelling overnight from Cairo disgorges its passenger list of American and Japanese tourists. Another Ahmed, in a fake Queens of the Stone Age T-shirt, and with a rotting front incisor, keeps me company on and off, hopefully pointing to any arriving rolling stock only to shake his head in disappointment almost immediately.

When the train does leave, Aswan disappears rapidly, its last remnants a level crossing where a camel and its owner wait patiently next to a Peugeot for the train to move on. The Nile appears on my left with a thin belt of vivid green, that sometimes the line cuts in two. It then acts as the border between the fertile belt of farms and the desert hills on the right of the line.

At 10 pm, I find, as I am shaken from sleep and turfed out of first one seat and then another, that Arab hospitality doesn't extend as far as Egyptian trains. Buying my ticket from the inspector on board rather than the station booking system, I have no seat reservation, and therefore no seat. The train is completely full – every seat in standard class taken. I spend the next five and a half hours in the vestibule at the end of the carriage, standing in the fuggy atmosphere beside smokers that come in and out from the carriages. I reach the stage of falling asleep on my feet; waking to catch myself as my knees buckle, before advancing to a spot on the floor, among the cigarette butts and other rubbish, on a sheet of newspaper given to me by a man in a similar position; forced to move every time the thick metal doors are hauled open at the next station.

When the doors are hauled open at Cairo's Ramses Station just before dawn, I sleep on a platform bench until the flies become bothersome in the early morning light, landing regularly on the back of my hands. Leaving the gaudy new station concourse for the busy elevated highways and pedestrian bridges outside, I make my way to downtown Cairo by taxi, ignoring the offers for trips to the pyramids in Giza, a Cairo suburb.

A year and a half after the overthrow of Mubarak's government by popular revolution, on the day Mohamed Morsi takes the oath of office as the short-lived first democratically elected leader in Egypt's history, the protest camp remains in Tahrir – meaning Liberation – Square; its brightly decorated tents and stalls forcing traffic into a bottleneck. The paving slabs that covered the pavements around the entrance of the monolithic government building on the square have been ripped up and used as missiles, leaving only the sandy base below. As I look for a gap in the traffic that would allow me to cross the road's multiple lanes a Cairene jokes 'it's best to close your eyes and pray to Allah'. There are 234 accidents in Cairo each day, with one death and 25 injuries every 13 hours. But then Cairo is the largest city in Africa. Twenty million people live here; a quarter of Egypt's population. Most of them are on my train back to Aswan.

After an hour or so of standing in the vestibule I manage to bag a seat on a bin turned on its side, where I'm woken every

242

time I manage to drift off for a further ticket inspection or the offer of a cup of tea. There I remain fairly comfortable until the early morning, somewhere around Qena, where enough passengers leave the train for me to find a seat. As possibly the only foreigner on board I dabble with celebrity, talking to a number of people including David, an archaeology student heading on holiday with his mates. He's attractive, fashionable, and apologetic, when he hears I'm heading to Edfu to visit the ancient Egyptian Temple of Horus.

'Because I study in Alexandria, I research the Greco-Roman period. There are no pharaonic sites in Alexandria.' He turns his attention to more recent pharaohs, excitedly explaining the revolution that overthrew Mubarak as if I couldn't have heard about it.

Edfu's Temple of Horus is one of the best preserved in Egypt. Visiting is much more hands on than I had imagined, and I am free to wander as the only visitor, with the two pigeons, kitten, and the bat fluttering about the dark chambers lit only by small ancient skylights. A monumental gateway leads into two anti-chambers of tall columns, carved to represent different types of tree, the leaves of the capitals differing from each other amid the bright colours of surviving paintwork. The anti-chambers lead towards a sort of holy of holies surrounded by a series of small rooms, the walls of which are carved with figures a metre high surrounded by hieroglyphs.

Ignoring the tired horses of Edfu's *caleche* owners I take a *servee* minibus to the east bank of the Nile for transport to Marsa Alam 228 km due east, on Egypt's Red Sea coast. We cross the Nile's fertile belt on cracking tarmac before entering the Eastern Desert, where hills of stratified yellow rock rise out of the bare surroundings. There is not a single town until I reach Marsa Alam, a mining town that doesn't appear to have been finished yet. Buildings of multiple storeys lie in various states of construction: bare foundations next to concrete shells facing onto buildings that are just waiting for a paint crew to arrive. The Cyrillic language computer print outs across town suggest a Russian beach resort, yet even in its centre every second building is in need of completion. Tarmac comes to an end at road junctions, replaced by gravel. There is little traffic in any case, and fewer people, as I take in my first view of the Red Sea, the azure blue shallows topped with the unnatural white of luxury yachts. After the crowds of Cairo, where friends are easy to come by, it's a lonely day. I'm more than ready for the slow five minute walk to the transport stand, from where I get a shared taxi to Al-Quseir 120 km north.

We pass oases of manicured green tidiness in an otherwise desolate landscape: resorts belonging to international hotel chains dotting the coast all the way to Al-Quseir; a town much larger, and much more of a town than I imagined from my map and experiences of Marsa Alam. There's a basic beach front – some juice stalls on the sand – a short distance from the historic port dating back to Roman times. It became an integral port for both the international spice trade and Muslims making their way across the Red Sea to Mecca for the hajj pilgrimage. By the sixteenth century, under the protection of an Ottoman fort, 30,000 pilgrims were making the week-long journey annually. Those who didn't make it are immortalised in the shrines built around the town.

As it turns to evening I join the Egyptian families eating thawed out frozen fish on the front. The flat, pale ethereal blue sea meets a bank of lilac cloud on the horizon before melting into a sky that replicates the colour of the sea below. It almost feels like I am circumnavigating again, rather than jumping between obstacles further inland brought about by some hex in Kenya. I find it hard to believe I have been travelling for 10 months; my life a series of individual journeys that start and end with the beginning and close of each day.

The only public transport available for my next journey is running to Hurghada 140 km closer to home. It replicates all that I have experienced on my short time travelling along the Red Sea coast: mountains like film trickery looking inland from the smooth black tarmac, while a series of well-cared for all-inclusive resorts try to keep everyone else out on the coastal side. The water must get deep quickly, turning black while the shallows sparkle under a debilitating summer sun.

Hurghada is no different, with a long line of resorts hugging the coast from 15 km south of town. While Britons seek the sun across the water in Sharm el-Sheikh, Eastern Europeans come to the resorts outside of Hurghada.

'Fifteen years ago there was nothing here. 'urghada was just a small town' says my driver, handing me a can of Coke, as the endless row of resorts roll past the window. 'Big problems. Forty years ago the population of Egypt was 40 million people; now – 80 million; too many people.' Instead of one of the overpriced resorts fighting for sunlight and beach access, he takes me to a friendly place in the centre of Hurghada that he describes as an Egyptian hotel.

Behind a low-rise the sea lies at a distance, so I follow the road in the aim of meeting it through a part of town that's not yet been built up. Fires flare from piles of plastic rubbish dumped on waste ground containing abandoned watch towers I presume are left over from the time when Israel took control of the Sinai Peninsula opposite Hurghada after victory in the 1967 Six Day War. The road leads on to Sheraton Street, a long stretch of corniche lacking public beach access. All the seafront is private, with high-rise resort buildings looking for a sight of the sea in competition with one another. They stretch beyond my endurance, and I turn back. Bars along the street offer free shots of vodka with every meal. Having my first beer after legally dry Sudan, I notice the number of local men that walk intimately with women whose skins are so pale it can only mean they are holiday makers.

Awaiting the arrival of my new passport at the British embassy in Cairo I have no reason to hurry north, but I find it impossible to do anything else. The handful of towns that break up the 450 km between Hurghada and Suez – the largest Ras Gharib and Zafarana – are mining towns with their own transport and, I'm told, a complete absence of accommodation. I end up about three feet away from where I start the morning, angry at the taxi drivers taking advantage of my lack of knowledge to drive me unnecessarily from one depot to another for transport that doesn't exist.

'Where do you want to go?' asks another by the hotel.

'I'm trying to go north: Ras Gharib, Zafarana, Suez, it doesn't matter, but you people are just trying to rip me off because you know I don't have a fucking clue what's going on, and I'm fucking fed up with it.'

'You people?'

'No. I didn't mean...I meant the other taxi drivers' I say calming down.

The road north is hot and monotonous as far as the industrial hinterland around Zafarana, causing me to doze beside the Air Force officer sharing the passenger seat. Isolated resorts appear, along with building work to extend existing hotels and create new ones, stretching for miles along the coast. Offshore, beyond beaches made up of desert rubble, cargo vessels line up ahead of their transit through the Suez Canal.

The Suez conurbation that includes Port Tarfik develops out of a series of oil refineries and heavy industry. It has a pleasant, if tatty, promenade along the waters of the port; the canal-side full of warehouses and yards I cannot get past. Rows of tall tower blocks follow the curve of the promenade; their ground floor walls covered in quickly sprayed graffiti, *ACAB: all cops are bastards* the most prominent; coming alive with tea and popcorn sellers only late into the night.

At the opposite end of the 190 km canal, at Port Said, I get my first view of the Mediterranean Sea since leaving Tangier, from the veranda of my room at the Hôtel de la Poste. When it has cooled down to pleasant – my African thermometer starting at cool and moving through pleasant to bearable, hot, very hot, and blast furnace, ending with Wadi Halfa and Djibouti – I stroll the few paces that take me to the canal side. As with Port Tarfik it doesn't look promising, with metal fencing more likely seen at the presidential palace in Cairo. In fact, marble-faced steps lead to a promenade above independent shops, giving a good view of the canal and the elegant architecture of a mosque and its twin minarets in Port Faud opposite. As a ship sails by, it's like being approached by a tower block. I follow the canal to its entrance beside orange sand beaches on the Mediterranean. I can go north in Africa no longer, and turn west towards Tangier. At 6.30 families are still playing on the beach, the women fully clothed, their plumpness reminding me of the image of Russian dolls I first had in the souq in Agadir 10 months ago. Despite that, the feeling – brought about by the city's open and cosmopolitan atmosphere – that I have returned to Europe is strong. When Egypt's leader Khedive Ismail inaugurated the canal in 1869 he said: 'Egypt is henceforth part of Europe, not Africa', and he appears to have been right.

Turning to the west I take a bus to Damietta in the Nile Delta, a journey that doesn't take much more than 50 minutes. A working class town, Damietta appears to be the centre of Egypt's furniture making business, with carpenters carving Louis XIV-style sofas and bed frames all along the length of 'road no. 507', the sweet smell of sawdust masking the smell of the open drainage canal leading to the sea.

It's easy to forget Damietta's a working city on the roads lining the eastern branch of the Nile, as blue and attractive as at Aswan, leaving the children's high altitude kites, flown from the palm-fringed promenade, for its convergence with the Mediterranean at Ras el Bar. It's another short journey by *servee* to Ras el Bar, the minibus predominantly ferrying shawled women to the affluent spit of land where well-to-do families holiday politely. Though we share almost no language and very little else, our readiness to communicate means conversation comes easily.

I follow the Nile, still in its unearthly blue costume, from the beginning of the waterfront development, paved and crowded with stalls and restaurants. Before this point the riverfront is just the natural sandy banks of a river in front of people's homes. On a breakwater at its mouth is a beacon of pillar box red. It marks its end; the end of the world's longest river, or at least the end of the eastern branch of the world's longest river. I have roughly followed the path of the Nile since Ethiopia's Lake Tana, through Sudan and the length of Egypt, a path that James Bruce could only dream of. Yet it has only been a small part of my journey around the coast of Africa, a path I would have kept for another day had southern Somalia been at peace, Eritrea not been ruled over by a nervous megalomaniac, and Sudan not had a revolving door of regulation that would turn even the sanest man mad. A monument of inlayed marble at the town's northern tip, among solely Egyptian crowds, quotes the 55th *sura*, or chapter, of the Qur'an: 'He has let free two seas meeting together: Between them is a barrier they do not transgress'.

On the Mediterranean's Hawaii beach, breakwaters calm the incoming waves to allow yachts to moor, while a couple of blocks away on the Nile engine-powered fishing boats berth beside one another, their sterns pointing out into the middle of the river. The girl at the cafe's next table is persuaded by her parents to come over to me. She welcomes me to Egypt in English, and asks where I am from before shyly returning to her smiling parents.

Date palms heavy with half-ripened fruit make use of the Nile's fertility for much of the way towards Raschid and the western branch of the Nile. With the shared taxi heading for Alexandria, I'm dropped off at a junction five kilometres from town. I consider walking for about 200 metres, before the heat stops me, and I wait for a *servee* to pull up beside me on its way to the centre of a town most famous for a lump of carved black granite that hasn't resided here for over 200 years. Most Europeans know Raschid as Rosetta. Within minutes of arriving I have seen images and replicas of the Rosetta Stone, discovered by Napoleonic troops forming part of a modern wall in the fort at the mouth of the Nile. Three languages are written across it: hieroglyphs, Demotic – an administrative Egyptian text – and Greek. Knowledge of the latter enabled the language of the ancient Egyptians to be deciphered after millennia.

It's either 40 km or 60 km from ancient Egypt to ancient Greece – Raschid to Alexandria – depending on which of the road signs within walking distance of one another I choose to believe. Plantations of neatly aligned date palms sidle onto the road; large bunches of green fruit hanging from each one, while additional crops planted in the spacing between the trees await picking. A sprouting of industrial buildings replaces the palms as the kilometres tick down. It's easy to tell we are approaching Egypt's second city: the traffic grows to four lanes in either direction and simultaneously crawls to a standstill; men slide the door of the *servee* open to jump out and walk the rest of the way.

Alexandria's downtown area faces the expanse of the eastern harbour and Fort Qaitbey, built in the fifteenth century on the site of the *pharos* lighthouse, one of the ancient wonders of the world, at the mouth of the harbour. I walk beside the harbour wall towards it, passing the petrol pumps, police station, and boat-building workshops of the Pharos Scenic Path. From the height of the fort's outer walls, protecting the square main tower and the courtyard around it, the towering apartment blocks of Alexandria stretch east-west beyond the curve of the bay. Home to more than four million people, the city lines the Mediterranean for 30 km, from Abu Qir in the east – the site of the British victory over Napoleonic forces at the battle of the Nile – to the royal palace at Ras el Tin to the west.

Founded by Alexander the Great, on 7th August 331 BC, the original Greek layout of the city also had a main thoroughfare that ran east-west to the lighthouse; new Alexandria built very much over old Alexandria. Another ran north-south along what is now Prophet Daniel Street, the location of the mosque of the prophet Daniel. It is said to be the site of the tomb of Alexander, who is sometimes considered a second depiction of the prophet. I cannot see much of the mosque, hidden behind walls smothered with the usual debris of African cities: irregularly parked cars, beggars, market stalls of cheap plastic toys imported from China, carts piled high with prickly pear fruit, and banners celebrating the beginning of Ramadan, the Muslim month of daytime fasting. I continue away from the harbour and the monumental buildings of the old European quarter, through dirty backstreets overcast with the shadow of the apartment blocks, and a market alive with rabbits, chickens, geese, pigeons, and turkeys all balanced on upturned crates.

I should, according to schedule, have only 14 days left and be preparing to return to Morocco. Instead, I am still in Alexandria, more than three weeks after arriving. The irony is that for a continent infamous for the slow pace of its bureaucracy it is British paperwork that has been the only one to delay my scheduled return to Tangier. Taking out my Michelin *Africa North and West* map for the first time since folding it up in Cameroon, I come to realise the distance I still have left to travel; three feet of map, 3600 km of land. Yet there is no future planning I can do. I can feel the depression, anxiety, and stress settling over me. I wait for a call from the embassy to say my passport is ready for collection that I am no longer convinced I am going to receive. I feel trapped.

When the call from the embassy comes, I miss it. The day I should be leaving Gibraltar I am instead heading south, along the desert highway on a SuperJet coach to Cairo, a road lined by crash barriers and scrubby trees. A new passport in hand, but a new delay for a post-Gaddafi visa to Libya means the joy of finally leaving Alexandria has soon waned.

Dokki, separated from downtown Cairo by the Nile and Gezira Island, is greener and more suburban in feel, though just as dusty, polluted, and chaotic. Most of the tented city in Tahrir Square has disappeared in the intervening month, leaving only the uprooted paving slabs, and allowing multiple lanes of snarling traffic to return. An oil painting in the Museum of Egyptian Modern Art on Gezira Island depicts the Nile in 1947 by the bridge linking the island and Dokki. The palms and fertile greenery have been replaced with grey concrete and heavy traffic.

The traffic through the dry bare earth of the road to Saqqara, a short drive from Cairo, consists entirely of clean tour buses and city taxis shining with wax. Children take water from roadside pumps beneath lanterns celebrating Ramadan that have been cut out of old newspapers, a few hundred metres from the ticket office of Egypt's earliest pyramid. I spend the next couple of days moving through Egypt's ancient past, from the tiers of Saqqara's stepped pyramid to its first true pyramids at Dahshur and finally the great pyramids of Giza.

At Dahshur, I use the layers of block work to reach the entrance of the burial shaft – a gap of missing stones – midway up one face. The shaft leads steeply down inside the pyramid, the height forcing me to bend double as the humidity increases during the descent. The tomb chamber at the base of the shaft is so dark my small wind-up torch barely touches it. As far as I can tell the chamber is empty. I examine its walls, smooth to the touch and without noticeable joins, very aware of the tonnage of stone resting above me.

Seeking the small window of bright sunlight at the entrance of the shaft I bang my back on the ceiling repeatedly, my

251

thighs desperate to straighten from their crouch. The angry barking of dogs leads me towards Dahshur's other pyramid, the limestone facing stones of the bent pyramid, whose upper portion takes on a steeper angle that its base, making it look like it has been squashed from above.

'It's not Giza is it?' says my taxi driver, gazing at the pyramids through the windscreen and the late morning heat haze, eager to get back to Cairo. The 28 day Ramadan fast would come to an end at sunset, and families across Egypt would be coming together for celebratory feasting and the Eid ul-Fitr holiday. The holiday brings the city to a halt, though the 357 bus I want to the pyramids of Giza is running, roaring past me outside the almost pink stone of the Egyptian Museum.

It's difficult to find anyone within sight of Giza's plateau, just a few paces from Cairo's outer reaches, interested in doing anything other than get me on some sort of pack animal. It's little different inside the complex. The August heat is stifling, but I mind this far less than the constant offers of camels and horses or the ridiculously priced bottles of water.

The Eid holiday and high summer means Egyptians substantially outnumber foreign visitors. I circle the two larger pyramids on foot, to soak up the atmosphere of an Egyptian bank holiday at the only remaining wonder of the ancient world. It only succeeds in leaving me disheartened; that we can turn a place fundamentally aligned with human ability and endeavour to an ugly market of cat-calls for camels, rubbish-strewn ground and traffic jams formed out of visitors' vehicles. It's less an educational and historical site than an illustration of free market enterprise.

An article in the *Egyptian Independent* a few days later echoes my view of the pyramids – the Haram: 'There is something tragic about the Haram area – jumbled hotels, gaudy souvenir shops, skinny horses, tourist touts so desperate they fling themselves at moving taxis like moths at a lamp, sunbaked tourists smoking cigarettes crouched on hotel stoops rather than wandering around and risking getting accosted'. I leave disappointed, almost tearfully frustrated, and wish I could collect my Libyan visa and leave Cairo as well.

Returning from the Libyan embassy in Cairo's Zamelek district empty handed day after day a general malaise sets in. Cairo feels like an open prison; much like Khartoum had done. In two weeks only two people have spoken to me out of friendliness, and I begin to fear hearing the greeting *salaam alekum*, sure in the knowledge it will lead eventually to a papyrus shop. I start to imagine a sinister hand on my shoulder preventing me moving on as I complete a year of travel. Whatever I do I seem unable to break from the capital. Mr Hamis, my contact at the Libyan embassy, is reassuring, telling me: 'Wait, wait. *Inshallah*, your visa will be ready tomorrow'.

It would be easy to point out that the will of Allah has very little to do with it. I am beginning to know how Tantalus felt: desperate, depressed, hopeless, played, helpless, stuck, and bored out of his mind. At least Sisyphus had a rock to keep him occupied. I am fed up with waiting and hoping; events out of my control. It is not so much Encircle Africa as Rot in Cairo. I have been in Egypt more than two months. I begin to wonder for the first time since Congo whether I'll manage to achieve my return to Tangier.

I have a palpable sense of relief when I finally walk away from the embassy not needing to return the following day. I am desperate to avoid any more delays, aside from a 12 hour wait for the next coach from Cairo to Marsa Matrouh on the Mediterranean coast west of Alexandria. It marks the western extreme of pharaonic Egypt; the place Ramses II built a garrison to protect his kingdom from Libyan attack in 1200

BC. It still has a large military presence, with jets flying low over the desert throughout the day.

Sallum, on the Libyan border, lies 200 km further west. The queue of vehicles transporting goods across the border starts several kilometres from the steep gradient bringing the road onto the Libyan plateau, and continues at the top without break for the seven kilometres to the arches of Egypt's exit point.

I am made to get out of the shared taxi, and told the Libyan authorities are not allowing foreigners to cross.

'My orders are only Libyans and Egyptians go. No one from Italy, France…'

'I have a visa – for overland travel. It has taken me two weeks to get this from Tripoli.'

'Only Libyans and Egyptians…'

The Egyptians prevent me from talking with anyone from the Libyan authorities, and soon blank me completely, intent on getting rid of me as quickly as possible. There is nothing more I can do than plead my case to their backs, curse, and find transport back to Sallum, after an hour of being ignored. Men that freely cross the border mock me, saying 'hundred dollars, hundred dollars' before breaking into laughter.

A taxi takes me back to Sallum, and from there I travel back to Marsa Matrouh. It's a quiet contemplative trip. It feels like I have ended up face to the ground at the second to last hurdle; every force in the universe transpiring or conspiring against me. A failure this far into my journey seems unfair; stories do not end this way. While the first eight months of my journey were fantastic, nothing seems to have gone right since I left Lamu: prevented from entering Ethiopia overland or travelling in Sudan, teargassed and almost robbed in Khartoum, trapped in Egypt waiting for a new passport and visa, and now denied entry overland into Libya.

In Matrouh I catch a minibus to Alexandria, travelling another 280 km, bringing my day's total close to 750 km; one third of the length of Libya's coastline. Alexandria seems busier, maybe because no one ever manages to leave.

Waiting for the next free coach to Cairo, the crowds of passengers show distain for the men in white uniforms dismantling the informal refreshment stalls and loading a tired and dripping chest freezer unit onto the back of a flatbed truck. The other bus station traders quickly hide handmade display units behind the ticket windows, and load boxes of crisps and chocolate into concrete sheds. There are flies all over the part-shaded row of seats, giving me a headache from constantly needing to twitch my head to keep them from landing.

I close my eyes; the soft suspension making the journey along the desert highway feel more like one by sea than by road. I know I am not missing anything, having travelled this route before. My only way into Libya is via terminal three of Cairo International Airport.

An hour after my scheduled take off time the first announcements say the flight will be delayed for another hour. The small boarding gate fills with delayed passengers, so that people can do nothing but stand in the passageways between seats. As flights scheduled after mine take off: to Juba, Moscow, Malta, and Berlin, and as time moves on, I become convinced my flight is going to be cancelled. It isn't called for another three hours, making it one of my longest waits for transport. I don't relax until we take off two hours after that; the total flight time less than half the time I spend waiting for it. In total it takes as long as it would if had I arrived in Tripoli by road.

Libya – Tunisia – Algeria – Morocco

So we left that country and sailed with heavy hearts

Homer, *The Odyssey*

I have no sense of movement on the flight despite travelling at close to 800 km an hour. Travelling by road there is a momentum I don't feel in the air. From the window of the aircraft the vast dry expanses of eastern Libya around the troubled second city of Benghazi are surprisingly neat: comprising symmetrical squares of land given over to date palms separated by laser-straight tracks.

The streets of Tripoli's walled old city are not; winding between one another on the promontory leading to the harbour mole like the thoughts in a daydream. They are almost empty as I pass the open wooden doors of the old British consulate, from the outside just another wooden door in a street of doors, leading to an interior courtyard enveloped by the rooms of the eighteenth century Ottoman mansion. As I go further into the medina the paths get worse, with paving replaced by open drains and the dissipating water of dripping pipes. I stop at Midan Essaa, an attractive brick-paved square centred on a pale Ottoman clock tower overlooked by the rear of the red castle.

I take tea under the shaded umbrella of an outdoor café, paying with dinar printed with *9/9/1999* – the date of the Sirte Declaration that replaced the Organisation of African Unity with the African Union – and still bearing an image of Gaddafi as a thoughtful father figure on the reverse. Images of Libya's new flag, replacing the plain green of the Great

Socialist People's Libyan Arab Jamahiriya, are painted on every surface. After my time dodging needy Cairenes, the polite welcome of Tripoli's residents and the readiness with which vehicles stop at crossings is almost overwhelming. Serene and industrious, businessmen share mid-morning coffee with colleagues to the sound of metal being hammered into shape in the workshops of the metalworkers' souq.

Following the ancient walls of the medina to reach the harbour, I come across a group of street cleaners in orange overalls, the only men I encounter moving in the heat; every one a black migrant.

Come the cool of evening young families enjoy the bouncy castles, popcorn, and candy floss of Martyrs' Square – Gaddafi's Green Square – metres from the bullet-torn marble cladding of the pillar on the seaward entrance to the square, constructed when this area of Tripoli was still known as the *piazza Italia*.

The oldest colonial monument in Tripoli is the only remains of the ancient Roman city. Set in a hollow at one entrance to the medina the second century Arch of Marcus Aurelius stands squat and square like an undressed version of Paris' *Arc de Triomphe*.

In contrast, the modern town of Sabratha sits inland, leaving an entire Roman version on the shores of the clear blue Mediterranean. I have little choice but to continue west away from the trouble spots of Benghazi and Sirte that I witnessed from the air during my transit from Egypt. 60 km from Tripoli, along roads in perfect condition, it takes only an hour to pass the militia checkpoints, tank, and pro-revolutionary graffiti that makes Gaddafi look like a crazed Mick Jagger. The walls of modern Sabratha's buildings are bullet-pocked; its bank bearing the marks of a shell's impact. It's the first time I have to use a candle since Cape Town.

I'm dropped off at a row of Italian warehouses by a passing driver, two large rusting chimneys reaching skyward, having started my approach to the Roman city on foot. I can find no ticket into the ruins, slipping through the low dry gorse to the near indistinguishable low walls of houses and shops and the temples and bathhouses with greater confidence as time goes on without challenge. I greet everyone I see: a couple courting in a way I thought had ceased to exist with my grandparents' generation, a family who seem only too aware they shouldn't be in the tiers of the three-storey amphitheatre, and the half-naked squatters in the portacabins around the administrative block that use the mosaics of the fourth century bathhouse as a toilet.

Leaving the Roman city to its silent watch over the Mediterranean I barely catch sight of the sea again until the Tunisian border, my passage only slowed by the traffic of a couple of scruffy medium-sized towns and a three hour wait on either side of the frontier.

'It's full, full,' says my driver exhausting his English. Without shade, the vehicle moves only two car lengths in half an hour. Men crouch in the shadow of a wall, racing back to their vehicles and their families to launch forward eight feet before those behind them sound their horns, desperate for any sense of advancement. My patience turns to boredom and then irritation. My driver nervously eyes his emptying packet of cigarettes each time he races back to the wheel. Sadiq, an almost accent-free English-speaker appears at my window.

'The driver says you have no air conditioning in the car. If you would like anything – water or food – then please come to my car, I am behind you; that is my family. The Tunisians are taking extra precautions because of what has happened in Libya…you know…there are guns everywhere. But it gets better every day.' Three hours later the US consulate in Benghazi is attacked and the US ambassador killed.

*

259

'You're a journalist?' asks the officer clutching my notebook, the red and white Tunisian flag attached to the upper arm of his uniform. I shake my head.

'And what's this?'

'A microfibre travel towel.'

'Very James Bond. And this?' It brings a smile to my face.

'It's a fetish charm from Togo, for…for *bon chance.*'

'A souvenir?'

'*Oui.*' Despite the ridiculous questions it's good to be able to read road signs again, and communicate more easily. The creeping movement of my car also gets me into the same time zone as London.

The sea remains just out of sight until a little before the signs point to the six kilometre Roman causeway that still links the mainland with Djerba, the island of Homer's Lotus Eaters; the thigh-high scrub towards the stocky whitewashed walls of its main town Houmt Souq littered with scraped cars.

I spend the night in an old caravanserai taking up two sides of one of the oddly-shaped pedestrian friendly squares, avoiding the *zone touristique* 10 km away. The neat paving extends into an interior courtyard ringed with bougainvillea-covered barrel-vaulted rooms. Dark domes dot the souqs; the stalls of Berber women, wrapped in striped cream shawls and wearing flat-brimmed straw hats, spill out onto the cobbles.

I only see occasional strips of blue between the sky and flat stretches of uninteresting sandy scrub as I journey to Sfax by minibus – *louage*. Arriving in the late afternoon the shop owners in the well-maintained cobbled streets of the medina are taking down and packing up their wares. Squeezed between the stalls of clothes and perfumes is the ninth century grand mosque, its columned prayer hall visible through an open door ready for evening prayers. Outside of the colossal sand-coloured medina walls, the noise from nesting sparrows in the trees lining the main avenues is deafening. Swifts use the ancient walls to close in on insects; starlings form diffuse patterns in mid-air.

It's easy to find transport, though more difficult to remain in sight of the sea, there being a thin strip of land home to gnarled old olive trees separating road from shore all the way to Mahdia's thriving medina. Colourfully painted pottery knick-knacks aimed at visitors line the cobbles, contrasting the blanched white walls as I take an indirect path through the twisting alleys to the fort of Borj El Kebir. Surrounded by Muslim graves and sitting on evidence of earlier towns, it overlooks a Punic era harbour, a square of water cut out of the shoreline rock, a reminder I am nearing Carthage.

Returning from the fort promontory, it clouds over and the wind picks up. The weather becomes bad enough for the market stall holders to shift their pottery souvenirs inside, in heavy armfuls, hoping to avoid the first rain I experience since leaving Addis Ababa three months ago.

From the window of the train the country looks greener north of Mahdia, the bare orange-brown dirt between the gnarled olives replaced with tough grasses. The scenery becomes increasingly industrial on reaching Monastir, where the train reverses its way through the suburban build up to the gates of Sousse medina and port. Entering the medina at *bab el-jedid* gate I'm able to follow the turrets and stairways of the sand-coloured walls, planted with summer flowers where there's space. I begin to think I won't reach the end of the spiral stone steps when I reach daylight at the blustery top of the fortress, the strong wind pushing rain showers across the sky. The high round tower I climb rises from one corner of the square fortress, giving me spectacular views of the simple grand mosque and souq alleyways beyond.

Leaving the medina at its northern gate I follow the coast to the high-rise hotels of Sousse's *zone touristique*, Russians in hot pants standing outside smoking. From there I continue north by *louage*, a dull ride across a flat landscape to Nabeul, where I switch to a bendy bus terminating in the small town of El-Haouaria exactly on time at 2.30 pm.

Reaching El-Haouaria for 2.30 is about all there is to do here. Spread out among fields of chillies, tended by women in colourful shawls, it's difficult to know exactly where the heart of the town lies, and I trace a path through the mostly empty streets, dotted with garages and basic patisseries. A road uphill leads me to Africa's northern shoreline, close to the tip of Cape Bon, a finger of land extending towards Sicily. Mysterious-looking islands seem to send the waves colliding noisily with the rough rock – full of hollows – rising several metres above them while the wind whips at my hair and shirt.

I am the last to board a minibus to Tabarka, only four kilometres from the *frontiere algerienne*, past the turbines turning with the strong winds of the coast. The coast of Tabarka is protected by a stout Genoese fort, taking advantage of a natural rise just a short distance, through pines and other Mediterranean species, from the main street. Closed, with a *no trespassing* sign to one side, I am able to walk three quarters of its perimeter – the final section blocked by a shear drop. It's a peaceful place with a steady stream of visitors. They recover their breath by watching the local men fishing from rowing boats, and admiring the views of the open sea to north, west and east. The view south is blocked by the ridge of hills leading inland towards Jendouba.

The men at the *gare routiere* greet me with kisses to both cheeks as if I were a long lost friend. With little chance of permission to enter Algeria alone, I must continue eastward, inland to Jendouba and Bizerte, over hills that make me groggy from the winding path. As well as east I have travelled north, to the northernmost point of my journey, after over a year of travel.

Bizerte's two ports echo one another, the dog-leg entry canal into the old port cut from bedrock, and guarded on the one side by the walls of the Kasbah and on the other by Sidi el Hani fort, linked by a bridge. It is replicated on a grander scale by the canal linking the newer lake port with the Mediterranean, its entrance guarded by the *capitainerie*. The bridge connecting either side of the canal has a straight angular modern form, pivoting open twice a day to allow ships to pass through. A larger orange oil tanker – the *Hellen* of Singapore registry – is towed in by tugs and guided by the pilot's speedboat, after a small vessel registered to La Goulette – the port of Tunis – leaves.

The motorway to Tunis cuts across the olive-speckled hills of Cap Farina to the *gare de nord* on the capital's outskirts. The streets around it, at the closed *bab saaloum* tram stop are busy with locals trying to hail already full private hire taxis or fighting to board buses. I'm invited to join two friends through the hot covered souqs and narrow medina streets, that every so often open into a cobbled square used as a car park, to the defunct Porte de France, more a triumphal arch than a medina gateway, topped by a Tunisian flag wrapped tightly around its pole by the wind.

Wide boulevards run from the Porte de France to Avenue Habib Bourguiba, named after Tunisia's first president, who took office in 1957. The avenue is lined with a central row of tightly clipped trees, and a dozen or so tanks and riot vans protecting government ministries. Tunisia's second president, Ben Ali, only left power as a result of the Jasmine revolution, the revolt that ignited the Arab Spring. Roads around the ministries are barricaded with railings and razor wire. An olive green helicopter hangs low, performing tight circles over the centre. Within arm's reach of shoppers a policeman, masked by a black balaclava and armed with a shotgun, rages against a member of the public carrying the paper bags of designer stores. It would be comical if I didn't think at any moment, and under the slightest provocation, the police might start firing. A colleague, also in a balaclava, has teargas canisters hanging from his belt.

At the other end of the avenue, life is more normal, with families sitting at restaurants, and men ducking into what shade they can find away from the hot sun. The new president hides behind the high walls of his compound, barring views over the Antonine Baths of Carthage, separated from the chaos of central Tunis by a lake sharing the name of his capital.

A taxi takes me from the centre to the airy modern smoke free *gare maritime* at La Goulette on the banks of Lac Tunis. There is only one other foot passenger on the 11 deck *Carthage* to Marseille, a detour I come up with to avoid resorting to a further flight over Algeria, and its land border with Morocco, which has been closed for the past 18 years.

The Mediterranean remains fantastically flat, with just tiny undulations like the minute changes to the skin of some giant animal. The sun doesn't so much set as fade away, losing colour as it descends behind a thick low bank of cloud; a perfect end to my time in Tunisia.

When I get up to the open sections of decks seven and eight the next morning, land – Europe – is already visible as a fuzzy line on the horizon, as I have seen so many times during my journey. A yacht race is taking place around the low rocky island of If protecting Marseille's port, the gentle wind filling the sunshine-yellow jib sails. The bells of the Byzantine-style cathedral ring out for Sunday service. With one week of travel remaining I am on the wrong continent, and I'm eager to get onto the correct one again as quickly as possible. It may seem ridiculous to want to return to Africa for 100 km of Moroccan coast, before crossing back to Europe, but it is important for me to close the loop, and encircle Africa, by reaching Tangier's seedy depths once more from African soil.

By nightfall Marseille's *gare Saint-Charles* has emptied out and taken on a sinister air. Immigrants from Algeria and Morocco wander among the waiting passengers, offering hashish in spite of the Alsatians and uniformed police at the station's entrances. I don't feel altogether safe waiting for the first of four trains that will take me across the border to southern Spain.

Having lived all my life on a united island with indefatigable boundaries perhaps I overestimated the importance of boundaries to other nations and people. My journey suggests they don't really mean very much to local populations, who often cross without the visa formalities of foreigners like me. The big boundary lies between Africa's citizens and Europe. Most simply cannot get visas to travel as I have done on their continent.

There are about 20 coaches to the train departing Barcelona for Malaga, my destination in Spain. The coach computer shows an impressive 301 km/h across the late summer Spanish undulations, but the frequent stops make our top speed redundant. I see the Mediterranean and what I believe to be the Algerian coast in the distance, until I realise it's the reflected shadow of another passenger's head in the window. The tracks then leave the coast, following a line that divides Spain almost equally into an eastern and western half.

In the short time I am in Malaga, buying a ticket for the ferry *Juan J Sister*, it manages to remind me of Africa's Mediterranean coast. The same narrow streets lead to squares filled with outdoor cafés, where shoe-shiners carry their footstool boxes from a shoulder strap, peddling for work.

Having crossed the busy shipping lane separating Europe and Africa I am back on the African continent, but not out of Spain. I started the circumnavigation by leaving a British enclave on the Spanish mainland, and come close to ending it by entering territory in Morocco held by Spain since 1497.

My legs aren't too interested in Melilla's hilliness. I take a direct route to what I had considered the fort, in fact Old Melilla, a series of four fortified precincts providing layer after layer of defence. It's not so much an old town as a giant castle rising and falling tiringly in the morning heat. Compared to the new town, outside the walls, it's quiet, with few cars and fewer people on the narrow streets.

The bus ride to the Beni Enzar border post takes only 10 minutes from Plaza Espana, and border formalities not much longer. I leave fortress Europe – high walls and higher razor wire fences – for a dirty rubbish-strewn concrete mass. Desperation seems to trickle from the air like the early morning drizzle. After sunny Spain-in-Africa, it's grey.

I take a shared taxi to Nador only a few minutes south of the enclave; Morocco's answer to the port in Melilla. It's brighter here, the sun breaking through the cloud to glint off the Mediterranean. I'm able to catch another shared taxi to El-Hociema, following the folds of the coast for almost the entire 120 km; the whole of Morocco's northern coast laid out in front of me.

I leave El-Hociema by the same road in which I enter, joining the main road west, through patchwork hills coloured with blocks of forest, scrub, bare earth, and blood-red soils. A road, a broken line on my map, follows the coast for the much of the journey through El-Jebha and Oued Laou to Tetouan. The former capital of Spanish Morocco, Tetouan is only eight kilometres from the coast, and 100 km from Tangier. The multiple requests for money take the shine off the impressive theatre of jagged Rif mountain peaks acting as a background to the whitewashed Moorish architecture.

My last leg in Africa, the 100 km to Tangier, I complete on a leaky bus that shudders with the force of the idling engine. We pass the turn off for Tanger-Med port around 14 km outside of the city. Sitting on the bus I realise I have a vague recognition of the streets. I have been to Tangier before – I have done it – I have Encircled Africa.

Gibraltar

I did not fully understand the dread term 'terminal illness'
until I saw Heathrow for myself

Dennis Potter

I have to guess my way from the port in Algeciras to the bus
station, where an electronic board displays the times of the
next bus to *La Línea* and the border between Spain and
Gibraltar.

There are queues of weekend traffic into Gibraltar
extending out along the Spanish corniche of Gibraltar Bay,
and even on foot I'm struggling against the flow of Saturday
strollers. The African migrants have left their shelter in the
Landport gate tunnels by Casemates Square, where I burn my
fingers on fish and chips from the same shop I visited on the
first day of the journey, eating them on the same end of the
same bench.

My original plan was to return to Europa Point and look
across to Africa again, but all my reserves of energy are
spent, and it is consolation enough to know that all that
separates me from Africa is 14 km of often still water, after
having travelled the equivalent of the earth at the equator.
There are too many tourists enjoying the late summer sun for
me to be an exception, for anyone to ask why I might be in
Gibraltar, in the way I was asked almost continuously in
Africa, so I stay quietly on the bench and think about my first
sight of England in 13 months. Reaching into my bag I untie
the Togo fetish charm, letting my wish return to Legba, the
words 'what now? What's next?' running through my head.

ebook editions of this title are available, including editions
containing 120 of Ian's photographs

www.encircleafrica.org